T0327303

"A powerful and important account of the role data plays in shaping everyday life from a world leading researcher with decades of experience in the field."
James Ash, Newcastle University

"Rob Kitchin is engaged in making our datafied world more liveable. He asks not just how our digital selves are constructed, managed and marketed by others, but how we might connect to that process and influence it."
Linnet Taylor, Tilburg University

"We all use data to tell stories. In this tremendous book, Rob Kitchin tells stories too, prompting us to reimagine how data lives and how we live with it."
Paul Dourish, University of California, Irvine

"Data Lives is the ultimate resource for all of us who have wondered what happens to our data after they enter the ether beyond our digital devices, where we only briefly encounter data along what are revealed to be complex and often surprising trajectories."
Agnieszka Leszczynski, Western University

DATA LIVES

How Data Are Made and Shape Our World

Rob Kitchin

BRISTOL
UNIVERSITY
PRESS

First published in Great Britain in 2021 by

Bristol University Press
University of Bristol
1–9 Old Park Hill
Bristol
BS2 8BB
UK
t: +44 (0)117 954 5940
e: bup-info@bristol.ac.uk

Details of international sales and distribution partners are available at
bristoluniversitypress.co.uk

British Library Cataloguing in Publication Data
A catalogue record for this book is available from the British Library

ISBN 978-1-5292-1514-4 paperback
ISBN 978-1-5292-1515-1 ePub
ISBN 978-1-5292-1564-9 ePdf

Cover design: Liam Roberts
Image credit: 123RF / 84671628
Bristol University Press uses environmentally
responsible print partners.
Printed in Great Britain by CMP, Poole

Contents

List of Abbreviations   vii
Acknowledgements   x

PART I: Introduction
1   Data Stories   3

PART II: The Life of Data
2   Blind Data   17
3   The Nature of Data   23
4   Gridlock   31
5   In Data We Trust   37
6   How to Lose (and Regain) 3.6 Billion Euros   45
7   Harmonizing Data is Hard   51
8   Open-and-Shut Case   61
9   The Politics of Building Civic Tech   69
10   So More Trumps Better?   79
11   Hustling for Funding   85
12   The Secret Science of Formulas   95
13   The End of the Data Lifecycle   101

PART III: Living with Data
14   Traces and Shadows   111
15   Recommended Life   121
16   The Quantified Self   127
17   Fighting Fires   137
18   Management Through Metrics   143
19   Guinea Pigs   153
20   Big Brother is Watching and Controlling You   161
21   Security Theatre   169

22	When a Country Ignores Its Own Data	175
23	Data Theft	183
24	Data for the People, by the People	187
25	Black Data Matter	197

PART IV: Conclusion
| 26 | A Matter of Life and Death | 207 |
| 27 | Data Futures | 219 |

| Notes | 229 |
| Index | 255 |

List of Abbreviations

AIRO	All-Island Research Observatory
ANPR	Automatic Number Plate Recognition
ATM	Automated Teller Machine
BAME	Black, Asian and Minority Ethnic
BCD	Building City Dashboards
CBRRO	Cross-Border Regional Research Observatory
CCTV	Closed-Circuit Television
CSO	Central Statistics Office
DCC	Dublin City Council
DBEI	Department of Business, Enterprise and Innovation
DEHLG	Department of Environment, Heritage and Local Government
DES	Department of Education and Science
DPER	Department of Public Expenditure and Reform
DHO	Digital Humanities Observatory
DRI	Digital Repository of Ireland
ED	Electoral Division
EPA	Environmental Protection Agency
ECB	European Central Bank
EU	European Union
FIPPs	Fair Information Practice Principles
GDPR	General Data Protection Regulation
GGD	General Government Debt
GIS	Geographic Information System
GLAM	Galleries, Libraries, Archives and Museums
GNIB	Garda National Immigration Bureau
GPS	Global Positioning System
GSM	Global System for Mobile Communications

HEA	Higher Education Authority
HFA	Housing Finance Agency
HSIS	Humanities Serving Irish Society
HSS	Humanities and Social Sciences
IMF	International Monetary Fund
IQDA	Irish Qualitative Data Archive
ISSP	Irish Social Sciences Platform
iOS	iPhone Operating System (also underpins iPad and iPod Touch)
KPI	Key Performance Indicator
LGBT	Lesbian, Gay, Bisexual and Transgender
MAC	Media Access Control
MAPC	Metropolitan Area Planning Council
NAVR	National Audio-Visual Repository
NIRSA	National Institute for Regional and Spatial Analysis
NISRA	Northern Ireland Statistics and Research Agency
NPM	New Public Management
NTMA	National Treasury Management Agency
NUTS	Nomenclature des Unités Territoriales Statistiques
OECD	Organisation for Economic Co-operation and Development
OSI	Ordnance Survey Ireland
PIIGS	Portugal, Ireland, Italy, Greece and Spain
PRTLI	Programme for Research in Third Level Institutions
PRO	Public Records Office
PSRA	Property Services Regulatory Authority
RFID	Radio Frequency Identification
RIA	Royal Irish Academy
RPPR	Residential Property Price Register
RTE	Raidió Teilifís Éireann
SAPS	Small Area Population Statistics
SEUPB	Special European Union Programmes Body
SSAI	Social Science Assessment Instruments
TDR	Trusted Digital Repository
TfL	Transport for London

TRIPS	Travel-time Reporting and Integrated Performance System
UNDRIP	United Nations Declaration on the Rights of Indigenous Peoples
WHO	World Health Organization
WWW	World Wide Web

Acknowledgements

As the essays in this book attest, I have collaborated with dozens of people on research and writing projects over the years, each of whom have helped shape my thinking and praxes concerning data. I'll not name them all as it would be a long list, but I would like to thank them for the conversations, debates and camaraderie. The analysis and stories presented in this book reflect my thoughts, recollections and interpretation of events. I would like to thank David Butler, Dana King, John Green, Justin Gleeson and Sandra Collins who gave useful feedback on the stories and essays, and the anonymous reviewers of the book proposal. The Irish translation in Chapter 12 was kindly undertaken by Gearóidín McEvoy via Elizabeth Mathews. At Bristol University Press, I'd like to thank Paul Stevens, Kathryn King, Leonie Drake and Freya Trand for commissioning a book that takes a slightly different approach to communicating scholarly ideas and shepherding it through the production process.

The essays and stories in *Data Lives* draw on research conducted over the past 30 years across a number of funded projects:

Building City Dashboards (2016–20), Science Foundation Ireland (15/IA/3090);

Getting Smarter About Smart Cities: Improving Data Privacy and Data Security (2015), Department of the Taoiseach;

The Programmable City (2013–18), European Research Council (ERC-2012-AdG-323636);

Crosplan 1 (2009–11) and Crosplan 2 (2012–14), Interreg, Special EU Programmes Body;

Digital Repository of Ireland (2010–15), Programme for Research for Third Level Institutions Cycle 5, Higher Education Authority;

Creating All-Island Datasets (2008), Strategic Investment Board;

Irish Social Sciences Platform, Programme for Research for Third Level Institutions, Cycle 4 (2007–12), Higher Education Authority;

Cross Border Regional Research Observatory (2005–06), Special EU Programmes Body;

International Centre for Local and Regional Development (2004–09), various awards, Department of Education, Department of Foreign Affairs, International Fund for Ireland, and InterTradeIreland;

National Institute for Regional and Spatial Analysis, Programme for Research for Third Level Institutions, Cycle 4 (2001–05), Higher Education Authority;

Issues of Validity and Integrity in Cognitive Mapping Research, (1992–95), Economic and Social Research Council.

PART I

Introduction

1

Data Stories

Data. Big data. Open data. Database. Personal data. Data-driven. Data brokers. Data analytics. Data is the new oil. Data plan. Data deluge. Data activism. Data science. Data infrastructure. Data justice. General Data Protection Regulation. Data. Data. Data …

A decade ago, the word 'data' seemed to be largely the preserve of researchers and a few professional administrators and workers. Now, it has entered our everyday lexicon. We are aware that our data are routinely harvested, that our digital world generates and consumes vast volumes of data, and our economy and government are becoming data-driven. Yet, it is not always clear what data are, how best to make sense of them, and what is at stake.

Before this data revolution, data were largely treated in a common sense way. They were gathered facts about the world; the raw material generated through scientific measurements, government surveys, administrative systems, academic research, explorations and fieldwork. They were the building blocks that enabled the creation of information and knowledge. However, just as we pay little attention to the bricks that enable us to build complex buildings, which collectively create vibrant cities, we rarely focused critical attention on data. Consequently, we have found ourselves living in a data-driven world that, on the one hand, seems intuitive to navigate – we use digital technologies, click here and there, fill out online forms, agree to terms and conditions, share our thoughts and photos. On the other hand, we have little comprehension as to the full spectrum of data harvested about us, what happens to them, and how they are used.

Digital systems are often black-boxed, meaning we have little sense of how they work beyond their interface and immediate effects. Data-rich organizations, such as private companies, data brokers or state bodies, are by design secretive, either to protect commercial advantage, hide their activities, or to protect the integrity of their work. We simply have to trust that they are only generating the data they need, and are treating, using, and acting on these data in ethical ways.

In recent years, this trust that has been eroded. Our faith in digital systems and data-rich organizations has been undermined by a series of scandals and data hacks. The Snowden revelations exposed how our data are being gathered on a massive scale by governments in order for them to be able to spy on their own and other nations' citizens. The Facebook/Cambridge Analytica scandal demonstrated how the data profiles of millions of people were used to target them with posts designed to shape their voting preference. Not a week seems to go by without a major data breach in which millions of personal records are accessed, including sensitive ID and financial information.[1]

Despite these events, the data revolution continues apace, and we remain either largely ignorant or indifferent to their consequences, or feel impotent to be able to do anything about them. We have little choice in our interactions with government if we want to receive entitlements and services and comply with legislation. Data is the price we have to pay for using commercial platforms, or receiving benefits and rewards for purchases. The only alternative appears to be to avoid the use of digitally mediated transactions, which is all but impossible when we routinely shop online, pay with credit/debit cards, use mobile phone apps and converse with friends using social media.

While most people interested in data are focused on how to use them productively in their work – as a means to create insight and innovation, gain efficiencies and optimization, extract value and make money, and manage and control systems – a number of academics, journalists and civil rights advocates have started to question the logics and consequences of the data revolution. Under the banner of critical data studies they focus their attention on the nature and production of data, and how everyday life is being transformed by data.

Rather than seeing data as simply the raw material – the bricks – used to create information and knowledge, they cast data as a manufactured material that intrinsically has value. Data, they argue, is never raw but always cooked to some recipe. Data do not pre-exist their generation; they are not simply waiting to be collected or harvested in a technical, passive and objective manner. Instead, they are produced – that is, actively created via procedures and instruments of our devising. Through their handling and sharing data can mutate, becoming cleaned, wrangled, transformed and combined. Ultimately, they can be deleted, completing what can be a complex data life cycle.

Data then are not benign, neutral measures that reflect the world as it is, within technical constraints. What data are generated, and how they are produced, handled and used, is the result of choices and decisions by people. These, in turn, are shaped by intended outcomes, theories and concepts, research designs, procedures, protocols, standards, resources and finance, regulations and laws, organizational processes, ethics reviews, political context and so on. The cooking of data does not take place in vacuum, but within context. Data-driven endeavours are not simply technical systems, but are socio-technical systems. That is, they are as much a result of human values, desires and social relations as they are scientific principles and technologies.

The sociality of data is also evident with respect to how we have come to live with data. The data revolution has been transforming work and the economy, the nature of consumption, the management and governance of society, how we communicate and interact with media and each other, and forms of play and leisure. Our lives are saturated with digital devices and services that generate, process and share vast quantities of data.

We carry smartphones around with us, using an array of apps and games throughout the day. We communicate using email, messaging, video calls and social media. We employ computers and digitally controlled technologies to perform work tasks. We monitor our health and activity using self-tracking devices. We drive around in cars chocked full of computers that mediate our driving experience, even if we're not aware that they are doing so. Our homes are increasingly full of digitally mediated appliances from personal assistants such as Alexa and Siri, to smart TVs and home management systems. We pay for goods and services using electronic cash, often to buy digital products (games, streaming services, books). Even if we try to live analogue lives, we cannot escape surveillance systems and the databases of governments and companies with whom we have to interact.

The result is we leave a series of data footprints (that we choose to create) and shadows (that are captured whether we want them to be or not) as we live our everyday lives. These data are valuable commodities and are used for a range of purposes, including verification, profiling and decision-making. They are shared and traded, feeding into a vast global data market. Our data now often precede us, influencing what adverts we routinely see, whether we are approved for a loan, or tenancy, or job, and whether we receive special offers and rewards. As such, our data can be used to empower us, but also exploit, discriminate and persecute. Much of this consumption and monetization of our data is hidden from us, and many of us barely know the extent to which it is influencing outcomes critical for our future well-being. Consequently, while some of our life with data is clear, much is opaque.

Recognizing the sociality of data, and comprehending data and data systems as being socio-technical in nature, provides a conceptual position for challenging the teleological mantra of the data revolution. That is, it provides a platform to contest the seemingly inevitable, pre-ordained data landscape and how data-driven systems work, and to envisage different data futures. A critical aspect of divining such futures is to actively explore moral and ethical questions with respect to how data are produced, shared, traded and protected. Indeed, several debates – some of which are happening in the public eye, some behind closed doors – are ongoing about how data should be managed and governed through rules, principles, policies, licences and laws, and under what circumstances and to what ends data can be employed (GDPR (General Data Protection Regulation), for example, is a result of these debates). There are no easy answers, and the suggested approaches and outcomes are strongly contested by different parties given what is at stake. Yet, the results of these debates will have an effect on our data-driven world.

The objective of *Data Lives* is to reveal the myriad, complex, contested ways in which data are produced and circulated, and the consequences of living in a data-driven world. What follows reveals our data world to be full of potential dangers, but also benefits and hope. The life of data and living with data is bound up in contingencies and is open to new configurations and possibilities. And while the data revolution seems to have a relatively robust path dependency, it can be diverted onto new routes. We can create our own data lives.

Telling Stories

The usual approach to writing an article or book that examines the praxes and politics of data is to produce a rather sterile narrative that weaves together the theories, observations and findings from the academic and policy literature with empirical evidence and conceptual musings of the author. The voice is most often in the third person, impassionate and distant. The aim is to create a convincing argument in a neutral register that displays a strong degree of objectivity. I've written plenty of such accounts, which are usually impersonal, full of jargon and conceptual musings, and are aimed at academic peers.

In *Data Lives* I take a different approach to examining data, using the more familiar narratives of personal reminiscence, journalistic-style essays, and short stories. Rather than writing from a detached academic position, I adopt a different kind of voice and point-of-view to personalize the narrative both with respect to the writer and reader. In essence, I employ a more reflexive standpoint that draws on my many years of experience of researching and writing about data, building data infrastructures, serving on the boards of institutions that produce government data and telling data stories to influence public policy. The chapters that follow tell a set of interconnected stories about how data are produced, processed and interpreted, and the consequences of living in a data-driven world.

Storytelling has always been a powerful way of communicating ideas and providing a critical lens to consider society and social processes and change. Short stories, novels, comics, documentaries, biographies, television dramas and movies provide media that can be more provocative and playful than academic accounts. They can set out different views and explore values, conflict and consequences using various forms of narrative devices. For example, science fiction uses extrapolation and speculation to explore possible futures given present trends. In particular, SF employs the tactics of estrangement (pushing a reader outside of what they comfortably know) and defamiliarization (making the familiar strange) as a way of creating a distancing mirror and to prompt critical reflection on society.[2] These tactics were used to good effect in a book I edited recently – *How to Run a City Like Amazon, and Other Fables* – in which the contributors used short stories to explore what cities would be like if they were run by, or using the business model of, different companies.

In what follows, the essays are more akin to personalized documentaries or memoir, or short explanatory accounts. The stories are purely fictional tales or modified dramatizations of events. Both the fiction and non-fiction are rooted in my own experiences, though they also draw from extensive wider research and reading. The use of personal recollection and reflection might create the impression that there is a somewhat anecdotal quality to the message. Undoubtedly, it is the case that some of the material is circumstantial; they are specific stories about data based on personal interactions and various kinds of data work. Many are data tales that I have told others over coffee or in a bar after workshops or to illustrate a point in the classroom; little vignettes of practices and encounters that I have found illustrative, disturbing or humorous.[3]

Some readers might be wary of this approach, casting it as 'unscientific'. It's certainly the case that the arguments presented are not based on the use of a rigorous, systematic, scientific method involving a representative sampling frame, impartial and rote analysis, and impassionate, descriptive interpretation (though some of the projects they describe are). However, I would contend that it does not render the arguments made invalid or without useful insight. Nor does it mean that the material and examples discussed are unrepresentative. Rather, what is presented are case studies/histories produced through a form of recovered auto-ethnography and contextualized with respect to the arguments and findings of the wider critical data studies and data science literature. These case studies/histories are illustrative of situations and processes that I have witnessed many times and will be familiar to those who regularly work with data, or are concerned with how data affect our everyday lives. After all, they are rooted in 30 years of real-world projects, academic research, knowledge of the field, practical experience of data work, and the politics surrounding data initiatives.

Like all researchers, I am familiar with generating and handling data. Academics are trained with respect to how best to collect, process and interpret data. Whereas other academics are mostly using data to understand and explain particular phenomenon, much of my focus has been on data themselves. My doctoral work in the early 1990s focused on whether the methods used to measure individuals' geographic knowledge about the world produced valid data, and if the statistical tests used to analyze them created accurate and reliable insights.[4] My approach was scientific, using quantitative and statistical methods to test the veracity of the data produced and the analytics used to make sense of them. My conclusion was that significant amounts of overlooked error and bias were being introduced through the processes of generating and analyzing data and these shortcomings were leading to findings that lacked integrity.[5]

I still believed in the usefulness of data and science, but my faith in them was shaken a little. As a result, I have long been interested in issues of data quality and veracity, undertaking a number of projects that examine these in different contexts. For example, a recent project has explored whether it is possible to use real-time data from smart city technologies to create new official statistics.[6] This has involved examining the data with respect to issues such as representativeness, access, coverage, accuracy, reliability, cleanliness, consistency, completeness, provenance and transparency. Collectively, these qualities concern trust: do we believe in the integrity of a dataset to tell us something meaningful about the world?

Much of my own empirical research in the 2000s, and that of my colleagues in the institute I directed, concerned social, regional and cross-border policy. Government data was essential for performing this work. However, it was often hard to access, or provided in formats that were difficult to use. As a consequence, throughout the 2000s and 2010s I was involved in a series of projects focused on creating open data infrastructures for storing and sharing data, as well as creating online interactive tools for visualizing and mapping data, including: the All-Island Research Observatory (AIRO) that compiles datasets that span the Republic of Ireland and Northern Ireland; the Irish Qualitative Data Archive (IQDA) that stores and shares qualitative social sciences data; the Digital Repository of Ireland (DRI), which is a national trusted digital repository for storing and sharing the digital collections of galleries, libraries, archives, museums and universities; and the Building City Dashboards (BCD) project which created the Dublin and Cork Dashboards that inform users how the cities are performing. Each of these initiatives has sought to formulate guidelines and best practices for building and maintaining data infrastructures. They are long-term endeavours and all still active.

From the late 1990s, I also became increasingly attentive to social theory and critiques of traditional science. My initial interest concerned the implications of the internet for everyday life and the nature of software. While I was trained to code as a key part of a Master's degree in Geographic Information Systems (GIS), and wrote dozens of programs to conduct my doctoral research, subsequently I learned how to deconstruct software and its embedded values and to think critically about what the code was being used for. In the early 2010s, my focus drifted from code to data, writing a book, *The Data Revolution*. This book adopted the lens of critical data studies to consider the nature of big data, open data, data infrastructures, and to map out their consequences for society. Just as the book went into production, I started a new five-year study, The Programmable City, which examined critically the role of software and data in managing and governing cities, teasing apart the discourses, technologies, practices and social implications of data-driven urbanism.[7]

In addition to academic work concerning data and data infrastructures, over the years I have served on various advisory boards/panels, such as the Data Forum of the Department of Taoiseach (Irish Prime Minister's Office), the Irish Census Advisory Board, the Irish Research Council, Dublinked (Dublin's open data portal) and Smart Dublin (the city's smart city body), the Audit Committee for the Irish Central Statistical Office, the Irish Social Science Data Archive, and the National Consultative Panel on Open Data. I have also conducted public-facing data work. For example, between 2009 and 2015 I regularly wrote data stories for the blog *Ireland After NAMA*,[8] presenting just-in-time data analysis on topical issues – mainly housing, planning and population change. This involved undertaking and publishing an analysis of government or industry data within a couple of hours of its release. This was often followed by discussions with print journalists and radio interviews.

Data Lives

The aim and the challenge of this book was twofold. First, to translate my knowledge of working with and thinking about data and recast it into stories that are more likely to chime with people's own experiences. Second, to use the essays and storytelling to highlight why we need to think and act critically with respect to data, both in terms of how they are produced and used. These ambitions to playfully and critically examine data is captured, I hope, in the title of the book, '*Data Lives*'. It is intended as a kind of pun, with 'lives' rhyming with both 'gives' (as in life of data) and 'hives' (as in living with data). About a third of the chapters discuss initiatives located in Ireland. That is inevitable given I have spent my entire career on the island, two years in the North and the rest in the Republic. The themes discussed in these essays and stories are equally applicable to elsewhere, as the other illustrative material related to the United Kingdom, United States, China, Hong Kong and Australia make clear.

Part II reveals the cooked nature of data and details the praxes and politics that shape the data life cycle from generation to destruction. It's divided into 12 short chapters, six of which are short stories and six essays. The part opens with a blind date between two researchers who have very different notions about the nature of data and the ethos and practices of science. An essay examining the nature of data from an etymological, philosophical and technical point of view then follows. 'Gridlock' charts the data journeys and transformations that take place across the network of cameras, sensors and software that makes up a traffic control system. Issues of data quality and veracity in open datasets are then examined using a variety of examples from the Irish data system. 'How to Lose (and Regain) 3.6 Billion Euros' imagines a conversation between two senior civil servants when they realize that the Irish government has lost 3.6 billion euros through a spreadsheet error (which really happened and wasn't noticed for over a year). Data interoperability and the difficulties in harmonizing data across jurisdictions is explored using Ireland/Northern Ireland and Metropolitan Boston as case studies. A conversation between open data advocates and a civil servant in charge of the process reveals the challenges of getting government data made open. The technical and political trials involved in building a suite of open data tools is then scrutinized by charting the development of the Dublin Dashboard. This is followed by an argument between two researchers concerning the epistemology, methodology and ethics of data science versus traditional science in studying fertility. The role of finance and the politics of collaboration is made clear through charting the development of the DRI. How choices and decisions concerning the analytics applied to data shapes outcomes is revealed in an account of a working session between academics and a government minister to devise and implement an 'objective' method for allocating government funding. The final essay examines the transitory nature of data and its deletion, by either design or accident.

Part III details what is at stake living in a data-driven world. The part opens with an essay that charts the transition from an analogue to a digital world, its effect on data footprints and shadows, and the growth of data brokers and government use of data. How profiling and social sorting shape consumption and entertainment through recommendations and nudges is then detailed. This is followed by an account of sousveillance and how we produce, monitor and react to data relating to ourselves, thus creating a quantified self. The consequences of dataveillance is explored with respect to how personal data shadows led to unemployed, volunteer firefighters in Australia's recent fires losing their benefits. 'Management through Metrics' charts how public and private sector organizations are increasingly using key performance indicators and technocratic procedures to manage work and workers and its consequences. The implications for citizens of data-driven management is examined by charting the issues of living in a smart city testbed area, demonstrated through a walking tour for local residents, led by a public official. How these technologies are deployed as mass surveillance and social credit scoring in China and their threat to democracy is then examined. This is followed by charting the Kafkaesque procedures involved in data-driven airport security. The benefits of evidence-informed policy over anecdote is explored through an account of the financial crash in Ireland and the effect of creating public data stories. 'Data theft' details the consequences of data breaches for a company and its customers. How citizens can take a more active role in using data for the public good through civic hacking, citizen science and data justice initiatives is then examined. The final story charts how a group of citizens seek to challenge systemic and institutional racism within their city by building their own datasets and tools.

Part IV opens with a chapter that pulls together the themes explored in Parts II and III in a discussion of the life of COVID-19 data, how it has been used to reshape our daily lives by directing intervention measures, and how new data-driven technologies have been deployed to try and help tackle the spread of the coronavirus. As a whole, the book argues that it is crucial to appreciate the praxes, politics and effects of both the life of data and living with data if we are to imagine and create different kinds of data-infused lives. Hopefully it prompts, on the one hand, a critical reflection on the role of data in your own lives and the data-driven world we are living in, and on the other, an impetus to take a more active role in shaping the terms in which those data are produced and used. With respect to the latter, the final chapter examines what kind of data future we want to create and strategies for realizing our visions.

I have tried to structure the book so that it can be read from cover to cover, with a long arc of argument threaded throughout, but also so that the reader can dip in and out and engage with particular issues and themes. Hopefully the essays and stories resonate and provide insight and food for thought in navigating your own data lives.

PART II

The Life of Data

2

Blind Data

Emma stared out of the café window at two gulls fighting over a burger carton. She'd no idea what had possessed her to tell her mother that she'd be bringing a date to her sister's wedding. Or why she'd let Tracey take charge of solving her dilemma, other than the ceremony was in a week's time and there was no way she was asking one of her exes to play the part.

'One grande cappuccino.' Julian placed the coffee on the table and slid into the seat opposite. 'And one black tea.' He took a sip. 'Lovely.'

Emma tried not to cringe. They already seemed mismatched. She was wearing a crumpled Joy Division T-shirt, black jeans, and blood red Doc Martins. In contrast, his blue dress shirt and tan chinos were pressed and his white Nikes scuff-free.

She pulled a weak smile. 'Thanks. So, how do you know Tracey?'

'School. When she lived in Dublin. You?'

'University. In London. We shared a bedsit in Crouch End.'

'You're *that* electronic engineer?' Julian laughed.

'What's so funny?'

'Nothing. I mean, you know, she's told me a few stories. Like how you wired the windows to stop thieves and electrocuted the landlord.'

Emma shook her head. 'That's not entirely true. I made some adjustments to an existing system and that creep deserved the shock.'

'Sounds like I'd better behave myself then.'

'Always a good idea on a first date, Julian. Any date, really. So, tell me about yourself. What do you do?' Please be normal, she thought to herself.

'I'm an anthropologist.'

Emma was reasonably certain she'd caught the eye-roll in time.

'I work in an interdisciplinary research institute,' Julian continued. 'Technology and Society. I study how digital tech is built and used. My thesis examined the politics and praxes of a couple of start-up companies who were developing new apps.'

'The politics and praxes?' Emma sighed. Only Tracey would think a preppy anthropologist who saw politics everywhere as a suitable wedding date for her. She was an engineer. Creating an app was code and applied maths.

'You know, all the pressures shaping how a company operates – raising finance, legal compliance, relationships with investors, in-team relations, trying to create a new market. And how people work with each other and with technologies to design and build a product. All the choices and decisions made. The negotiations. What data they use. How it is processed. What they do with it.'

Emma took a sip of her cappuccino, sorry that she'd asked. This was her own fault. She should have just said she was going to the wedding on her own. But no, she didn't want to seem like Emma No-dates. She was just going to have to grin and bear it. At least her mother would be delighted if she turned up with a 'nice boy' like Julian.

'And you?' Julian enquired.

'I work on sound sensors.'

'Building them?'

'And testing them in the field. We're creating a sound sensing network for monitoring and modelling background noise across the city.'

'Okay, so now I know why Tracey thought we'd be a good match. You build tech, I study how tech is built. Voilà.'

'Voilà?' There was no voilà here, Emma thought. There is bleak acceptance of fate.

'I bet she thought that we might be able to work with each other. Or I could study your work. Or at least we'd have something to talk about.'

'So, I'd be your lab rat? I don't think so.'

'I'd be more interested in the processes and messiness of the science than studying you per se.'

'So you're saying I'm not interesting enough to study?'

'I'm not walking into that trap.'

'You already have. And there's nothing messy about what we do.'

'Well, I don't mean messy messy; I mean all the contingent intricacies that shape the tech you create and the data you produce.'

'Contingent intricacies?' Despite her intentions, Emma's heckles were now up. 'I forgot that they make everyone in the humanities swallow a dictionary. And we're collecting data, not producing it. And for the record, it's all rooted in established science, though we're pushing boundaries as well.'

'I'm sure you are,' Julian said, holding his palms up, 'but you're definitely producing data not collecting it. Data doesn't pre-exist their generation. Your sensors create them.'

'You're saying there's no sound to collect?'

'No, I'm saying there's no data. You create the data. Via your sound sensors.'

'But the sound is the data. It's an electromagnetic frequency.'

'Which you measure with a sensor and record as data entries. Probably in decibels, right?'

'Yes.'

'Which is a made-up scale. Invented by somebody.'

'Bell Labs. In 1924. Deci being a tenth of one bel; named in honour of Alexander Graham Bell.' For the first time in the conversation, Emma felt on safe land. 'It's a logarithmic scale: a change in power by a factor of ten corresponds to a ten dB change in level.'

'Right. So, sound does not pre-exist as decibels. You've assigned that unit to it and that's what you record in your database. If the scale was different it would be recorded differently.'

'But it would still be measuring the same thing.'

'Is it though?'

'Yes!'

'But would you always get the same readings?'

'Yes. We're practising science. It's rational, logical, objective. The whole system has been carefully set up to ensure we get the best readings.'

'But you've had to make choices and compromises, right? You've chosen which sensors to use. You've chosen how many they'll be, where they'll be and their scan rate.'

'But that's all been done rigorously. There was a lot of thought and planning involved to make sure we comply with EU guidelines on standards and placement.'

'But you'll have still made compromises. They'll have been cost constraints. Permissions needed for siting them. Logistical concerns. And those standards and guidelines have been created by committees through negotiation. How's it configured?'

Emma felt at sea again. This was never going to work. It was hopeless. They'd be stuck together at the wedding for hours. If she had to listen to this kind of nonsense all day she'd go mad. They'd end up like those seagulls fighting over scraps. As they were already doing.

'Humour me,' Julian cajoled.

She wanted to scream, 'I am.' Instead, she said, 'Fine. We have a network of 16 Sonitus EM2030 sensors that measure sound readings every five minutes, pinging the data back to our server via GSM.'

'Why every five minutes?'

'To save on the battery life and the network communication costs.'

'But you could do it more frequently?'

'Every second if we wanted. Though the data would also get noisier.'

'So there's noise in the data?'

'Yes, but we control for that using a smoothing algorithm.'

'In other words, you've compromised on the sampling rate and you transform the data to deal with residuals or errors. You're generating not collecting the data.'

'Jesus, Julian!' She'd finally reached her limit. 'This is your idea of a date?'

He didn't seem phased by her outburst. 'We're both researchers. We're discussing research. It's common ground.'

'You're trying to undermine my work.'

'No. No, I'm not. I'm not saying it's not good. It might be brilliant. And it's no doubt very useful. I'm making a point about scientific practice. At best, you're practising mechanical objectivity – trying to minimize biases, errors, calibration issues and so on – but it's still set up in your vision, based on your education and experience, and compromising for circumstance. You're still making choices that influence the outcome. The data isn't raw, it's cooked to your recipe, using instruments that you picked, which will have their own quirks.'

'Of course, but by your logic you can't get better than mechanical objectivity and we strive for that and the sensors we use are excellent.'

'But would every sensor produce the same results?'

'Any good one, yes.'

'They'd be no variances between them?'

'Maybe very minor differences, but nothing statistically significant.'

'And this would still be the case with cheaper sensors?'

'That's why it's important to use a decent sensor.'

'So the instrument makes a difference to the veracity of the data. Okay, so let's try a thought experiment.'

'Let's not. Look, I need to get going.' Emma finished most of her remaining coffee. She was just going to have to swallow her pride and go to her sister's wedding alone. This had been a bad idea from the start, especially letting Tracey set her up with an anthropologist. A preppy anthropologist who probably thought Joy Division was a branch of happy mathematics.

'Really?' Julian said, genuinely surprised. 'This is just getting interesting.'

'You think?'

'Yes. Absolutely. Okay, say we had a sound monitoring station in situ for 30 years. Every five years we updated it to the latest technology. For the first 20 years, the data are collected by hand. A person visits the station on the hour, views a needle that varies position with decibel level, and writes down a reading. For the last ten years, the process is automated, with the reading taken automatically and the data transmitted via a mobile phone network. Given that the instrument and method of recording changes over time is the data the same in nature? Is it equivalent in accuracy and quality?'

Despite her antipathy, Emma felt compelled to defend her work. 'Yes. Because they will have controlled for all the things you're insinuating.'

'I'm not insinuating anything. I'm …'

'Julian. Just drop it. The only person you're convincing with this nonsense is yourself. Sound exists. We measure it. Scientifically. With integrity.'

'That's what I've been saying. Except science is contingent and relational not essential and determined.' Julian leant back in his chair.

'Whatever the hell that means.'

'It means that decisions, equipment and context make a difference. You know, if this were a romcom we'd probably be making out right now.'

Emma rolled her eyes. 'If this were a romcom I'd be forced to ask you to be my date to my sister's wedding, where I'd stumble from one embarrassing scene to the next.'

'Well, I'd be delighted to be your date. This is the best conversation I've had in ages. Have you not felt a certain frisson in the air?'

'Frisson? No wonder most people in the academy see anthropology as a pseudoscience if that's how you interpret signals. And God knows how you even measure signals.'

'Well, that proves my point: data are sketchy and interpretation is in the eye of the beholder.'

'The data were clear,' Emma said, standing. 'You tried to mansplain – incorrectly – my own discipline and research practices to me. I've no idea what Tracey was thinking … what I was thinking. This hasn't been so much a blind date as blind data!'

'So you don't want me to be your date at the wedding?'

Emma headed for the door, then stopped. What would be worse: the shame of no date, or the date from hell? Was that an experiment she really wanted to conduct? She glanced back and sighed. No way was this going to turn into a romcom. Murder without the mystery perhaps.

3

The Nature of Data

The divergent positions of Emma and Julian in the previous chapter are illustrative of the different ways in which data are conceptualized within the academy. For Emma, data are straightforwardly raw pieces of information about the world, which she collects through her sound sensors. Sounds pre-exist their capture, and her measurements are directly representative of audible electromagnetic frequencies present in the atmosphere. In this sense, data seem unproblematic and commonsensical. They are benign, objective and non-ideological in character, reflecting the world as it is subject to technical constraints; they are raw measures that exist independent of philosophical thought. It is the job of the scientist – or government bureaucrat or business process controller – to collect and record data using suitable instruments and processes, and to use them to make sense of, and act in, the world. There is no politics or other agenda at play and the data collected can be taken at face value. The sensor simply measures sound, where the phenomenon measured is independent of the measuring process. By following established procedures and acting rigorously, high-quality data are captured.

Emma does not deny that there can be issues with integrity in data collection, but believes it is the job of the scientist to find the best, most representative way of capturing data, and to develop and apply techniques to effectively nullify any noise, errors or gaps in the dataset. In this way, the validity (represents what it is supposed to), veracity (accuracy and precision), and reliability (consistency over time) of the data, and any analysis undertaken using then, can be assured. In other words, for Emma, it is only the uses of data that are political, not the data themselves or the science used to collect and analyze them. This is reflected in the technical terms used by scientists to describe their data processes: 'collected', 'entered', 'compiled', 'stored', 'processed' and 'mined'.[1]

Julian has a fundamentally different view. He understands data as being produced not collected. Data do not pre-exist their generation, but are created through the process of conducting science. Decisions by scientists concerning the general methodological approach, specific techniques, instruments and their calibration, sampling frames and so on, make a difference to what data are manufactured. While the scientist can seek to be rigorous, exact and objective, acting with integrity, nonetheless there are choices and compromises made shaped by resourcing, practicalities, regulatory/legal requirements and differences of opinion. And there are intrinsic politics at play in terms of how a project is framed and contextualized with respect to how it seeks to advance a field and the questions it aims to answer. After all, the same phenomena can be measured and recorded in numerous ways, for different ends, each approach providing a different set of data that can be analyzed and interpreted through varying means.[2] Once data are generated they are processed and transformed by practices of data cleaning and wrangling designed to deal with any noise, errors or gaps and to render them into a form suitable for any analysis. As such, for Julian, data are always cooked to some recipe.[3]

This cooking – as with in a kitchen – does not always follow the recipe exactly or produce a dish that matches what is in the cookbook. This is because it takes place within and is shaped by a wider socio-technical context.[4] This context includes the system of thought, forms of knowledge, learned behaviours and scientific conventions that have influenced a researcher's approach to an issue (what they have been taught, how they have been trained, what they have read and heard and their experience). But also the form of funding that might drive a particular focus or agenda (research grants, government contracts, venture capital, philanthropy); the need to comply with laws, licencing regulations, standards and protocols, and intellectual property regimes; access to equipment, materials, space and suitable personnel; negotiating differences of opinion within teams and across collaborative stakeholders; and if the data is underpinning economic enterprise, marketplace conditions and expectations. For Julian, data form the heart of a data assemblage[5] that is contingent, relational and contextual in how it operates. That is, there is nothing fixed or sacred with respect to data and science. Rather how data are manufactured and used to make knowledge is mutable and political, shaped by praxes and choices that are influenced by a range of factors (that themselves mutate over time as new ideas and knowledges emerge, technologies are invented, organizations change, business models are created, the political economy changes, regulations and laws are introduced and repealed, skill sets develop, debates take place and markets grow or shrink). In other words, the cooking of data does not take place in a vacuum or highly controlled environment, as Emma believes.

My own position is closer to Julian than Emma's. I do believe there is a world that exists outside of our conception of it. There is sound, and light, and atoms and molecules, landscapes, people, wildlife, objects, movement and so on, and these exist independently of measurement. In this sense, I'm a realist that believes that if a tree falls in a forest and no one is around to hear it, it does make a sound.[6] However, I also believe that phenomena do not possess ontological security; that is, they do not possess fixed, inviolate natures. Thus, what is understood as constituting sound, or a tree, or a forest is not intrinsically and universally agreed upon. Indeed, there are varying definitions of each of these, which have evolved over time through new thinking and debate.[7]

The same is true of data. What is understood to constitute data has changed with the passage of time. In fact, the word 'data' was first used in the English language as late as the 17th century to refer to anything widely accepted as given, granted, or generally known.[8] Interestingly, the term was inverted from its etymological roots. Data is derived from the Latin *dare*, meaning 'to give'. Data are that which can be abstracted and measured in some way. In general use, however, data refers to those elements that are taken. Technically, what is understood to be data are actually capta (derived from the Latin *capere*, meaning 'to take'); those units of data that have been selected and harvested from the sum of all potential data. As such, this book would be more appropriately titled '*Capta Lives*'. However, trying to get everyone on the planet to switch terms when 'data' is so thoroughly embedded in our lexicon is not a battle worth fighting. In the 18th century the definition and use of data shifted with the rise of modernity and growth and evolution of science, and the move from information and argument embedded in theology, exhortation and sentiment to facts, evidence, experimentation and discovery.[9]

It is no coincidence that the use of the word 'data' emerged during the Renaissance. At this time, there was a flourishing of scientific innovation with respect to philosophy, equipment and analysis that led to new discoveries and theories across the academy and new inventions in business, and transformed the world (leading to colonial expansion, new business and trade, and modern systems of bureaucracy). Forms of statistical analysis started to be developed. For example, the French philosopher René Descartes (1596–1650) developed a rectangular coordinate system to visualize and graph observations. William Playfair (1759–1823), an engineer and economist from Scotland, created a suite of data visualizations that are still commonly used today. A range of new statistical map techniques, such as thematic choropleth and isoline maps were developed in the 19th century. Over time, science evolved as new epistemological positions developed that set out how best to investigate the world.

In the 18th and 19th centuries, the use of the term 'data' extended from mathematics and natural philosophy to economics and administration. During this period, data are generally considered to be pre-factual and pre-analytical in nature; that which exists prior to argument or interpretation.[10] In the 20th century, data came to mean any information stored and used in the context of computing (data are input for coded algorithms), and its uses multiplied beyond science and administration.[11] As information philosopher, Luciano Floridi[12] notes: from an epistemic position, data are collections of facts that provide the basis for further reasoning or constitute empirical evidence; from an informational position, data are information that can be stored, processed and analyzed; and from a computational position, data are collections of binary elements that form the inputs and outputs of computation. In other words, data cannot be treated in a straightforward, non-philosophical way, because they are intrinsically understood and treated differently by scholars (as with Emma and Julian).

Beyond how we understand what data are, and returning to the example of a tree falling in the woods, like Julian, I believe that capturing the sound and the trajectory of the fall as data is not straightforward. The process by which we create data, extract information and produce knowledge is constructed, not simply observed. They are shaped by education and convention, and mutate over time. Established wisdom on practising science is not the same now as it was in the past: new ideas, instruments, techniques, methods, approaches, concepts and theories emerge that change how we frame scholarship and measure, handle, analyze and interpret data.

Jim Gray[13] argues that there have been four dominant scientific paradigms (generally agreed conventions and theories shared by scientists[14]) centred on epistemological approaches (ways of making sense of the world). The first of these he terms experimental science, which existed pre-Renaissance and tended to describe natural phenomena through an empiricist (weight of evidence) approach. The second was theoretical science, which was dominant throughout the Renaissance until the mid-20th century. Here, experimentation was used to test and derive theories in order to explain not just describe the world. Computational science, which seeks to simulate and model complex phenomena developed with the digital age. Here, the data employed might be synthetic, simulated and derived through modelling processes that extrapolate from base 'raw' data, for example in scenario building in weather and climate change forecasts, or predicting traffic patterns. Gray's most recently identified paradigm is exploratory science, a data-driven rather than question-driven approach to research.

Most academic scholars conceive of exploratory science as retaining core elements of an experimental approach, but it differs due to an initial step that seeks to generate hypotheses and insights 'born from the data' rather than 'born from the theory'.[15] It does this by using new forms of data analytics, including machine learning (a form of artificial intelligence), to mine data and identify patterns, associations and relationships that might be worth exploring in more detail. The process is guided in the sense that existing theory is used to direct the process of knowledge discovery rather than simply hoping that all relationships found within a dataset are meaningful in some way. Further attention, using the conventional hypothesis testing of the experimental approach, is then focused on those relationships that seemingly offer the most likely or valid way forward.

In contrast, some data scientists and business practitioners practise a form of exploratory science that is more rooted in empiricism. In this case, there is a belief that in the age of machine learning and big data (massive volumes of real-time data) data can speak for themselves free of theory. There is no need to interrogate datasets with particular techniques, or within specific theoretical context, in order to answer specific questions. Rather, multiple techniques can be applied to datasets to discover patterns that would not be identified with conventional approaches. Algorithms will spot patterns and generate new theories unguided by previous studies.[16] Such an approach has been used in marketing and retail where companies now have billions of records of purchases and online store searches. In one study, a supermarket chain analyzed 12 years' worth of purchase transactions for possible unnoticed relationships between products that ended up in shoppers' baskets.[17] Discovering correlations between certain items led to new product placements and alterations to the organization of shelf space and led to a 16 per cent increase in revenue per shopping cart. There was no hypothesis that Product A was often bought with Product B that was then tested. The data were simply queried to discover what relationships existed that might have previously been unnoticed. Proponents argue that this open, rather than directed, approach to discovery is more likely to reveal unknown, underlying patterns free of the constrictions and group think of established scientific practice and knowledge.

What this discussion reveals is that not only is data manufactured, but the approach to and process of manufacturing has changed over time. There are presently a number of different epistemologies employed in science in order to generate evidence and makes sense of the world. Moreover, it is clear that there are different ways to think about data themselves. Indeed, while we have so far mainly considered data from a philosophical, technical and etymological point of view, we can also think about them from ethical, political, economic, geographical and historical positions.

Data can concern all aspects of everyday life, including personal and sensitive issues, and they can be used in all kinds of ways, including discriminating against and persecuting people. Given the explosion in data generation and use in recent years, there are a series of ongoing debates and initiatives related to how data are produced, shared, traded and protected; how data should be governed by rules, principles, policies, licences and laws; and under what circumstances and to what ends data can be employed.[18]

Data are framed by political concerns related to how they are normatively conceived and contested as public and private goods. The open data and open government movements, for example, cast data as a public commons that should be freely accessible for anyone to access and use.[19] Business, in contrast, views data as a valuable commodity that, on the one hand, needs to be protected through intellectual property regimes (copyright, patents, ownership rights) and, on the other, should be exploitable for capital gain.[20] Data are a commodity that can be used by companies to reshape operating procedures and organizational structure, identify new products, segment markets, reduce uncertainty and risk, and increase efficiency, productivity, competitiveness and sustainability.[21] The ethics, politics and economics of data vary across jurisdictions and mutate over time.

Data then are manufactured in a context, form the heart of data assemblages, and they have a life cycle. They are made, processed, transformed, stored, analyzed, shared, circulated and destroyed. Data are cleaned, wrangled and transformed (converting from one form or format to another). Derived data are produced from other data – through generalization (aggregation, abstraction, sampling, categorization), calculation (statistical output, standardization) and combination (linking, merging). Metadata – data about data – are created to enable others to understand their characteristics and how they were manufactured. Data are stored on various media (paper, magnetic tapes, hard disks) in various forms (files, tables, lists, databases), and can be preserved in archives and specialized data infrastructures. Data circulate across networks and institutions (where they can be transformed into derived data, which also then circulate, and be used for diverse purposes). In fact, digital networks pulsate with data flows, as illustrated in the next chapter which explores how a data-driven traffic management system works, and occasionally go a little haywire. In this system, as with others, insight, information and value is extracted from data through many different forms of analysis. Mistakes and fudges are made, errors overlooked and poor decisions taken in all these activities. And data are deleted because there is a legal mandate to do so, or they have outlived their utility, or they are too costly to process or store, or simply by accident. The data life cycle is imbued with various praxes, choices and politics, framed within a socio-technical context.

4

Gridlock

Walter wasn't sure of the reason, but there was definitely something odd happening. Congestion in the north of the city had started to build half an hour earlier than usual and was also heavier. Numerous junctions had become bottlenecks and long tailbacks were growing everywhere like coral tentacles.

He glanced up at the wall of screens at the front of the control room, each showing a live camera feed of a different junction. All of them were clogged. Around him, his fellow controllers were busy at their desks, each surrounded by three screens, in their hands a console with a joystick and number keypad.

Each morning was a battle to keep the traffic flowing. Usually the control room didn't do too badly given the legacy road infrastructure – a medieval core, primary roads following old horse-and-coach routes, and inner suburbs laid out before mass car transit – and that four times as many vehicles than ideal were trying to traverse the network. But today they were losing the fight. Or at least, the traffic management system was.

'Walter,' his supervisor called, 'look at camera 153!'

He tapped in the number bringing up the video feed on his left-hand screen. The junction was at a total standstill.

'Do you see the black Merc,' the supervisor said, 'heading south, its nose in the yellow junction box? That's the Dutch Prime Minister's car. He's meant to be giving the opening address at the European Commission's meeting in the Mansion House in 30 minutes' time. Somehow he's got separated from his police escort. They're stuck at the next junction.'

'Yeah, I can see him.'

'I need you to get him back to his escort then green-light them through the centre of town.'

'I don't know if that's going to be possible,' Walter said, toggling quickly between cameras located at several nearby junctions. 'It's chaos all around him.'

'I don't care how you do it, Walter, just make it happen.'

'I'll do my best, but …' He didn't finish the sentence, already lost in the task.

Whatever the problem was it probably lay with Travista, the traffic control system, which would almost certainly be the answer as well.

Seemingly muttering to himself, but actually chatting to Travista, Walter scanned through the lane flows and traffic light settings in the junctions surrounding the one that had trapped the Dutch Prime Minister.

'What are you up to, Travi?'

Walter liked to think of Travista as sentient. Not alive as such, but knowing and omnipresent.

Simultaneously, she knew what was happening with traffic across the entire city. Instantaneously and continuously, she gathered and processed thousands of data points from inductive loops embedded in the surface of the road, cameras and radar scanners mounted on poles, and transponders fixed on buses, pinging them in packets across a dedicated intranet to a central server. There, the packets were re-joined and fed into a database, more valuable derived data produced, and raw and transitory data deleted.

And she had recognizable thought patterns: logic and rules that directed reactions to unfolding situations. She imported the derived data and used them to calculate how best to optimize traffic flow and balance competing demands by synchronizing the timing of signal cycles and phases of the traffic lights at three levels: a single intersection, a subsystem and across the entire system, where a subsystem was a group of closely related junctions sited around at least one critical intersection. At the same time, it was possible to converse with her; to suggest alternatives and tweak how she functioned.

In real-time, she actively shaped the progress and routes of hundreds of thousands of people in cars and buses as they made their way to and from work and school. Or, in the present case, sit motionless.

Walter turned to his left-hand screen, flipping through a sequence of camera feeds.

'How did you let this happen, eh? There has to be a critical accident neither of us can see. Or you've made a hash of the phasing somehow.'

He turned his attention to the right-hand screen and the readings for the surrounding subsystems.

'Maybe it's just a volume issue? Is that it? It didn't matter what you tried to do, you were overrun? But still … this phasing and cycle sequence is a … very odd choice.'

Like every sentient being, Travista occasionally got confused or overwhelmed. Which was what Walter was reasonably certain had happened that morning. Her calibration settings had encountered a novel scenario and been uncertain how best to react. The result was several subsystems becoming overloaded with traffic causing system-wide congestion.

'Travi, Travi.' Walter scratched his head. 'Whatever it is you're trying to do might work eventually. … Or not.'

'Well?' Walter's supervisor said, standing at his shoulder.

'It's a mess,' Walter replied, continuing to shuffle through junctions. 'I'm not sure what's she's up to. Even the bus lanes are blocked.'

'But you can get him there?'

'I can try, but it's going to take a while and it'll mean manually controlling the cycles and phasing in the area.'

Walter was conscious that while he might be able to untangle the knot by intervening, he'd be working against Travista's calibrations across all three levels, which would likely cause knots elsewhere to tighten further. And there'd be no going back. Any additional chaos would just have to work its way out over the next couple of hours.

'That's fine. You've got 20 minutes.'

'Twenty minutes! Is there any chance of getting the police on the ground there? It'll be easier to thread that one vehicle through than getting a whole lane moving.'

'How are they going to get there?'

'I don't know. Send a motorcycle, maybe?'

'I'll see what I can do.' The supervisor started to move towards his cubbyhole at the side of the room.

'And George?' Walter said, without looking up.

'Yeah?'

'I'm going need Janice to help.'

'I'm already up to my eyes,' Janice said. 'It's like every person in the north of the city has decided to drive to work today. It's a giant car park out there.'

'Help Walter, Janice. Apparently it's super-important this guy arrives on time.'

'Seriously? We're going to re-organize the city's traffic around one politician?'

'Janice, just do it. This has come from on high. It's just the usual routine for anyone with a police escort with bells on.'

'Okay, but this is a crazy thing to be doing right now. So, Walter, what's your plan?'

'We find an open channel we can direct traffic into and then work back along the subsystems to the Prime Minister's car.'

'We can use the interactive road signs to flag up the diversion,' Janice added. 'Also radio and social media.' She jerked a thumb over her shoulder. At the rear of the room were three traffic journalists who fed regular live updates to local and national radio stations and also posted them out via Twitter and Facebook.

'Good idea. I'll take south and east if you take south and west. See if we can find a candidate junction.'

Walter started to scan across junctions and subsystems viewing derived data from three sources: inductive loops that showed the number of vehicles passing through a junction by direction and lane and the temporal spacing between them; camera feeds from which machine vision algorithms extracted vehicle movement and also their type; and a smaller number of radar scanners that performed the same role.

Hopefully, these data would flag up a nearby intersection where at least some traffic was managing to pass through.

'Come on, Travi,' Walter muttered. 'There has to be somewhere not yet gridlocked. Any luck, Janice?'

'No. It's a disaster everywhere. You?'

'Not yet, but the bus lane frees up two intersections ahead of him.'

Walter opened up the bus map, which showed the location and progress of each of the buses active in the city, tracked using transponders. If needed he could contact any of the bus drivers to ask what was happening on parts of the road network out of camera view.

'It blocks again in the next subsystem down,' Janice said, 'but not if we direct the traffic left.'

'And after that?'

'It's free for two more subsystems.'

'And the diverted traffic will still be able to loop back to head south again?'

'I guess? Maybe check the model?'

Walter opened up their morning heavy congestion traffic model produced using automatic number plate recognition data which showed route flows and speed of movement compiled by scanning and tracking licence plates as vehicles passed through the network of cameras. Zooming in on the candidate junction and potential bus lane, he examined the pattern of flow. While not ideal, traffic would be able to turn right at three downstream junctions to get back on track.

'It's possible. But the bus lane might become a car park.'

'Well, they can be in a car park there, or where they are now.'

'Okay,' Walter said. 'I'm going to change the phasing and cycles to feed the bus lane traffic left and free up that laneway back to our Flying Dutchman. Can you manage all other movement back along and off the route?'

'I can, but Travista isn't going to like it.'

'No, she won't,' Walter said.

While they were overriding one part of the system, Travi would still be calculating and controlling the phasing and cycles across the rest of the city.

Within a couple of minutes, through a lot of chatter and coordination, Walter and Janice had got the traffic moving along the desired route. Eight minutes later the free flow had finally worked its way back to the Dutch Prime Minister's car, which slowly started to crawl forward.

'This is Houston, you are cleared for take-off,' Janice said loudly.

'Thanks, Janice,' Walter said, holding up a hand for a high five he knew wouldn't arrive since his colleague's attention was still glued to her screens.

'Well done, guys,' George called from his cubbyhole. 'Walter, keep clearing a path for him.'

'Once he gets to his escort they should be able use their lights and siren to do the rest.'

'Still, keep an eye on it. Janice, pick a knot, any knot, and start to unpick it!'

'You're not going to believe this,' Walter said, leaning back in his chair, stretching to ease out the gnarled ropes in his shoulders.

'What now?' George said, heading for Walter's desk.

'The traffic lights on Telegraph Road have just gone down.'

'What! That can't be right. Have we been hacked?'

'I don't know. I think she's just having a really bad day.'

'Who?'

'Travi. The data's all corrupted, or she can't think straight.'

'It's not a she, Walter, it's an it. And it's definitely not coping right now. What's he doing now?' George leant over Walter's shoulder and pointed at the screen.

A man had stepped out of the Merc and was hurrying to the pavement.

'It looks like he's going to hoof it the rest of the way.'

'He's heading for the bike station,' Walter said.

'He's going to cycle there?'

'He's Dutch. If this was Amsterdam he'd have probably cycled in any case. And he could just make it. Or at least only be a couple of minutes late.'

They watched the man swing a leg over the bike and set off along the pavement.

'Well, I'll be …' George stood up straight and clapped his hands. 'Okay, folks, let's try and get Travista thinking straight again and everyone else moving. And Walter, make sure a repair team has those traffic lights working within the hour. What a morning!'

5

In Data We Trust

In October 2012 the Property Services Regulatory Authority (PSRA) in Ireland launched the Residential Property Price Register (RPPR). Up until this point, there had been no official government dataset of individual residential property sales prices across the country. The lack of such data was a significant gap in housing information and the launch was welcome, even if it was happening several years too late. In 2012, Ireland was nearing the bottom of a massive housing crash. House prices were down over 50 per cent, and apartment prices by over 60 per cent, from their height in 2007.[1] House building had dropped from 88,000 new units in 2006 to a few thousand.[2] The RPPR tracked all residential property sales from 2010 onwards, giving address, date of sale and price, though missing other useful information such as property type, floor size or number of bedrooms.

Along with one of my colleagues, Eoghan McCarthy, I started to examine the dataset keen to see the geographic pattern of prices.[3] It quickly became clear that there were some issues with the data. Within half an hour of its release, Eoghan had already found over 200 suspected errors in the data. Most were identified by simply sorting the data by price value. For example, a semi-detached house in Limerick City was recorded as selling for €18m in 2010.[4] Our assumption given the property type and location was that two additional noughts had been added to €180,000, or a decimal point had been omitted. The other end of the sorted spreadsheet showed that some houses in very desirable parts of Dublin had sold for just a few thousand euro rather than hundreds of thousands. In other cases, multiple transactions had been lumped together. For example, one transaction of €4.5m was for 30 apartments. It would have been more appropriate to record 30 entries of €150k given that all the other transactions were sales of individual properties. Ronan Lyons, a real-estate economist working with a property company (Daft.ie) spotted the same errors and when he and his colleagues compared the dataset to their nationwide sales dataset they ended up removing 7.7 per cent of properties where there was a significant difference between the sale price as advertised and recorded.[5] Eoghan also had a go at mapping all the properties, but this proved difficult because the PSRA had not used Geodirectory, the national address database, to clean, standardize and geocode their address format. Instead, there was a variety of address formatting and many spelling mistakes. Attempting to match PSRA addresses with Geodirectory for Dublin only produced a 60 per cent match (and it was much worse for rural areas that do not have house numbers or street names).[6]

Used to working with and advising government departments and agencies on data issues we contacted the PSRA to point out the initial errors we'd discovered. We thought if they reacted quickly, they could pull the dataset, fix the most obviously glaring mistakes and then re-release it an hour or so later, thus minimizing any loss in confidence in the data. This is what the Department of Environment, Heritage and Local Government (DEHLG) had done the previous year when we'd spotted errors in the National Unfinished Housing Survey – the dataset was pulled 45 minutes after release, the errors we'd flagged corrected, then re-released shortly afterwards. Similarly, in the hours leading up to the 2011 Census being launched, Eoghan and his AIRO colleagues in their role as the visualization/mapping partner with the Irish Central Statistics Office (CSO), spotted errors in the census tables, which were then quickly fixed by CSO staff before publication the following morning.[7] In the case of the RPPR however, the PSRA thanked us for our feedback but declined to make any corrections as the integrity of the dataset was the responsibility of a third party (The Revenue Commissioners).[8] The consequence is that errors persist for some time and some may never be corrected.

This is not the only case of data errors we have spotted in official datasets failing to be addressed. For example, in a study examining travel to work patterns in Ireland, my colleague on the Dublin Dashboard project, Gavin McArdle, spotted thousands of illogical travel times.[9] By calculating distance between home and work address and then comparing with journey time, the analysis showed that a great many people were apparently travelling to work at above 120km per hour (the road speed limit). In fact, a couple of thousand were apparently travelling at above 1,000km per hour, some above 4,000km per hour. Our conclusion was that some people were residing in a different place to 'home' during the week and this was creating many of the errors (along with administrative errors). For example, my home is 80 miles from the university where I work, but I do not commute every day. Instead, during the week I live locally to the university. It takes me one hour 50 minutes to drive from home, and eight minutes from the local residence to get to work. If home and work-based residences are confused then errors are introduced into the dataset. We pointed this out to the CSO and they declined to make corrections, most probably due to size of the task and the limited number of users of the dataset, all of whom have the data skills to screen out such data.[10]

Similarly, we pointed out errors in the TRIPS database released through Dublinked (Dublin's open data portal) to Dublin City Council (DCC).[11] TRIPS provides road speed times, but has a number of errors in the database; for example, the inclusion of a false road segment that reduces a 6km journey to half a minute. Likewise, we reported errors regarding the coordinates of traffic sensors, which when mapped were out of position by 100 metres or more. While the engineers were responsive and conducted their own analysis on the dataset, no solution was found and it remained flawed. In all these cases, we had to try and fix the data ourselves. Indeed, data wrangling – checking, fixing, transforming and re-structuring data to deal with errors and make datasets more amenable to other processing and analysis – is a critical skill for all researchers handling complex or flawed datasets. Our solutions stayed local to us, meaning that others working with the datasets had to find their own fixes.

In other cases, it can take a bit of time and negotiation to get corrections made. A colleague working on the Building City Dashboard project, Oliver Dawkins, had spotted errors in a boundary dataset provided by Ordnance Survey Ireland (OSI), which had omitted former town boroughs from local authority boundaries. Customer services denied there were errors, despite repeated attempts to explain the issue. After a couple of months, an email to the OSI director got the file corrected. Repeated claims by housing specialists that there were issues with Irish housing completions data took years to get resolved. In the absence of a formal survey, new electricity connections are used to identify newly built properties. However, if a property did not sell and was disconnected, and was subsequently reconnected, it could be double counted as a new property. In the end, a review of the methodology used to generate the data was conducted by the CSO, concluding that the critics had been right to question the veracity of the data,[12] with new dwelling completions overstated by nearly 60 per cent.[13] As a result, a new methodology for determining the number of new dwellings was created and the figures corrected from 2018 back to 2011.[14]

At times, trust in data can be so thoroughly undermined that its status is downgraded to 'fairy tales'. This is what happened to crime and police statistics in Ireland in 2014. There are a number of issues with Irish crime data, such as crimes being recorded in relation to the police stations that handle them, rather than the location they are committed (with some stations specializing in some crimes, such as murders). As a result, when mapped the geographic patterns can give false impression of the distribution of crimes. There are also issues in the standardization of crime categorization, with some police officers recording the same crimes in slightly different ways, and also in timeliness of recording. And there are difficulties of retrieving data from the crime management software system, which is designed to manage individual cases and to limit file access to selected personnel and is not configured to create aggregated statistics. Such was the concern over data quality[15] that in 2014 recorded crime statistics data were suspended and placed under review by the CSO.[16] Since 2015 the data have been published with the guidance *'Statistics Under Reservation'*, with the CSO working with An Garda Síochána (the Irish police force) to improve data recording and statistics production (the statistics were suspended again briefly in 2017 due to issues with homicide data).[17]

In addition, there are suspicions of falsification of some data. For example, in a high-profile example, An Garda Síochána revised the number of breathalyser tests performed between 2012 and 2016 down from two million to approximately half a million.[18] While part of the discrepancy between claims and reality was administrative error and careless data recording, it's also clear that there was deliberate inflation of the numbers to make it appear that more was being done to tackle road safety. It is going to take some time for trust to be rebuilt with respect to Irish crime and police data, and even then their utility for certain kinds of analysis such as mapping will continue to be limited.

In addition to errors, every dataset has issues of representativeness – that is, the extent to which the data faithfully represents that which it seeks to measure. In generating data, processes of extraction, abstraction, generalization and sampling can introduce measurement error, noise, imprecision and bias. What instruments are used (for example, sensors or survey questions), what their settings and parameters are, and how they are deployed can influence the data recorded.[19] While some datasets might have very large sample sizes, such as everyone who shops in Walmart or uses Twitter, these do not include everybody. Indeed, neither are representative of wider demographics.[20] Not everyone shops in Walmart, and those that do are not drawn evenly from across the socio-economic spectrum. Very few people over the age of 65 are on Twitter. Moreover, there are hundreds of thousands of fake Twitter accounts producing tweets that seek to influence opinion and direct traffic to other sites. Even the accounts of genuine Twitter users are curated by them to try to create a particular impression, rather than forming a transparent window into their thoughts, values and opinions. How data are calibrated and classified can introduce ecological fallacies (false conclusions) in data analysis. Some phenomena can be difficult to measure because they are intangible in nature or not directly observable and indirect proxies are used instead. For example, we might use the number of patents filed as a proxy for innovation. In other cases, the cost of generating data might be too expensive, so a pre-existing or cheaper surrogate is chosen instead. For example, we might want to undertake a household survey about poverty, but due to the cost of administering the research a selection of related census variables is used instead. In addition, what data are generated are shaped by external factors, such as the regulatory environment with respect to privacy, data protection and security, which might limit what data are generated, how they are treated, analyzed, stored and shared.

These issues and experiences have taught me to be cautious with respect to data quality and fitness for use. Yet internationally there has been much work expended on formulating data quality guidelines and standards, trying to get those generating and sharing data to adhere to them,[21] and promoting the importance of reporting this information to users. Typically, data quality measures include veracity (accuracy and precision), completeness (sampling frame and extent of missing values), validity (represent what they are meant to measure), timeliness (are not out of date and are regularly sampled), coverage (the extent of that which is being measured), accessibility (access rights and openness), lineage (history of the data including method of generation and processing) and provenance (who created the data).[22] These measures should be provided to users in associated metadata to enable them to assess the suitability of the data for their intended analysis, to formulate any wrangling work, and to contextualize any interpretation or use of the data.

Some agencies are much better than others at adhering to guidelines and standards and ensuring high-quality data. This is especially the case with those dealing with personal and financial data where mistakes are more likely to be noticed by those they affect and can be costly (for example, health, welfare, taxation, education, banking and shares), and for agencies that specialize in data generation and management which might be audited by others, such as supra-national agencies and standards organizations. These bodies (for example, national statistics organizations, national mapping bodies, environmental protection agencies (EPAs)) employ data specialists, they have established data methodologies and practices, including quality review, and public trust and confidence is usually very close to the top of their risk register. In other cases, agencies have become lax or never had good data practices to begin with. They might contribute a limited amount of data into official statistics, or their data is less personal in nature or less critical to their core business, or they lack specialized staff, or they are simply more sloppy in their work and do not place special value on maintaining high-quality data.

Despite the drive to improve data quality by organizations, the open data they make available often have no guarantees or information about their veracity, continuity or lineage.[23] Portals typically do not report enough metadata to enable consumers to make a reliable judgement regarding data quality. In a review in 2016 of the open data portals of London,[24] Paris[25] and Dublin,[26] and the World Council of City Data (which reports data for 253 cities in 80 countries)[27] myself and Gavin McArdle found neither general nor specific measures of data quality reported beyond some details on data lineage, such as details of the data provider and date generated.[28] Instead, users are asked to trust that the data are valid, comply with established data standards, and any subsequent analysis or decisions made on the basis of the data are robust.

In a study in 2019, myself and Sam Stehle examined the data quality of 16 sources of real-time transportation and environmental datasets we were using in the Dublin and Cork Dashboards, nearly all of which were available through open APIs.[29] Our aim was to assess whether the data would be suitable for creating new official statistics. The data streams were bus locations, real-time passenger information provided at bus/tram stops and railway stations, road travel time, inductive loop counters, free car park spaces, flight locations, flight arrivals/departures, maritime boat locations, bikeshare, CCTV cameras, sound levels, air quality, pollution levels, tide level, river level and weather. Given we had very little metadata for any of the sources, we assessed the data by playing with them, hunting round websites for information and talking directly to data providers. For each dataset, we assessed it with regards to 15 measures: access, spatial and temporal granularity, spatial coverage, methodological soundness, measurement validity, fidelity, cleanliness, consistency, completeness, metadata availability, provenance, privacy, permanence, relevance and credibility. We rated each of these as 'good', 'fair', 'poor' or 'not ready'. 'Fair' denoted that the dataset had an issue that users were made aware of and were able to fix. 'Not ready' indicated an issue that could only be solved by data providers. Only the weather data was rated as 'good' across all 15 measures. There were relatively few instances of 'poor', but lots of the datasets had a smattering of 'fair' and 'not ready' ratings. We concluded that while the data might be good enough for the job for which they are employed, one would be cautious about using them as the basis for official statistics.

The fact that myself and my colleagues continually struggle to discover such information and have to extensively practice data wrangling has made it clear to us that there is still a long way to go to improve data quality and its reporting. This is somewhat of a worry in a data-driven world. How much analysis is suspect or faulty due to flaws or biases in datasets? How much scientific and policy interpretation is invalid? How many decisions are being made sub-optimally or on false pretences? In our social science research using secondary datasets we're left with no choice but to use what data is available, wrangling them as best as we can. While the old maxim 'garbage in, garbage out' holds, we work on the premise that datasets are good enough for the purpose for which we are using them. We cannot be 100 per cent certain of this, but judge this on the basis of our experience of working with data supplied by different agencies, and working directly with the agencies on projects. In general, we find there is a strong degree of integrity in data production, despite some of the flaws I've discussed. Those flaws, though, means it pays to always be cautious, to thoroughly assess datasets prior to use and to wrangle them where necessary. The cost of poor data practices is explored in the next chapter, where a spreadsheet error literally wiped €3.6 billion euros from Ireland's national accounts.

6

How to Lose (and Regain) 3.6 Billion Euros

The Assistant Secretary couldn't help feeling like a schoolboy every time he entered the General Secretary's office. The man was perfectly polite, but in a way that made it clear where power resided. And one didn't get to be head of the Department of Finance without knowing how to protect one's position or the most effective way to stick a knife into a colleague. Arguably it was the most powerful post in the civil service, controlling the purse strings for every cent of public sector spend in the country.

The great man had made a show of staring at the spreadsheet. Now he slowly raised his gaze. 'Three point six *billion* euros?'[1]

'That's correct,' the Assistant Secretary confirmed, resisting the temptation to look away.

'You're telling me, Peter, that the Department – *our* department, lost three point six billion euros?'

'Well, gained it really. We double counted it.' Even to his own ears his repost sounded weak.

'Except it was debt. So, we double counted the debt. We doubled how much we owe.'

'Yes.' Peter tried to inject a bit of positivity into his voice. 'But by finding it, we reduce government debt by 2.3 per cent.'

He really wanted to run a finger round his collar. This whole mess could be career-ending. Right at the point where the Gen Sec in Agriculture would soon be retiring. The vacant post would be the perfect opportunity to step up to the top table. Besides, the buck should stop with his boss; he was ultimately responsible for everything that happened within the Department.

'Two point three per cent. God, Peter, that's huge.' The General Secretary's frown deepened. 'And all because of a spreadsheet error by a staff member in *your* division?'

Peter inwardly cursed. The old bastard.

'It was a relatively simple mistake to make. The accountant wasn't sure how to classify a loan to the HFA from the NTMA. They'd assumed that it might be adjusted for elsewhere in the GGD calculations. It wasn't. So it appears twice in the national accounts, once as an asset for the NTMA and once as a liability for the HFA.'

'A data entry error then,' the General Secretary conceded. 'Why wasn't it picked up by their line manager? How come it never worked its way up to *you*?'

And there was the knife. Slid delicately between ribs.

'I'm … we're not sure. The person responsible sent an email to their supervisor on 23 August last year, and another on 1 September before they went on holiday, but it appears they never got a response.'

'This happened a year ago and it's just being dealt with now?'

'Well, we …'

'And I'm just finding out?'

The Assistant Secretary had hoped that he could sort the mess out and quietly brush it under the table. There was fat chance of that now. And the stakes were high: someone was going to have to take the blame and be thrown under the bus. He decided to tackle the question he'd started to answer.

'Well, there was some correspondence with NTMA and HFA, and with the CSO – they have a statistician seconded into the Department – but somehow it got passed over.'

'Passed over?' The General Secretary arched his eyebrows.

'Everybody assumed that somebody else had dealt with it. The accounts got returned, nobody spotted the mistake and everyone moved onto to other tasks. The change in the relationship between the HFA and NTMA confused things, I think. Rather than the NTMA acting as an agent for the HFA, it shifted to loaning directly to it. Plus, it was a crazy time. We were preparing for the bailout. We were all up to our eyes in ledgers, spreadsheets and forecasts.'

'Do you think the press or the public will care about how busy we were? The country's bust – don't quote me on that – and *you* managed to lose another three point six billion euros through a sloppy data error. Yet it's taken more than a year to discover.'

The Assistant Secretary was unsure what to say, so stayed silent.

The General Secretary let the pause grow. Eventually, he said, 'Well?'

Slightly flustered, the Assistant Secretary decided to let the second bomb drop.

'TV3 have got wind of the error and have put in a freedom of information request.'

'Well, isn't that wonderful. And they knew before both myself and the Minister.'

'I ... We ...'

'Plus *you* have a leaky division. How in God's name did that happen?'

The Assistant Secretary shrugged hopelessly. 'Somebody has a cousin working there, or saw a way to make a few extra euros, or felt it was in the public interest. You know what it's like. Especially now.'

'No, I don't know what's it's like. This is just what we need on top of everything else, trial by media. You've taken the media training course, I take it? Even if you have, they'll eat you alive.'

The Assistant Secretary could sense that he and the bus were destined to collide. The old bastard was already outmanoeuvring him. Which wasn't difficult given how badly he'd played this disaster so far. There had to be a trick to passing the buck upwards. No doubt the General Secretary could probably tell him how to pull such a move.

'How did you imagine your efforts to fix this were going to play out?'

'We,' he made a point of saying 'we', 'were hoping to get it fixed quietly before anyone spotted it.'

'How?'

'By simply updating the spreadsheet. A couple of clicks and we're €3.6b richer.'

'€3.6b less in debt.'

'But the kink is we'll need to get the CSO to resubmit the national accounts to Eurostat.'

'They'll want a full explanation as well. And no doubt the IMF, ECB and EU. There was no way that this could have been kept quiet, Peter. Your handling of it is going to make us look like fools.'

'I'm sorry, Sir.' He really did feel like a naughty schoolboy now. It just felt so unfair. He was going to be thrown under the bus for something he didn't do. Admittedly he was in charge of the systems that were meant to prevent these kinds of mistakes happening, but could he really be held be responsible for everything his staff did?

'You're going to have to explain all this to the Minister,' the General Secretary said gravely. 'He's going to have kittens. There'll be opposition questions. Media interviews. A blame game. There'll be calls for an inquiry.'

'An inquiry?' There was no way he'd be promoted to Agriculture after this scandal.

'The opposition will demand it. It's an enormous sum of money. Seven per cent of a year's tax take! There's a good chance there'll be calls for people to face penalties. Even lose their job.'

'I'm not sure that's fair on the individual involved, Sir. He did seek guidance.'

'I'm not talking about the individual. I'm talking about you. And the Minister.'

'Me? The Minister?' The bus was now approaching at speed. 'What about you?'

'Me?' The General Secretary placed a hand on his chest. 'I'm not the one who kept this under wraps for over a year. And the Minister is ultimately responsible for what happens in the Department.'

'But you're the General Secretary.'

'There'll have to be some continuity in leadership; a safe pair of hands to clean up and oversee the internal investigation.' The boss leant back in his chair and pulled a weak smile.

'You're expecting me to shoulder the blame?' Peter felt thoroughly outmanoeuvred. There had to be a way out of this mess, but he was damned if he could see it.

'It did happen in *your* division. And a year later it is still hasn't been resolved.'

'But I'm not the only one culpable,' the Assistant Secretary moaned. 'The HFA ...'

'So you're admitting culpability?'

'I meant we, *we're* not the only one at fault. The HFA, NTMA and CSO were also involved.'

'You're suggesting that we shouldn't take responsibility?'

'I ... if we play it right then the HFA will blame the NTMA, who'll blame the CSO, who'll blame the HFA, and we can stand on the sidelines.'

'I think you'll find that they will all blame us.'

'The blame would be shared.'

'You might yet have some promise, Peter. This is what I want you to do. First, you're going to take charge of sorting this mess out. Start by drafting an account for the Minister that thoroughly muddies the water and shares the blame around. Then draft a press statement along the same lines.'

Despite his distaste at the sensation, the Assistant Secretary felt gratitude well up inside him. He was being invited to try and solve the trolley problem: direct the runaway bus so nobody onboard got injured but folks at a bus stop took a tumble. 'I'll get to it right away.'

'And keep me in the loop. Don't do anything without clearing it verbally with me first. You have my mobile number. And leave the Minister to me.'

'Yes, Sir.'

'Three point six billion euros. A data error.' The General Secretary shook his head and waved a hand towards the door.

He waited until the Assistant Secretary had opened it before he spoke again.

'You need to up your game, Peter, if you want that job in Agriculture. I could do with a man I can trust there. I can put my trust in you, can I, Peter?'

The Assistant Secretary knew he'd just sold his soul. It didn't feel like it was worth 2.3 per cent of the national debt.

Harmonizing Data is Hard

'I've completed that audit on the census data.'

'And?'

'Of the 1161 SAPS variables[1] in the Republic's census about 32 per cent of them are directly comparable to those outputted in the North,' says Justin Gleeson, a researcher on what was then named the 'Cross-Border Regional Research Observatory' (CBRRO) project.[2] 'Another 31 per cent can be partially matched with a bit of fiddling around. The other 37 per cent have no equivalent questions.'

'So, we'll be able to do something. There's, what, 300 ... 350 variables that match, plus the ones we can part match.'

'Yeah, but the ones that match are all concentrated on certain topics and the part matching isn't going to be straightforward. If the CSO or Northern Ireland Northern Ireland Statistics and Research Agency (NISRA) are prepared to disaggregate their data and re-aggregate into the other agency's classes that would help, but I don't think that's likely to happen.'[3]

'But we could do some of that if we needed to?'

'Yes, but only by merging classes together to create common ones. We'll be losing detail.'

It's 2005 and we're discussing the possibility of creating an all-island census dataset, joining together data from the Irish and Northern Irish censuses. A joint project between Dundalk Institute of Technology and Maynooth University,[4] the CBRRO had been funded by the Special EU Programmes Body (SEUPB) to scope out the potential for a data portal, including a suite of interactive data tools, which could provide an evidence base for planning, assessing and tracking cross-border initiatives.

In the wake of the Good Friday Agreement and the peace process in Northern Ireland, cooperation between public sector bodies in the North and South had increased enormously. A huge amount of funding was being invested by the Irish and British governments and the EU to support shared services, joint infrastructure and common development plans. However, there was a dearth of cross-border datasets to formulate policy and inform decision-making. Indeed, at the time, it was rare to see cross-border data visualizations or maps. And those that had been produced usually came with a warning about interpretation as some element had to be fudged in order to create them.

Our idea, drawing on the concept of the Regional Research Laboratories in the UK,[5] was to try to address this lacuna by conducting data audits, creating cross-border datasets, and building prototype tools for displaying the data. To that end, we had hired a smart GIS specialist, who fortunately for us wanted to return to Ireland from the UK. Justin had experience of managing regional and national datasets and building online interactive mapping tools. He quickly set to work on a data audit, examining datasets produced by the CSO, NISRA and other government agencies. Ideally, we wanted to be able to create cross-border maps that displayed the data at a sub-regional scale.

It quickly became apparent why there were few, detailed cross-border data visualizations and maps – it was very difficult to create single, common datasets. Regardless of what the data referred to – health, economy, enterprise, transport, environment, planning and development – there were incompatibilities between the datasets. Just about the only maps one could make were at a coarse regional scales (what are called NUTS[6] 2 and 3 regions[7]) using Eurostat data,[8] where Northern Ireland was a single NUTS 2 region and five NUTS 3 regions, and the Republic was composed of three NUTS 2 regions and eight NUTS 3 regions.[9] Anything with a finer spatial granularity seemed to be just about impossible to produce.

We identified a number of problem issues.[10] Different kinds of data are generated in each jurisdiction. For example, the questions asked on household surveys can differ, or the data recorded by administrative systems might vary. Data can be recorded using different data units (for example, euros instead of pounds sterling, kilometres per hour instead of miles per hour), or classified into different data classes.[11] The spatial units used for reporting data are organized at different scales. At the time, in the Republic there were 32 local authorities for 3.9m people, in the North there were 26 district councils for 1.68m people. At a finer spatial granularity there were 3,414 electoral districts in the Republic whose average population was 1,062 and average size 20.4 km². The closest equivalent unit in the North were wards, of which there were 582 with an average population of 2,895 and average size of 24km². Data for wards then referred, on average, to three times as many people than for electoral districts. There are similar issues for health, police, education and other statistical geographies, and for political constituencies.[12] Metadata standards also vary, making it tricky to assess and compare data attributes. Likewise, accessibility to data can differ, with some datasets being openly available in one jurisdiction but closed in another. Fundamentally, two related but different approaches and geographies for generating official statistics had developed on the two parts of the island.

The most promising option given our desire for granular data appeared to be the census. However, as the opening conversation started to elaborate, significant differences between the Irish and Northern Irish censuses became apparent.[13] The Irish census takes place every five years, whereas the one in the North every ten, and at the start of the new millennium they were misaligned with a Foot and Mouth outbreak delaying the Republic's census by a year (2002 as opposed to 2001 in the North). The Northern Ireland census is aligned with the other two UK censuses (England and Wales; Scotland) in terms of the questions asked. Certain questions are the same or very nearly the same on both censuses as they are core concerns or are common across the European Union in order to provide European-wide, base demographic, social and economic data (as mandated by Eurostat). Other questions are similar and broadly measure the same phenomena, though subtle differences in question phrasing or data classification mean caution needs to be exercised in undertaking direct comparison as the data are not like-for-like. Both censuses have issues with continuity. Questions change between censuses, and therefore the number of variables released can vary quite substantially.[14] The spatial units used for organizing and reporting data can be changed to reflect new patterns of population or a re-organization of political geographies, and are published at different scales in each jurisdiction. At one level, it seems to make sense for the CSO and NISRA to work together to try and align data production. However, neither jurisdiction wants to alter key questions as they will lose their time series and the ability to see how the country has changed over time.

Working around these issues, we created an online interactive mapping tool and a set of online interactive data visualizations. Care needed to be taken when interpreting the maps and visualizations as they suffered from an ecological fallacy issue – the spatial scale was different on either side of the border (electoral divisions in the Republic and wards in the North). Nonetheless, a workable, if flawed, solution had been produced for creating cross-border datasets. In 2008, we published *The Atlas of the Island of Ireland*,[15] the title reflecting the politics of jointly naming both jurisdictions.[16]

In the late 2010s, I revisited creating cross-border datasets again, scoping out the possibility of assembling a selection of comparable key indicators for an area spanning the border in the north-west of the island. In part, the project was driven by the Brexit agenda given the centrality of the Irish border to the negotiations between Britain, Ireland and the EU, and the potential consequences for communities and broader society and economy of a hard border. The idea was to move beyond census data that could only be compared every ten years, to find datasets that would enable annual or sub-annual tracking of performance across different sectors – population, housing, economy, education, health, crime and policing, environment, and transport – at a local scale. If possible, we also wanted to find some data relating to cross-border movement and trade, preferably including real-time data of cross-border travel flows. We would then create common datasets that spanned both jurisdictions, displaying them using a dashboard interface.

Our hope was that in the intervening decade some of the issues we'd previously encountered might have been addressed. Two of my colleagues, Stephanie Keogh and Oliver Dawkins, spent some time hunting through online data repositories and conducting a data audit. They struggled to find comparable data that matched temporally and spatially (many of the desired indicators are not produced annually at a suitable spatial scale in the Republic; they are published at a regional scale and it is not possible to disaggregate the data[17]). Nonetheless, they started to assemble some datasets, though neither were comfortable with what they created given the variances in data production in each jurisdiction.[18] Myself and Martin Charlton, the deputy director of the National Centre for Geocomputation, spent a number of days replicating and extending their work, and Oliver had another go at assembling workable datasets. Despite our labours, we could only create a handful of comparable datasets that had some integrity, and even then there were issues.[19] Reluctantly, we abandoned the project, concluding that it was not possible to produce a meaningful, fit-for-purpose cross-border dashboard.

Rather than a trying to create a dashboard with existing data, what was needed first was a data harmonization project where agencies on either side of the border worked together to create comparable datasets. Data harmonization is a key concern of the EU in order to be able to monitor and compare phenomenon and change over time across Europe. Eurostat, the supra-national EU statistics body, works with the national statistics agencies of EU members to align data production methodologies and outputs. The INSPIRE directive seeks data harmonization for spatial data.[20] What is clear from our research is that, despite these initiatives, there is a long way to go to create comparable, cross-jurisdictional datasets at a sub-regional scale that can guide local planning, development and shared services.

Similarly, at a global scale, data harmonization is also a key concern for bodies such as the United Nations and its various agencies[21] in order to be able to compare and track key phenomena across countries. In 2014, an initiative sponsored by UN-Habitat, the World Bank, the World Economic Forum, the Organisation for Economic Co-operation and Development (OECD) and the Government of Canada, led to the publication of a new ISO data standard, ISO37120:2014 (Sustainable development of communities – Indicators for city services and quality of life). The ISO standard is designed to produce comparable, verifiable, transparent and trustworthy global urban data which are certified by the World Council on City Data.[22] To gain certification, cities are required to produce and report up to 100 indicators with respect to 17 themes concerning city characteristics, services, infrastructure and quality of life.[23] The standard was created because initial research had shown that it was difficult to find equivalent data across cities. This was borne out when Gavin McArdle and myself conducted a data audit to see if Dublin might apply for ISO37120 certification. We could only find suitable data at the right spatial scale for 11 indicators. While some of the required indicator data is not produced in Ireland, or is held by private entities (such as energy data), much of it is published at regional not city scale. Benchmarking Dublin against other cities then is not straightforward.[24] Nor is changing the data regime to ensure that Dublin is ISO37120 compliant.

One might expect these jurisdictional data issues to exist between countries given that each developed their administrative systems and national statistical services for their own ends. Within a country, however, data harmonization would seem a reasonable expectation. Certainly, one would anticipate it being the case for a city. I was therefore somewhat taken aback when visiting Boston to find a highly fragmented data landscape. I'd travelled to the city in April 2016 to undertake fieldwork on smart cities and data-driven urbanism as part of The Programmable City project.[25] In the month I spent there, I interviewed 37 stakeholders who were active in urban data initiatives. One of the first things I discovered is that the City of Boston (with a population of 653,000 in 2013) is one part of the wider Metropolitan Boston area (population 3.2m) that is composed of an additional 100 other cities and towns. Together these 101 municipalities formed a large contiguous built-up area, and as one travels through the urban environment there is nothing to denote that several different political administrations are being traversed.

I quickly learned that each of these 101 cities and towns had local autonomy, ran local government services, and had different forms of governance, with some being run by elected mayors, others by appointed city managers; some fully staffed by professional workers, others also relying on boards and commissions made up of citizens serving in a part-time or voluntary capacity. At the same time, there is no regional government with executive powers that oversees, directs and coordinates the cities and towns. Instead, they all act largely independently of each other and there is little history of cooperation. What this means is Metropolitan Boston has 101 local government departments for planning and development, parks and recreation, health and welfare, waste, public safety and emergency services, housing and property, arts and culture, education, environment, transport and so on.

It also means it has 101 data regimes.[26] The City of Boston is highly data-driven and well organized with respect to managing and utilizing municipal data. It has a number of specialist data teams (mapping, open data, performance management, civic tech) and a data coordinator within every city department. Cambridge, the second largest municipality in Metro Boston, has a relatively large GIS team and an open data coordinator, but at the time of my interviews had not embraced performance management and had relatively little data analytics capability. Somerville, the sixth largest city in Metro Boston, was the first municipality to embrace data-driven performance management in 2004. SomerStat,[27] a team of five people, employs performance analytics on operational data to supervise the work of city departments, guide budgetary planning and create community data profiles. In 2016, it was still in its infancy regarding open data provision. While the three cities share borders with each other they have very little interaction regarding data. The other 98 municipalities seemed to have significantly less data programs and capabilities. Newton and Lowell had some experience in using performance management analytics, and some departments across all municipalities are data-led and proficient, but generally they had very basic open data sites and weakly coordinated data systems.

The result is a fractured, uncoordinated data landscape with each municipality creating their own datasets. Even when data concerns the same phenomenon, they might employ different data ontologies (recording/classifying the data in different ways). What this means is that, with the exception of data required for state/federal reporting, it is impossible to join datasets together to create comparable metro-wide datasets. This has a number of consequences, reducing spatial intelligence about the characteristics and performance of the city-region, fostering back-to-back planning, limiting potential data-driven innovations to urban governance and management, and stifling the benefits of open data.[28] In addition, scales of economy are not being realized through shared data services, with there being duplication of effort across Metro Boston, along with significant gaps and inefficiencies where cities and towns have less capacity and resources to produce and manage data.

When I tried to suggest that the cities and towns work with each other with respect to data, I was told quite firmly by everybody I spoke to that this was unlikely to happen. Indeed, most did not want it to happen. When I suggested that they could be compelled to adopt common data standards, one public servant explained that politically such a move would be blocked: 'You can't mandate to the municipalities, they will just tell you to get lost; it will never get through the legislature.' Several times I used the example of the four local authorities in Dublin, which are also autonomous and have no executive regional body overseeing their work, who collaborate with each other on open data and data services. One city official responded: 'In the case of Dublin you do need that unified portal of all four. It is not like Boston and Cambridge. If I am interested in Boston, I am interested in Boston, or I am interested in Cambridge, but in Dublin you kind of need that whole picture. We don't care once you go across the river!' There was a strong sense that Dublin was one city split into four parts, whereas Metro Boston was 101 separate cities and towns despite sharing a common urban footprint. Even policies like responding to emergencies such as flooding, or planning evacuation routes, stopped at municipality boundaries rather than being coordinated across the metro-region.

To try to combat this fragmented landscape and provide some consistency and coherence in urban data across Metro Boston there are some active cross-cutting initiatives, though each has constraints. At the state level, Mass GIS (Bureau of Geographic Information)[29] provides a state-wide database of geospatial information and a standardized set of turnkey solutions (pre-prepared online GIS) for smaller municipalities who lack the resources to build their own. Initiated in 2008, New England StatNet works with municipalities on a voluntary basis to address resource and data skills issues and promote the use of data-driven performance management. The MAPC is a quasi-state planning agency created by Massachusetts legislation in 1963. It works with municipalities in the metro-region to produce a non-statutory, non-binding regional plan, facilitates shared procurement of services and provides a standardized set of administrative and statistical data compiled by state and federal bodies. It has no authority and a weak formal mandate with respect to municipalities. The Boston Area Research Initiative set up in 2011 is an inter-university initiative that works with the City of Boston, and to a lesser degree with Cambridge and Somerville. Its primary remit is to conduct academic and policy-led research using Boston as a case study, rather than to provide data services or act as a coordinating data infrastructure for the metro-region. While each of these initiatives has value, they do not address the fundamental problem of a lack of a coordinated approach to administrative and operational data across Metro Boston.

What working on the Island of Ireland cross-border data projects and the Metro Boston interviews have taught me is that while we increasingly live in a data-driven world, much of that data generated and deployed is fragmented and difficult to join together, even when it concerns the same phenomenon. And it will remain that way for the foreseeable future despite data standardization initiatives. This is because data production is intrinsically institutional in nature, created and corralled by organizations (municipalities, government agencies, supra-national bodies) that do not necessarily span multiple jurisdictions. This is as much the case with scientific data as it is statistical, administrative and operational data. Science follows data standards and practices that are set by international and national organizations, and some of these might be in competition with each other. One only has to look at how references are formatted in academic papers to know that there are multiple conventions on recording publishing metadata. Data is shaped by territorial politics and systems of governance. We might strive for data harmonization, but achieving it in practice is difficult. And as the next chapter highlights, often the first hurdle is to get access to the data in the first place.

8

Open-and-Shut Case

'The key thing here,' Professor Sarah Jenkins said to her colleague, 'is to try and get the Department to take open data seriously. It doesn't matter if it's through us or others, or even themselves. We just need them to get their act together and to make more data accessible.'

They both knew that wasn't quite true. Without an injection of funds their own open data initiative, the Regional Data Lab, was in danger of winding down. They weren't quite at the make-or-break point, but it was always hovering nearby.

Dr McNeill nodded. 'I'm not holding my breath.'

He'd been banging the open data drum for a number of years. In his experience, government had very little interest in making their data available, and even less enthusiasm for spending money during austerity. And open data was not free data; somebody had to pay for the labour of preparing data for release and building the necessary data infrastructure.

A middle-aged man poked his head out of a nearby door. 'Professor Jenkins? I'm Paul Lester, the principal officer for open government. Come in, come in.'

The room was small and cramped, overfilled with bookcases and filing cabinets. The dirty window provided a view of another office building.

Lester retreated behind his desk. 'The unit was only set up a few months ago, so we're still finding our feet. I know you met one of my colleagues at the open data consultative panel; he said you've got a proposal concerning open data tools for the public sector?'

'That's partially why we're here, but also to get a sense of what you do and the roadmap for making more government data accessible,' Professor Jenkins said. 'I'm not sure what you know about us, but basically we work with local authorities and government departments to create open data tools – mainly interactive maps and graphs – to aid their work. And we're always looking for more data to plug into our tools.'

'That's the Regional Data Lab website?' Lester said, aware he should have taken a closer look at the site before the meeting.

'That's us. What we do is take what data are already openly available and make them useable for those that lack the skills to build their own tools so they can use them in formulating policy. There's a *lot* of duplication in the work across agencies. Rather than negotiating separate contracts every time, it would make more sense to simply centrally fund the RDL to provide a suite of core data services.'

'You're looking for funding?'

'Funding would be great, but that's not why we're here. We're more interested in the development of a national open data repository and access to more data, and a coordinated approach to providing data analytics for the public sector. We can do the latter, or another dedicated unit can.'

'You're suggesting that the public sector doesn't know how to analyze data effectively?' Lester said, defensively.

'Well, some departments are well organized,' the professor conceded. 'Especially those that specialize in statistics and mapping, but most are well behind the curve. There are issues across the board – data management, data quality, analytics, sharing and interpretation. We wouldn't be getting contracts to help them otherwise.'

'But departments and agencies are functioning fine as it is.'

'Well, that wouldn't be our experience,' the professor said. 'Every agency we work with has data issues. They're either missing key datasets or not making effective use of what they do have. They don't have the literacy or analytics capabilities, or the data are locked within units when they could be used across the organization and by others elsewhere. That's the kind of work we help them with.'

'I think you might be overstating the issue somewhat,' Lester said, smirking. 'Government's been working fine with the data it has and without open data. Officers on the ground know what's happening in their areas and department officials have a good sense of the broader picture. The system works.'

Professor Jenkins sighed. For the head of a unit in charge of opening government data, Lester seemed quite resistant to the idea. Any chance of funding for the RDL seemed remote, but more importantly the whole open data agenda seemed at stake.

'It works inefficiently and without detailed insight,' she countered. 'People on the ground might have a rough feel for what's going on, but gut feeling is not hard data. And what they do know isn't feeding into policy and practice, either locally or nationally. What's been happening with housing would tell you that.'

'I'm not sure ...'

'Either people knew what was going on and ignored all the warning signs,' she continued, 'or they didn't know or didn't understand. Either way, the market imploded. And if they do know and understand things locally, they don't know how their area is performing compared to other areas around the country and how that's been changing over time. I'm not talking hunches and intuition here. I'm talking facts and figures. If we'd been taking notice of the data ...'

'The same thing would have happened,' Lester interrupted. 'The data wouldn't have stopped the party: developers building, banks lending and investors purchasing. And nobody wanted to be a party pooper.'

'But evidence-informed policy could have lessened the excesses.'

'Perhaps, but the boom and bust would have happened anyway. Look, anyone who knows what they're doing can access relevant data. Those working on housing policy have access to it. They did all the way through the boom.'

'But not everyone involved in housing. Voluntary and community housing bodies. Buyers. Renters. Ordinary investors. Politicians. Academics.'

'You've just said that the key group are those that make policy. Besides, a lot of data is already available through the national stats site or the department websites, or if they've a legitimate interest they can work with the data holders or request the data.'

'That's not ...'

'And they should have the skills to be able to process and interpret the data,' Lester said, raising his hands. 'Most professional staff in the public and voluntary sector have degrees. They have reasonable technical and analytical skills, especially those dealing with data or formulating policy. I access and analyze our data all the time.'

'Again, that's not our experience,' Professor Jenkins said, trying to project a placid demeanour despite her annoyance at Lester's reasoning. 'If it were, we wouldn't need to exist and we wouldn't be working with so many agencies or have a waiting list for our training sessions. Just because *you* can access and make sense of the data doesn't mean everyone can.'

'Also, improving data management and making data open will help fulfil the open government agenda,' Dr McNeill added, sensing the need to try and move the conversation on. 'It'll help create transparency and enhance accountability. Plus it'll foster the formation of an open data economy and create jobs.'

'I'm familiar with the arguments for open data,' Lester said, tersely. 'But it's not at all straightforward to pursue. People trust us to protect their data. It's often personal in nature and they don't want it in the public domain. There are a range of issues around privacy and data protection and commercially sensitive information that all need to be worked through. We can't afford a scandal that will shut it down before it gets going.'

Dr McNeill snorted and shook his head. This was going nowhere. It had taken less than 15 minutes for the official to play the get out of jail card for government: our data is too sensitive to share.

The professor, however, was not yet ready to throw in the towel. 'Nobody's expecting personal or commercially sensitive data to become open. All the data already in the public domain is aggregated in some way into classes or categories, or by geography. That's some of the work we do for government departments – we anonymize the base data and aggregate them into units for analysis and sharing.'

'*You* have access to the base data?'

'Yes. We're contracted to help ...'

'But ...'

'We've all been cleared as official statisticians of the state. And we take data security seriously and work with the Data Protection Commissioner's office to make sure they're happy with the process and outputs.'

'That's still not ...'

'Look,' Professor Jenkins continued, 'this kind of work should be going on across the whole public sector, but it can't because of a lack of knowledge and skills. You're already using resources to generate the data in the first place and it's a waste not to extract as much value as you can from them.'

'It's not that simple though, is it,' Lester replied, trying to rally, now aware that the two academics had much better knowledge of government data and what went on behind the scenes than he'd anticipated. 'All that additional work of aggregating and checking to make sure it complies with data protection costs money. As does producing and maintaining data repositories. Plus we're already getting value out of the data we produce and I'm finding little evidence we'd leverage further value in excess of the price of the additional work. It's difficult to see how it might generate an open data economy beyond consultancies taking our data, fiddling with it and then trying to sell it back to us.'

'But you're not factoring in all the savings you'll make through the improved government services that the data will enable,' Dr McNeill countered, 'or how better evidence-informed policy will grow the economy and increase efficiency and productivity and improve social conditions and quality of life.'

'That's all aspirational. Policy is much more about politics than evidence.'

'Nor are you placing a value on the public good produced by making the data open,' Dr McNeill continued, undeterred. 'The spillover effects of open data and data-driven government are potentially huge and should easily cover the costs of production and maintenance. Plus you'd be getting additional taxes from any products and services created by private companies.'

'I'm familiar with the rhetoric,' Lester said, rolling his eyes, 'but there are few documented cases of it working in practice. What open data portals there are seem to be little used. Some datasets are barely downloaded and there are few cases of data being successfully monetized except for high value datasets such as real-time transport and weather. Governments have spent a lot of money, but have little to show for it.'

'Well, the RDL is pretty well used,' Professor Jenkins said, 'and we work with lots of public sector bodies who are interested in open data and are spending money on it. By centralizing and consolidating all the multiple bits of work we and others do through a centrally funded unit we reckon you'd save hundreds of thousands, possibly millions, in paid data services.'

'Unless you're creating new jobs without the need for a new budget line then we're unlikely to be able to help.'

And there was the bottom line, Dr McNeill thought. All that mattered in the current climate was job creation. Unless they could demonstrate in tangible terms open data producing new jobs they were wasting their time.

Professor Jenkins, however, seemed determined to prove a point. 'Even though we'd be saving you direct costs and producing an evidence base that will produce efficiencies across the public sector through better service delivery and policy?'

Lester shrugged. 'Where's the proof that the evidence we use at present is insufficient, or that new evidence will lead to significant efficiencies and savings?'

'I'd say the fact that we're in the middle of the biggest crisis in the state's history because a massive property bubble was allowed to develop because nobody was taking a blind bit of notice of the data, and our planning and development policy was being guided by stakeholder interests rather than by evidence-informed policy is a good place to start.'

'We're going round in circles. And besides, that's not entirely true,' Lester countered. 'Our spatial strategy and development plans were evidence-informed.'

'Both were corrupted by political interests and they were rolled out after the horse had bolted.'

'Regardless,' Lester said, seemingly conceding some ground, 'the efficiency argument will be difficult to sell to the Minister. Given austerity, he's only interested in programmes that are going to create new jobs and inward investment. Savings have to be demonstrable cutbacks – calculable reductions in spend, whether that's salary, capital or other costs – not in intangible efficiency gains that will be difficult to prove. He wants hard numbers.'

'Changes in policy will lead to changes in hard numbers,' Dr McNeill said. 'The gains will be evident in the data.'

'But not as hard cash, or clear economic benefit such as jobs.'

'But that's a false economy.'

'That's reality.' Lester brushed a piece of fluff from his sleeve. 'And besides, just because more data might be available doesn't mean that it'll drive policy making. That's not how we typically make policy here.'

'But it will still better inform policy making,' Dr McNeill pressed. 'And without it how can we transform policy making into something more sensible than anecdote and political interest?'

Lester laughed. 'You're assuming that's something that politicians and the public actually wants! My experience is that isn't the case. And even if data were to shape policy, most of our policies are short-lived, or they aren't implemented or enforced.'

'So, you're saying that there's no point pursuing open data because evidence-informed policy is a pipe dream?'

'I'm being a realist.'

'But you're responsible for the government's open data agenda?' Professor Jenkins said.

'I am.'

'You don't seem to be very in favour of it.'

'What gives you that idea?' Lester seemed genuinely perplexed by the accusation. 'It's my job to examine how best to open up Irish government data when it makes sense to do so.'

'So you're planning on opening up government data?'

'Absolutely.'

'On what basis?'

'On the basis that it is government policy to do so as part of the open government agenda and it will be beneficial to society and the economy.'

Dr McNeill snorted again.

'You've just been arguing the opposite,' Professor Jenkins said.

'No, no, I haven't. I've been saying that it won't be easy. There are lots of things to consider.'

'In other words, you'll spend the next two years preparing a report that will then go to a cross-department committee, followed by six months of review and revision. It'll then need political approval, followed by consultation with stakeholders and further revision. Eventually a watered-down policy will be produced. If there's a change of government in the meantime, the process might survive or it could be dropped. But it doesn't really matter because, as you've just noted, it won't be implemented.'

'Well, that's a cynical way of looking at it.'

'The RDL was born out of such cynicism. It'll probably die from it as well. Look, thanks for your time. It's been an enlightening if dispiriting conversation. We'll see ourselves out,' Professor Jenkins said, rising to her feet, her passion having run its course. What hope she'd had on arrival had evaporated. Lester and his unit were an exercise in being seen to be doing something while not actually doing it. Like many government initiatives. They would spin a line, paying lip service to international debates, and do the minimal amount possible.

Lester appeared surprised by the sudden end to the meeting. 'You're leaving?'

'There's nothing left to say. Until you or the Minister become open data advocates we'll just keep limping along as we are. And so will the country.'

The Politics of Building Civic Tech

Open data can be used to build all kinds of civic tools, one of which are city dashboards. These use a suite of interactive, often interlinked, visualizations (graphs, charts, gauges and maps) to display time-series data about the performance of a city.[1] The idea is to enable users to see the present state of play and the historical trend with respect to different aspects of urban life: economy, labour market, demographics, transport, environment, housing, health, education, crime and emergency services. In some cases, benchmarking is used to show how a city is performing with respect to other cities, or how neighbourhoods within a city compare to each other. Ideally, the data displayed are as timely (real-time, weekly, monthly, quarterly, and preferably no more than annually) and spatially (exact location, neighbourhood, district) resolute as possible, and are typically operational and administrative in nature. Cities generally use dashboards as informational tools to help shape and monitor policy interventions; some also use them as management tools to monitor and guide performance of city services and staff.

Building a city dashboard is a good way to gain an in-depth knowledge of how civic tech can be created using open data, and the politics and praxes involved. This was a strategy we adopted on 'The Programmable City' project,[2] which sought to examine how city processes are captured within code and as data, and how these code and data are then used to manage our cities. For most components of this project, research was carried out by conducting interviews with key actors and spending time working with smart city initiatives. However, for the city dashboard to work, rather than seeking to understand an initiative from the outside, our plan was to immerse ourselves in the process from the inside by creating the technology.

At the initial meeting in November 2013 between myself and Gavin McArdle,[3] a computer scientist hired to build the dashboard, we started to map out an initial requirements analysis for an operational system. We discussed the possible scope and organization for our proposed dashboard, identified desirable datasets and their necessary characteristics, explored potential software options, sketched out a basic strategy and timeline for development, and set out what research needed to be undertaken over the next few weeks.[4] By the close of the meeting we had a reasonable degree of consensus. Based on our deliberations, our initial aim was to try and combine design and approach elements of the London city dashboard[5] developed by the Centre for Advanced Spatial Analysis at University College London that displays real-time data for the city, with aspects of the London Dashboard[6] that displays public administration and statistical data.

Our plan was to create a city dashboard composed of a number of modules that would display key performance indicator data.[7] These data would enable a user to answer three questions. How well is Dublin performing? How does Dublin compare to other places? What is happening in the city right now? The first two questions would be answered through displays of administrative and statistical data, the latter by visualizations of real-time data. Where possible we would try to use open source tools, and we would only use open data, meaning that others could replicate our work but also create their own tools. We also wanted the tools to be accessible and easy to use for people with little visualization skills; and also be interactive allowing users to explore the data.

We also mapped out a program of initial research, consisting of three tasks. First, we would conduct a detailed data audit of the city, identifying what datasets existed, their temporal and spatial characteristics, their formats and standards, who owned them and whether they were available as open data. We were guided in this task by previous audit work for AIRO,[8] our exploration of the London Dashboard, and the 100 key indicators detailed in what was then the forthcoming ISO37120 standard[9] (see Chapter 7). Second, we would explore other city dashboards to examine their content, design and ethos, and get a sense of what we felt worked well, what to avoid, and what approaches and tools we might productively borrow. Third, we would produce an initial mock-up of what a Dublin Dashboard might look like and how the site might be organized. This would capture our initial design thinking and give us a starting point from which to iterate.

From a critical data studies perspective, this initial meeting immediately revealed the contingent nature of producing new data-driven technologies. We were not following a pre-ordained scientific path; making sure we were approaching the task in the correct or optimal way. Rather, we debated different viewpoints and options, seeking to settle our differences and negotiate common positions. Our varying stances were shaped by our prior practical knowledge and experience, technical expertise, knowledge of the literature and other city dashboards, and expectations. Our initial decisions and program of tasks created a pathway for the dashboard development, opening up potential build parameters with respect to content, design and tools, while closing down others. If other key actors had been involved in the process (such as stakeholders or potential users), or a different set of ideas and ideals been proposed or decided on, or different dashboards been used as inspiration, then the project would have unfolded in an alternative fashion.

The absence of other actors in our planning and deliberations was a flaw in our approach. Our plan had been to build a prototype then to approach DCC with a view to forming a working relationship with them. We thought it would be easier to get them involved and to leverage additional operational datasets from them if we had something tangible to show. We didn't seek the views of potential end users, principally because what we were trying to do was exploratory research, we didn't have a clear sense of what we would ask them, and there were time constraints. Before we had a chance to make much progress the key potential stakeholder, DCC, came to us. In mid-December, the Office of International Relations and Research Office in DCC informed AIRO that it was in the process of putting together a tender document for the possible development of a 'Data Visualisation of a Dublin Indicator Database'.

Just at the point where we had made a start on creating a city dashboard, it appeared that DCC was thinking of commissioning one. Five days later, we had our first meeting with a DCC staff member in their offices. Both parties explained what they were hoping to achieve. We agreed that we would continue to develop a prototype dashboard for Dublin, and DCC would supply a spreadsheet of the 37 indicators across ten themes they were hoping to include in their data visualization project (identified as desirable indicators in a recent sustainability report[10]). We would examine whether it was possible to source suitable data for these indicators. This meeting redirected some of our data audit work, but not in a significant way. Our initial ideas concerning principles, design and tools, however, stayed the same. In February, DCC became a partner in our project, offering resources in kind (staff time for consultation and additional data). Significantly, DCC had different views, priorities and expectations which had to be accommodated into the endeavour.

By the end of January 2014 we had compiled an initial database of publicly available data related to the city. We had also downloaded samples to examine the characteristics and suitability of the data for inclusion in the dashboard. Of the 37 indicators desired by DCC only ten were available at a Dublin city or more granular scale on an annual/sub-annual basis.[11] Our audit revealed that sourcing suitable, public data for some indicator themes, such as education, health and demography was impossible beyond the five-yearly census data. Sourcing real-time operational data was also proving to be difficult, limited to some transport and environment data.

Given the data limitations and to widen the appeal and utility of the dashboard, a decision was taken in March to broaden the scope beyond indicator and real-time data visualizations. Instead, we would seek to include as much data concerning the city as possible through a wider set of visual analytic tools. Some of these tools had already been developed by AIRO, such as interactive mapping modules of census, housing, crime, welfare, planning, land use and services data, or by other third party actors, such as city benchmarking sites, city apps and crowdsourced reporting of city issues. Other new tools would need to be developed, for example relating to social media data. The AIRO tools would be included directly in the dashboard, whereas we would redirect users to the third-party tools. We would also provide a portal to the data sources.

This was a significant decision as it shifted the aims and purpose of the project, as well as having consequences for design and analytical tools. Two new framing principles were added: to include as much data as possible; and re-using existing resources if they did a good job. The system requirements were altered to include being able to answer other questions: Where are the nearest facilities/services to me? What are the spatial patterns of different phenomena? What are the future development plans for the city? How do I report issues about the city? How can I freely access data about the city? At this time, we also had a discussion with DCC staff about possibly including targets to denote whether the city was performing as desired. Such targets are common in other city indicator systems, such as CitiStat[12] used in some American cities.[13] This suggestion was not pursued, however, because of the absence of established criteria for satisfactory performance and the political implications of imposing targets which might have an effect on the management of relevant staff (see Chapter 18).

By this stage, we had also recruited an ethnographer, Sophia Maalsen,[14] whose role was to independently document how the project was unfolding. Sophia was to follow the project for six months, attending our internal meetings and those with DCC and other stakeholders, taking notes concerning the conversations and decisions taken. She also had access to the email exchanges. The aim was to record how the project was being developed, charting its evolution and making sense of the processes behind the decision-making. One of the difficulties of researching an issue when performing it personally is maintaining sufficient distance to be able to impartially identify the key processes and patterns. Sophia's involvement as a kind of fly-on-the-wall observer ensured some distance and independent perspective on the praxis and politics involved in the initiative. And it was clear that there were politics at play as all the parties involved sought to influence how the dashboard evolved. Instructive meetings included those where we discussed with DCC staff data visualizations that showed Dublin was under-performing and how best to present that data to the public, or whether it should be included at all.[15]

Over the next few weeks, the prototype dashboard was reconfigured as new and existing tools were incorporated into a newly designed interface. There were several internal and external meetings, which included discussions and decision-making with respect to data for inclusion, site organization and interface design. Choices had to be made concerning the visual analytics to be used and how they would be configured. We continued to try to source new data and discover existing data tools for the city. Gaining access to datasets was a perpetual problem, with access blocked by a lack of resourcing to make them open, or fears over data protection, data security and data quality. By the end of July we had a functioning system, though only eight of the planned 12 top-level modules were substantially complete and there were still many snags. Nonetheless, our preference was to seek an official launch of the site in the next couple of months in order to try to leverage additional datasets and build working relationships with other data providers. Our hope was that by having the site live it would let reluctant data managers see that there were few risks and many benefits in making their data open. We continued to tweak the design and tools of the site right up to the launch of the Dublin Dashboard on 19 September 2014. At that point, the site contained or linked to 56 sets of data visualizations organized within 12 modules, providing hundreds of interactive graphs and maps for the city.

After the launch, we continued to maintain and develop the site. We also started to write articles and book chapters detailing our thoughts on city dashboards. What was clear to us was that a lot more research and thinking was needed with respect to their development. Consequently, we applied for further funding to undertake a larger, four-year project titled Building City Dashboards. The project proposal argued for systematic and rigorous research on how best to create city dashboards, paying particular attention to three core issues. First, data problems concerning processing, quality and veracity, and archiving. Second, visualization and interaction problems and how to produce effective visual analytics, optimize them for different devices and platforms, create multi-modal displays including 3D environments, and improve user experience. Third, analytics/ modelling problems, moving beyond visual analytics to perform data analytics, statistical modelling, predictions and simulations. In this sense, the project sought to tackle a set of fundamental, technical and practical questions. To do so, we would continue to develop the Dublin Dashboard, but also a develop one for Cork, using a lighthouse/follower approach (build one and see if it can be replicated for another). We also made a commitment to use an open science approach, wherein the data used and code produced would be openly accessible.

The application was funded by Science Foundation Ireland and we started work in September 2016. Unlike the development of the initial dashboard, a key aspect of the research was that we would be guided by much more comprehensive user requirements. To that end, we interviewed potential users of the dashboard about their views and experiences of the Dublin Dashboard, plus three other dashboards (London, New York and Hawaii). We also used a think-aloud protocol method, where users would state their thoughts while they navigated and used each site.[16] Our respondents divided into three types of users: novices, who had little experience of dashboards and typically had low levels of data literacy; end-users, who had some familiarity with dashboards through their work and moderate levels of data literacy; and advanced users, who were very familiar with data visualizations and how to produce and interpret them, and had strong data literacy. Novices found city dashboards to be quite challenging to use: they often found the visualizations confusing and the site difficult to navigate. End-users tended to have specific issues with site organization, visual design, and interpretation. Advanced users felt that the dashboards did not provide sufficient data analytics to perform the kinds of tasks desired, and they often just wanted access to the data so they could undertake their own analysis.

The feedback revealed that the Dublin Dashboard was too confusing in terms of the modes of interaction and navigation used, diversity of modules available and the data visualizations presented. Many of the tools, especially the mapping modules, were too taxing as they were not intuitive to use. There was no consistency in module design and interaction, little information presented beyond the visualizations, and users often found themselves outside the dashboard on another website. Not including potential dashboard users in the planning and design of the original Dublin Dashboard was a serious mistake. We had pulled all the data of the city together and allowed people to explore it, but in a sub-optimal way.

Using our findings we decided to fundamentally change our approach to designing and building a city dashboard. First, using the characteristics of our three groups of respondents we created three personas: Josh (novice), Jane (end-user) and Geoff (advanced).[17] We mapped out fairly detailed profiles for each of these personas in terms of their work, interests, data literacy, skill levels and typical data tasks. We then charted the characteristics of a city dashboard optimized for each persona. For Josh, a dashboard would need to provide defined routes, use simple visualizations, and these be supported by plain-English explanation that aided interpretation. In other words, provide curated data stories. Jane needed a clean, simple, well-organized dashboard with basic visualizations that provided only the information she needed to complete specific tasks (like sourcing evidence for formulating policy). In contrast, Geoff required more advanced tools that let him query and analyze the data and answer more complex questions. This provided a bit of a conundrum – could we cater for all three users through a single dashboard?

Our solution was to parcel the site into three sections: data stories, tasks and tools. All users land on the same opening webpage and are directed into the part of the site most suited to them, or they can simply explore the data by theme. In addition, to ensure continuity of design and that all components are open access, the site now only includes content produced by the team, with a separate portal page created to point people to other related resources. To a large degree, this reversed our original decision in March 2014 to widen the scope of the dashboard. We developed a set of guiding principles, drawn from our research and the human-computer interaction and web design literature, and used these and our personas to develop a new beta version of the dashboard. Part of our specification was that the dashboard would work well on different types of devices, such as laptops, tablets and smartphones. The new beta site was then tested with a new set of beta users, using the feedback to further refine the design. This was used to guide the development of the Cork Dashboard.

In addition, we started to experiment with other visualization tools. In particular, we were keen to explore displaying the same data used in the dashboard in 3D environments. Working with surveying company, D3D, and OSI, we created a 3D model of a 7km by 4km section of the centre of Dublin. We built a virtual reality (an immersive game space) and mixed reality (both the virtual model and real world are visible at the same time) environments and a set of associated tools viewable using specialist headsets. Rather than looking at a map, users could see a 3D landscape of the city which they could walk or fly around. We chose to focus on a planning and property related theme, allowing the user to add new buildings, view building shadows, run flood simulations and view data related to planning applications, land zoning, house prices and the census. We also commissioned a 3D printing company to create a 3.5m by 2m physical 3D model (a 1:2000 scaling), which we could then project data onto from above. Taking a more creative approach, we also worked with three data artists – Cordula Hansen, Conor McGarrigle, and Jeffrey Weeter – to explore alternative ways to make sense of urban data.

Like the process for creating our original city dashboard, the redevelopment of the Dublin Dashboard and production of the Cork Dashboard involved a significant amount of planning, negotiation, and trial and error, amongst a much larger team (four principal investigators and 13 researchers over the course of the project) and group of stakeholders. There were team meetings every fortnight, along with numerous informal meetings and conversations between team members, and meetings with stakeholders and suppliers. The production of the dashboards was a collaborative endeavour, not simply a technical production. There was nothing inevitable about how the dashboards were designed and built, or their content and tools. Rather they were assembled and evolved over time through debate, play, trial and error, testing and feedback, and decision-making that took place within the terms and conditions of the funding, technical and data constraints, social, political, legal and financial context, and the power dynamics of the team and between stakeholders.[18] Just as these processes and institutional landscape have an effect on how a dashboard is created, the collective manufacture of dashboards reshapes institutions and their practices. Through our interactions with them our stakeholders changed their data management and practices, including their attitude to open data. In turn, our engagement with the stakeholders shifted our thinking with respect to the work of local government and the mechanics and politics of data-driven governance, which altered how we approached the task of designing a city dashboard (for example, making us wary of management through metrics; see Chapter 18).

What this contingency means is that how users come to know the city through a dashboard is mutable. How we design dashboards, and what data are included and how they are displayed, influences what knowledge is learned and how it is applied. Importantly, given that dashboards are a key means by which operators monitor urban infrastructure within control rooms, this mutability directly shapes the nature of data-driven urbanism and how our cities are managed and run. Indeed, as discussed in Part II, running a city in a scientific, technocratic way – driven by data – does not mean that the city is run in a neutral, value-free, non-ideological way. A city can never be run in such a fashion because the data themselves, the technical systems they operate within, and the context in which they are deployed have a politics. Data and systems are cooked.

10

So More Trumps Better?

Selena placed her coffee on a tall table and rolled her neck. She was still perplexed by a presentation she'd just witnessed and was torn between approaching the speaker to discuss their study and shying away.

A recently submitted job application to work in the same institute as the presenter was holding her back. She was reasonably certain that critiquing the research of a professor who could well be on the hiring panel would be an ill-judged move. And she was well aware that she had a habit of becoming immersed in a debate, which was fine if the aim was to win an argument and not care about the consequences, but less so if it jeopardized potential employment.

'Dr Russo?'

She turned to the voice. The professor had found her.

'Professor Brown! I was just at your talk.'

'And what did you think?'

She'd set that up just perfectly. A couple of sentences and they'd already reached dangerous ground.

'It … It was fascinating.'

He tilted his head, sensing her unease. 'In a good way?'

And now she was trapped. If she answered 'yes', she'd have to spin a web of lies to justify the answer. If she said 'no' she'd have to explain her discontent. Neither seemed like an attractive option. Instead, she plumbed for: 'Did you not think of using data from official sources?'

'The whole point of the project was to try an alternative source.'

'But why would you use Twitter data to examine fertility?' There, she'd said it. She'd tipped herself over the edge and there was no going back.

'Because Twitter's a really rich set of social data,' Frank said, smiling. He was still feeling upbeat after the positive feedback in the session. 'There are 330 million active users globally and they're tweeting about all kinds of issues, including health and family.'

'But are they really tweeting about fertility?' Selena pressed. 'About children being born?'

'They tweet about everything!' Frank laughed. 'About what they had for lunch, football matches, breaking news, celebrities, fashions, you name it. And about if they had a child.'

'But you can hardly get a good sense of fertility rates from that, or reasons for the rate,' Selena persisted.

'Well, you can use it to calculate a proxy rate, comparing rates of women with and without children, looking at family changes, mapping geographic patterns of the tweets, but we're only partially using the data for this. We're mainly interested in soft measures concerning fertility, such as attitudes, values, feelings and intentions.[1] And about related issues such as family planning, abortion and overpopulation. In particular, we can get a sense of sentiment: whether people are positive or negative about parenthood, whether they are tired, over-joyed, depressed.'

Selena shook her head and sighed.

'You're not convinced?'

'Not really, no.' She knew that she should probably play it safe and retreat from the debate, but the professor's justification for using Twitter data had gotten under skin. 'My approach to understanding fertility starts from a very different place. It's driven by theory and hypotheses. If there's something I want to find out more about, I formulate a research question, then I look for a dataset that might help answer that question, or devise a method that will produce the required data. You seem to have started with the data. You have a dataset and you're trying to find a question that you might be able to answer with it.'

'Well, kind of, yes,' Frank said. 'The data revolution is producing this deluge of data, right? Masses of it. Gazillions of records. Real-time streams of data exhaust; data that are largely by-product of the system. So, just as a car produces exhaust fumes, digital technologies produce data fumes. I'm interested in how we might be able to repurpose those fumes. Re-use them in a productive way. In our case, to examine aspects of demography.'

'But you're a data scientist, right? Not a demographer?'

'I'm a data scientist that works in a social sciences institute.'

The mention of the institute barely registered with Selena. She was centred solely now in the debate.

'So, you're coming at this as a data problem,' she asserted. 'You've no detailed knowledge of demography or demographic research?'

'Well, we did do some background research,' Frank said, trying to counter the thrust of the critique. 'We didn't approach the issue completely in the dark.'

'But you're not steeped in the field though, you …'

'But we don't need to be,' Frank interrupted. 'What we're trying to do is open up new avenues into fertility research. Enable demographic researchers to exploit new sources of data. Very large samples of social data. Enable them to ask different kinds of questions.'

'I get that, but it seems to put the cart before the horse. We already have good demographic data – from the census, household surveys, public administration, health and welfare records. We know what the fertility rate is, we know what health issues might be associated with that, such as post-natal depression. We have good factual data for entire populations. And we could administer household health surveys through family doctors with a structured set of standardized questions.'

'But the latter would be expensive and only for a sample of people.'

'Yes, a *known* sample,' Selena stressed, 'where we have specific, associated data such as age, health history, social class, education, occupation. You don't know any of that from Twitter data. Just gender. Assuming the person hasn't set up a false account. And Twitter is full of fake and bot accounts. Plus Twitter itself is a sample – an unrepresentative one. Not everyone has a Twitter account and those that do are more drawn from certain age groups, occupations and social classes.'

'But we have a massive sample to work with. Millions of users and billions of tweets. And the data are being continually produced, whereas a survey might be just conducted once, or every few years due to its cost to administer and process.' Frank shook his head. He found it baffling that somebody wouldn't want to use such data.

'But the survey data would also be standardized,' Selena pressed ahead, 'meaning we would have comparable data between the people in the sample. Whereas, as I understand it, you are using machine learning to extract sentiment from the tweets, then trying to identify patterns within that sentiment. No question has actually been asked. Meaning is inferred.'

'Yes, that's the case. We're looking to extract meaning from tweets.'

'But what about sarcastic tweets? Say one that says "God, I hate being a mother!" Which sounds like the person really regrets having a child. But an attached photo shows her smiling, holding a baby pulling a funny face. Which suggests she's actually delighted.'

'We try to find ways to spot those quirks within our natural language processing by using supervised training,' Frank explained. 'In other words, we try to teach our algorithm to recognize intent. An exclamation mark after "mother", for example, might indicate irony or sarcasm. And in a sample of millions of tweets, the balance is going to be mostly the correct classification, or at least good enough.'

'So more trumps better,' Selena said, sarcastically, immediately regretting it. It hardly mattered though now, she thought, she was hardly likely to get the job after this conversation.

'Sorry?'

'Having a massive amount of poor, unrepresentative data is more useful than having small samples of carefully curated data?'

'We're not suggesting that one replaces the other. Rather they can be used to complement one another. We can see if the same trends are evident in each.'

'But to what end? And what if the trend isn't evident in each? Do you trust the higher-quality, tailored data more, or the Twitter data?'

'I'm pretty certain that they'll both have some utility.'

'But one would have a lot more utility than the other?'

'Well, that would be an interesting premise to explore. If we had survey data we could compare what they reveal with the insights from the Twitter data.'

'And what about the ethical implications? Nobody posting on Twitter thought that their data was going to be used for fertility research. That it would be used for research at all.'

'But it's public data.' Frank was genuinely perplexed. For much of the conversation he'd felt on the back foot, despite making what he thought were reasonable arguments. 'They share their views freely on a publicly accessible website.'

'Yes, to talk to each other. They are participating in social media, not filling out a health survey questionnaire. And it is not public data. It's owned by Twitter who allow researchers access to a sample of it.'

'But the important point is we have access to it. It's an unbelievable resource. And why should people object to their data being re-used for science?'

'The point is about consent,' said Selena, shaking her head. 'The data are being used for a purpose that users have not been consulted about or given permission for.'

The more the argument progressed, the more depressed she felt about the case being made to oppose her views and her foolishness for starting it in the first place. She should have just said the presentation was fascinating and left it at that. The professor just didn't seem to get the issues she was raising, or to have even thought about them, and he potentially held her future in his hands.

'I'm pretty certain it's covered by the terms and conditions people sign up to when they open an account,' Frank said.

'And those terms and conditions are probably a mile-long list of legal gobbledygook.'

Frank shrugged. 'That's not my problem. My problem is how to re-use the data to discover interesting things.'

'Things that you don't know much about.' Okay, that was definitely below the belt. Now she was just being self-destructive.

'You really don't like the idea of using Twitter data for social research, do you?' Frank laughed. 'Or that I'm not a demographer.'

'Well, using Twitter data and having limited domain expertise doesn't seem particularly conducive for drawing conclusions about fertility.'

'Ouch!'

'Sorry, I didn't mean ...'

'Oh, I think you did!' Frank laughed. 'Well, that was ... interesting.' He finished off his coffee.

Selena felt like she'd kind of won the battle, but lost the war.

Frank took a step away, then turned back. 'Do you think you could provide the domain expertise we're missing?'

Serena shrugged, suddenly unsure what to say.

'Maybe add some theory and hypotheses? Some ethics?'

'I ...'

'It might be good to have a colleague who's willing to speak their mind, though I'm not sure if I'm looking forward to your interview or not! By the way, that's why I came over; we shortlisted you for the post you applied for just before I travelled here. You'll be getting a letter shortly.'

Serena watched him wander away unsure whether to feel elated or deflated. Had she just enhanced or blown her chances? Either way, she doubted Twitter would have the answer.

11

Hustling for Funding

'We run out of money in a few months' time,' I say, trying to keep the tone of my voice neutral. 'We've researched over a dozen different ways of financing the project going forward, but the only sustainable way is core funding from government. Without that, the other sources we've identified are unlikely to happen.'[1]

It's 2015 and myself and two colleagues are having a conversation with a couple of senior civil servants in the Department of Education and Science (DES) about the future of the DRI.[2] It is part of a set of ongoing discussions we had been having with officials in four government departments, plus a couple of state agencies, over several months.

'As you know we're supportive of the DRI,' an official replies, 'but we haven't yet found a suitable mechanism or budget line. Have you tried the Department of Culture, Heritage and the Gaeltacht?'

'They directed us back to you. We were passed to them by DBEI,[3] who we were passed to by DPER.[4] Who you passed us to. We're going round and round in a game of pass the funding parcel. Everyone seems to agree that the DRI needs to be funded, but nobody wants to add it to their budget. In the meantime, our time is running out.'

'The problem is that you're not a neat fit into any one Department,' the second official says, 'and given austerity constraints we cannot add new line items to our departmental budgets.'

'Then why not add our funding to an existing budget line? Perhaps one of the universities, or any capital grant to the RIA?'

'It's not that simple. Plus, given the remit, there should probably be a contribution from all relevant departments rather than one covering all the costs.'

'Which seems to be impossible to coordinate.'

'Not impossible, but challenging,' the first official replies.

'And it seems unlikely to happen in the short term. If we cannot find the funding, then we're going to fold. The partners can't cross-subsidize and carry the costs. The €5m the government has invested in building a new national data repository will have been wasted. We'll lose our key staff and all their tacit knowledge, plus the infrastructure and the goodwill of the stakeholders. If you decide to do this again in a few years' time you'll be starting pretty much from scratch given a new team of developers and partners will be in place and the speed of tech development, and it will be incredibly difficult to persuade the stakeholders to come back onboard.'

'And there really is no other way of funding this?' the second official asks.

'There's no other country in the world that doesn't provide at least 60 to 70 per cent of core funding costs,' Dr Sandra Collins, the DRI director, answers calmly. 'And they gradually introduced other funding sources into the mix.'

'At the minute, we're expected to go from 100 per cent core funding to 100 per cent self-sustainable overnight,' I add. 'Yet, a stipulation of the original award was that the project would have an open data mandate, which means we cannot charge for use of the data. Trying to raise €600,000 a year to fund core staff and services when we have limited means of raising finance is basically impossible. In the original call, you asked for a 100-year project, but only allocated a five-year budget. The bottom line is, if the state wants born digital data created by state institutions to be available to our grandchildren and subsequent generations then it needs to sustainably fund a trusted data repository.'

For the six years I had been working on the DRI it had been beset with institutional politics concerning its framing, development and operation. The future funding issue was just the latest example in a long list of fraught exchanges that could be traced back to its original conception and funding mechanism.

The DRI was born out of a funding opportunity, but seemed destined to die due to a funding failure. Without a political solution, the data life cycle would turn full circle much more quickly than initially anticipated.

The first scoping meeting for what became the DRI was held on 3 December 2008. A number of senior academics and librarians from several Irish higher education institutions met at 19 Dawson Street, the home of the RIA, to discuss a potential funding bid to create a new national data repository for humanities, cultural heritage and qualitative social sciences data. The aim was to scope out the feasibility, and possible shape and partners, of such a bid in the context of a forthcoming funding call, The Programme for Research in Third Level Institutions, Cycle 5 (PRTLI5).[5] The call for proposals had not yet been announced, but there was plenty of speculation that it would happen shortly and what it would be seeking. Since building a coalition of partners and putting together an application was a complex process, the meeting sought to pre-empt the call and get the ball rolling by brainstorming initial ideas.

I attended the meeting wearing two hats. The first was as chairperson of the Irish Social Sciences Platform (ISSP), which had received €16.5m of funding under PRTLI, Cycle 4, to create a common programme of research in three areas (knowledge society, balanced regional and rural development, sustaining communities), as well as a shared doctoral training programme, across 19 disciplines in eight institutions. In total, ISSP funded 54 PhD students, 16 postdocs, a number of support staff and a couple of new building projects, and linked together three existing inter-institutional research institutes. ISSP included three data-focused initiatives: AIRO, see Chapter 7;[6] IQDA;[7] and Social Science Assessment Instruments (SSAI).[8] My second hat was as director of the National Institute for Regional and Spatial Analysis (NIRSA), itself established through PRTLI Cycle 2 funding, which had been developing the IQDA. My aim was to ensure that ISSP partner institutions and the IQDA initiative would be part of any consortium bid to develop a new national repository given our interests and expertise and the need to find funding for the next phase of our ongoing research.

Other attendees were representing other existing data initiatives in the humanities that had been funded by previous rounds of PRTLI or other funding sources. Since the policy of the Irish funding agencies and schemes (especially the PRTLI cycles) was to fund the scaling-up of initiatives and innovation, and not to fund existing enterprises and consolidation, attendees knew that the prime means of gaining a fresh injection of monies would be through a new round of collaboration between already large-scale enterprises. The meeting proposed to scale collaboration and ambition by bring together ISSP, the Humanities Serving Irish Society (HSIS) consortium (which included the Digital Humanities Observatory (DHO)), and several stakeholder partners from the GLAM (galleries, libraries, archives and museums) sector, drawing together digital data collections from across the partners into a single federated repository.

The Royal Irish Academy was chosen as the site for the meeting as it was considered a neutral venue and organization, and it had already been muted that it would act as the lead agency for the initiative. The politics of selecting a university from among the collaborating institutions to act as the lead partner would likely fracture the fledgling consortium before it started formally. My memory of the initial meeting was it quite a cagey affair. There were only two social scientists in attendance and we kept having to push to extend the scope of any bid from cultural heritage and humanities datasets and GLAM external partners to include qualitative social sciences data and other potential partners such as state agencies and NGOs. It was clear from the discussions that there were already divisions in how to approach the application and what would be proposed, and some attendees had met prior to the meeting to establish initial institutional alliances and formulate lines of thinking to try and guide how the outcome might unfold. Nonetheless, there was a reasonable amount of coherence in a vision for a new national data repository, in part because we were all familiar with the game of assembling bids for PRTLI funding and knew the government was only expecting one united bid that linked all relevant institutions. In addition, some next steps arrangements were put in place. These included three people being nominated to put together an outline proposal (myself, Susan Schreibman from the DHO, and Robin Adams,

Trinity College Dublin librarian), liaising with other attendees as they sought guidance from their own institutions as to their potential involvement in the project. We also had a working name: The National Audio-Visual Repository (NAVR).

Assembling a PRTLI consortium is a somewhat fraught business that involves a lot of political manoeuvring inside and between institutions. In the case of PRTLI5 and from my perspective, the politics were playing out at four scales. First, Maynooth University was unusual in that it would have two research institutes – NIRSA and An Foras Feasa (a HSIS partner institute) – as partners in the RIA consortium. This meant both units would have to form a united front to external partners, while internally negotiating their respect roles and anticipated funding streams from the Maynooth portion of projected funding. Second, NIRSA/An Foras Feasa were competing against other potential units in Maynooth University to be able to bid for funding. The university would set its own priority areas for seeking PRTLI funds, depending on its strategic ambitions and what senior managers thought was most likely to be funded, and they would set a cap on what funding could be sought. The fact that we had been accepted into the RIA-led consortium was no guarantee that we would be part of the final submission (indeed, other initial consortium partners, such as humanities/library scholars in Limerick University and University College Cork did not get through their internal competitions). Third, we were liaising with other ISSP partners about the RIA consortium, whether we would go with it or form our own IQDA consortium, or whether we could leverage other ISSP partners into the RIA consortium. Fourth, we were negotiating with the other RIA consortium members about our potential role in the project and our slice of the funding pie, and keeping our ear to the ground about other potential bids.

Before a coherent technical and practical vision of a potential new national data repository has been formulated, a frantic set of data politics was already playing out. My role was to represent the social sciences perspective and the interests of NIRSA and IQDA in shaping the bid and to make sure we were part of the winning consortium, with a share of the funding that would enable us to make a strong contribution to the initiative. Being part of the core writing team would help enable these outcomes, but ultimately the bid would reflect negotiation and decisions between partner institutions. Arriving at consensus – or at least a tolerated bid – in practice consisted of a lot of meetings and phone calls in which there was a great deal of negotiating, haggling, bluff, persuasion, proposal and counter-proposal, and horse-trading. This process intensified once the PRTLI5 scheme was formally announced by the Irish government on 8 January 2009.[9]

Such politics are vital, as which partners form the consortium, and what the arrangements are with respect to their roles, staffing and funding, will define what data repository is built in terms of vision, technologies and approaches taken, and what data it will house. At first, the RIA consortium and the initial vision seemed well supported across institutions. However, it became clear that there were two issues which might derail the bid. First, some institutions were not getting through their internal competitions, removing researchers with significant expertise and resources from the consortium. Second, and more problematically, one university decided to split from the consortium and submit its own rival bid. Significant efforts aimed at different levels of the management in this university to persuade them to re-join the consortium failed. Despite the government making it clear that it wanted inter-institutional collaboration, this rival bid set out a different vision of a single institution providing a service to all the others, rather than expertise from across institutions being used to create a shared service. This split was divisive, especially amongst the HSIS community that had a track record of collaborating with each other and were also collaborating on another bid related to graduate education. It also made signing up external partners from the GLAM sector difficult as they were being asked to choose which bid to back.

In the end, the RIA consortium consisted of five higher education partner institutions: The Royal Irish Academy, Dublin Institute of Technology, National University of Ireland Galway, Maynooth University and Trinity College Dublin. In addition, there was one devolved partner,[10] four no-cost university partners,[11] and 16 supporting stakeholder institutions.[12] By the time of submission, the proposal had been through several drafts and iterations. What we proposed to do was build a unified, robust, scalable, accessible and sustainable Trusted Digital Repository (TDR)[13] for the humanities and qualitative social sciences with common data and metadata standards, formats, access rights and research tools. The NAVR would provide an online, federated TDR for discovering, accessing, managing, preserving and interacting with a wide variety of multimedia resources (texts, images, photographs, audio files, video, architectural and engineering drawings, historical papers).

It would do this through intense collaboration across HSS, computer science, libraries, government and civil society agencies and working with Ireland's national cultural institutions with respect to metadata standards, policies (relating to access, intellectual property rights, file formats, governance and so on), and methods for digitizing, archiving and storing AV/textual data created in English and Irish, in conformity with best international practice. To ensure the project would be delivered there was a governance and management structure and ten work packages, organized into four strands.[14] Different institutions had responsibility for delivering the different work packages. To our delight, the Higher Education Authority (HEA) selected our proposal for funding.

The NIRSA role in the NAVR was specifically focused on work package 4, which concerned the development of a suite of policies and guidelines required to create a TDR, examine potential ways to source future funding and to take an active role in the management and governance of the initiative. Over the next few years, myself and Professor Jane Gray attended operational and management meetings, along with work package meetings, and Dr Aileen O'Carroll worked on developing the policies and guidelines. In addition, we would hold regular meetings with our An Foras Feasa colleagues involved in the project (who were based on the floor below us). Not long after the project started a decision was taken to re-brand NAVR as DRI.

Every meeting was an exercise in data politics. Sessions would involve imagining, suggesting, debating, persuading, campaigning, cajoling, pressuring, conceding and so on, as we sought to move the project forwards and deliver on our commitment to build a TDR. Sometimes our deliberations would go relatively smoothly as we quickly found consensus.

Other times it was a slog as different parties sought to advance or defend particular positions, relationships and technologies, and influence decisions and how the DRI was taking shape. Generally, despite these politics, the consortium was amicable and there was good camaraderie, aided by having excellent leadership through Sandra Collins, then Natalie Harrower. Occasionally, the atmosphere was soured, personal and institutional tensions arose, and other actors (for example, Deans or VPs of Research) would be called upon to try and move past stalemates or smooth over ruffled feathers. And gradually, the DRI got built and achieved TDR status (which is externally accredited). It was formally launched on 25 June 2015.[15] Just in time to be potentially shut down due to a funding crisis.

Which brings us back to where we started. Though it's important to note that there was more at stake than funding in the discussions about the future of DRI in terms of governance and operations and which partners would continue to be actively involved in building, maintaining and managing DRI, and would receive a portion of the funding allocation. The business plan we were seeking finance for in 2015 would shrink a team of over 40 active members down to six core funded staff, with other remaining staff funded through other soft monies (principally research grants). There were also potential financial risks to institutions staying in the consortium in terms of covering extraneous operational costs. Ultimately, however, sourcing finance is *the* key issue for *all* data initiatives. Unless there is a means of covering the costs for labour, equipment and other essential inputs, data are not generated or stored, and thus cannot be used or shared. Even in open data projects, the data might be free to use but they were not free to create, or to process and host. Somebody is paying for technologies, infrastructure and electricity, even if they are cross-subsidizing it from other sources and the labour is volunteered. Without finance, the life of data quickly speeds towards termination unless they can be rescued in some way, such as transfer to another repository.

In the end, after a protracted process, we were successful in getting the Irish government to continue to fund the DRI, which continues to go from strength to strength. The funding is not yet fully secure, in that it is renewed periodically as opposed to having an open, ongoing multi-annual funding as with other state-funded data initiatives, such as the National Archives or CSO. But it does have a firmer foothold on the budget balance sheet. Hopefully, it will remain a 100-year plus initiative so that future generations will have access to digital artefacts created today.

12

The Secret Science of Formulas

Karen clicked 'Apply' and the map redrew on the screen. The country was coloured in a patchwork of red and grey.

This pattern was at least the 20th iteration of the map.

Seated next to her, her boss rolled his neck and stretched his arms. 'Well, that's fixed the problem in the south-east,' Professor Butler observed.

They'd been hunched in front of a computer screen for the past two hours. The Minister stood behind them, mostly hovering, occasionally pacing. To their right, the Minister's special advisor scribbled into a spiral-bound notebook.

An anxious official from the Department leant against the wall by the window. He would have much preferred to have kept this exercise in-house than use outside experts.

Karen was torn between shoving the monitor off the desk and telling the Minister exactly what she thought of his 'scientific method' for allocating capital funding, and desperately wanting her home area to receive some of the investment. Her head was firmly with the former, her heart the latter. Some places were going to receive funding through this dodgy process, so why not hers?

The problem was that so far her area had more often been grey than red. If at the end of this charade it was still grey she might find it more difficult to hold her tongue.

'What happens if we add in another variable?' the Minister asked.

'It depends what it is,' Professor Butler said. 'What are you thinking of?'

'The Irish language.'

'For any particular reason?'

'Its decline is linked to population loss.'

'It's probably declined just as much in urban areas as rural ones, maybe more so,' Professor Butler said. 'I'm not sure it's a good indicator of development need beyond the necessity to invest in Gaeltacht areas to protect and grow the language.'

'But proportionally it will have affected rural Ireland more. It'll show where we need to encourage new social infrastructure, housing and population growth.'

This had been the pattern of conversation. The Minister making suggestions, the professor politely providing alternatives. The bullish former maths teacher with no background in spatial planning overriding the director of a regional development institute with over 20 years' experience. Occasionally, the special advisor chipped in with a political observation; usually that such-and-such politician or Minister was based in an area, or its local and national results from previous elections.

The nub of the problem was the Minister had a very particular outcome in mind. He wanted the investment from his new scheme to be spread across as many constituencies as possible, and certainly the ones that traditionally voted for his party or those that might swing away from the government. However, he didn't want to be seen to allocate the funding on political grounds, nor run the scheme on a competitive basis. Instead, he wanted to be able to say that the monies had been apportioned using a statistical formula that assessed need objectively.

Karen glanced over at her boss and rolled her eyes. It was obvious to the pair of them that adding the Irish language variable was not going to give the desired result. And from her own standpoint, her home area would remain grey.

'Minister, how about looking at some socio-economic variables instead?' Professor Butler asked. 'They'll give a better idea of present social and economic need.'

'Just add in Irish in for now.'

Creating a formula for producing a map that pleased the Minister was proving to be trickier than anticipated. In part, this was because he had his own ideas about which variables were good indicators of relative deprivation and need. The core variable he'd selected was population change from independence in 1922 to the present, with decline being taken to indicate a need for investment in infrastructure and regeneration.

Professor Butler had tried to point out that many areas which had lost population were now relatively wealthy, meaning the funding would be going to areas that did not need it. In return, he'd been schooled in an economic history of Ireland that was mostly rhetoric and discovered that population change as the base variable was non-negotiable. The fact that this excluded every city and just about any town from the scheme was a conundrum they hadn't yet solved.

Karen pulled down a menu, opened a pop-up box, added the new variable and altered the settings. The pattern on the screen changed.

'What happened to the areas here?' The Minister reached between the two of them and tapped the West coast.

'Since they have high levels of Irish speakers they've dropped out of the qualifying areas.'

'That's not what I was trying to do at all. The Gaeltacht areas should definitely qualify for funding. We want people and businesses to be moving to them.'

'At least it's had the effect of adding in some towns and city neighbourhoods.' Professor Butler pointed to the area south of Dublin.

'That's the last place that needs this funding!'

'Sin é dáilcheantar an Aire Airgeadais,'[1] the special advisor said in Irish.

'Maith go leor, go maith, tá roinnt leithdháilte ag teastáil uaidh; cathfaimid dara babhta cístí a fháil pé scéal é.'[2] The Minister laughed. 'Ach ní ar chostas na Gaeltachta.'[3]

This had been a common tactic throughout the meeting; swapping into Irish when they didn't want Professor Butler, who was Welsh, to understand.

While her Irish was somewhat rusty, Karen had been able to pick up the main gist of their exchanges. In this case, the advisor had noted that the area was the Finance Minister's constituency. The Minister had replied that it would need to have some allocation given the need to secure a second round of funds, but not at the expense of Gaeltacht.

She shook her head at another example of the Minister's notion of science in action. 'Do you want me to remove it from the formula?' she asked.

'No, no. We need to flip it round. Instead of low rates qualifying, it should be high rates.'

'If we do that then the qualifying scores for places with low rates, which is just about all areas outside of the Gaeltacht, will fall,' Professor Butler said.

'Let's try it and see.'

The new map was broadly similar to one they had created an hour ago, which had been rejected.

'Okay, that's better,' the Minister said.

'Ach níl áit ar bith i ndáilcheantar an Aire Airgeadais',[4] the advisor said.

'Tiocfaimid ar an méid sin.'[5] Swapping back into English the Minister continued. 'We need to find a way to join some of these areas up. We can't fund a cluster of two areas; they need to be sizeable enough to create some kind of critical mass.'

'We could apply some kind of adjacency rule,' Professor Butler said.

'We can't fund an area if it doesn't meet the qualifying criteria,' the Departmental official said, speaking for the first time in half an hour.

At last, Karen thought, the pen pusher had found his spine.

'Don't worry, Donal,' the Minister said. 'It'll all be covered by the formula. How about getting us some tea and coffee?'

'I'll ring down.'

'Or you could go yourself.'

Donal sighed. 'The same order as last time?'

'Yes,' the Minister said, without waiting for the others to confirm.

So maybe he hadn't found a backbone, Karen mused. They were all just passive dupes in this exercise. It was a textbook example of Gerrymandering,[6] and they were all complicit. She was clicking away as directed. The professor was trying to nudge and steer, but was a long way short of open resistance. The department official was playing waiter, and the advisor was a bought and paid for 'yes man'.

As the official left the room, Professor Butler took the mouse and started to explore the map. 'This isn't going to be easy,' he said. 'If we take these two clusters here. The only way to join them is to add these two EDs. But they have gained population, not lost it.'

'But only by a few per cent,' the Minister observed. 'If we were to add a rule that if an area is next to a qualifying one, and if its population growth is less than ten per cent, it also qualifies.'

'We could, but that will still exclude any town.'

'They're already getting private investment, but, okay, we could alter the rule so that you can add adjacent areas as long as the overall, larger cluster rate remains negative.'

'That could work,' Professor Butler conceded.

'Try adding that rule, Karen, and we'll see where that leaves us.'

Karen inwardly groaned. With this methodology, they would be here until midnight.

'We can't apply that as a global rule,' she said, looking over her shoulder. 'We'll need to review each adjacent area and manually add them and see what happens to the rate.'

She glanced at her boss, willing him to say something. Anything to make this charade end.

'Then that's what we'll do,' the Minister said. 'Perhaps we can try and get your home area funded this way as well.'

Karen took back the mouse, then paused. She was being bought. No, she was being coerced through the possibility of being bought and her home neighbourhood receiving sizeable investment. She could be responsible for that new infrastructure and jobs. Or not.

She cursed herself, then the Minister. If her home area wasn't red by the end of the session he could well be wearing the monitor as a helmet. And the chances of her ever voting for his party of gombeens was less than zero. If the Oireachtas[7] subsequently believed the funding was allocated scientifically they were bigger fools than she already thought they were.

The End of the Data Lifecycle

A couple of years ago I had a chat over coffee with a colleague about bidimensional regression. It is an analytic technique for regressing one set of geographic coordinates onto another. One use is to see how closely an old map aligns with a modern one, computing the variation in the position of locations and any translation, scale and rotation effects. In my doctoral research I used bidimensional regression extensively to statistically calculate how closely the cognitive maps (remembered geographic knowledge) of my study participants matched a real world map.[1] To do so I had written a computer program that performed the regression calculation and plotted the outputs as a map, along with the statistical values.[2] Inspired by the conversation once back in my office I decided to have a look at my original code and data, which I had been dutifully transferring from computer to computer for 25 years.

I immediately ran into a problem. Although I had digital copies of my program and data files, at some point I had compressed them to save space on storage. Most probably I did this to be able to get the whole archive onto a 3½-inch floppy disk, which only had 1.44 Mb storage (this took place a long time before storage became cheap and ubiquitous, when managing files to reduce their size was important). I had used a DOS[3] utility program called Pkpak to archive the files. Unfortunately, the corresponding program, Pkunpak, would not run on my laptop, which operated using Windows 7.

Stuck, I turned to an old 486 desktop computer from the 1990s. I already knew that if I did manage to unpack my files, the compiled, executable programs would not run on my modern machine so I'd kept the old computer in case I ever needed to run my analysis again. I knew that this somewhat ancient machine would probably unpack the files; in fact, they were likely to already be extracted from the archive and stored on its hard disk. I hooked the 486 to a monitor and turned it on. To my gratification it booted up. Disappointingly, however, it didn't have the required drivers to enable the monitor to show the interface. I'd kept the computer, but not a compatible monitor. A bit of searching on the internet and I discovered a program that would unpack the files on my laptop, but it only worked on a 32-bit machine, and mine was 64-bit.

I had locked my digital data beyond use. Moreover, I had a filing cabinet drawer full of non-viewable 3½ floppy disks, all storing old data from various projects. No doubt the dozens of Zip disks, CDs and DVDs in the same drawer will similarly become unreadable over time. With some more searching, I probably would have found an unarchiving program that worked, assuming that the files had not become corrupted in some way. I could have also located an old monitor to purchase. Instead, I abandoned the task and pulled down a box from on top of a bookcase.

The box contained all the original hard copy data from my doctoral research – all the maps and charts that my participants had drawn and the surveys they had filled out. The chances of me ever re-using these data are slim to none. I have already processed and analyzed them, extracting insight that was converted into information in the form of academic papers. Indeed, throughout history that has mainly been the fate of data: discarded after use with the more valuable information recorded in books and journals and stored in archives and libraries. Yet I'd never been able to bring myself to throw the material away. The data has little use or utility but they've not quite reached the end of their lifecycle.

In the data-driven world we live in, while it sometimes seems that data lasts forever, they all pass through a lifecycle. For the majority of data points, this cycle passes very quickly as the data are transitory – created, processed and deleted in micro-seconds. Value is extracted, or they are never examined or processed, and then they are discarded because they have little further utility and there's no point wasting resources storing them. A healthcare monitor in an intensive care unit measures in real time a whole series of different vital signs and related health data. The core data might be recorded for later analysis or playback if needed, but 90 per cent of the data is simply presented for display then deleted.[4] That deletion might be immediate in some cases, or after a few hours or days in others.

In some cases, useful data might be deleted accidentally, or without forethought. On 30 June 1922, munitions exploded in the basement of the Public Records Office (PRO) at the Four Courts in Dublin.[5] Anti-treaty forces in the Irish civil war had occupied the complex in April of that year. Despite being asked in person and in writing to ensure the safekeeping of the country's historical archive, they continued using the records office as an ammunition store. When Free State forces shelled the Four Courts, the administrative records of Ireland from the 13th to the 19th century were destroyed. These included property deeds and land transfer records, court records for criminal and civil cases, prison records and petitions, transportation records to the new world, financial statements and wills, ecclesiastical and parish records, and the original census forms from the early 19th century (returns for 1821, 1831, 1841 and 1851).[6]

By 1922, some of the original census forms had already been lost. The census returns for 1861 and 1871 were destroyed shortly after they were tallied and aggregated, derived data produced.[7] The 1881 and 1891 returns were pulped and the paper recycled during the First World War. Except for some census forms from 1821 and 1831 for particular counties, Ireland lost its entire original census forms and a rich source of demographic history. Today, the original census forms that are completed by every household are stored by the CSO in fireproof boxes in a secure warehouse outside of Dublin for 100 years before being handed over to the care of the National Archives. The PRO fire of 1922 was a key inspiration for the DRI (see Chapter 11) – if born digital data are to be available to future historians then they need to be preserved within a trusted data infrastructure. Another key project is 'Beyond 2022'[8] which seeks to discover duplicate records in other archives, particularly in the UK since Ireland had been a British colony until 1922, digitize the documents, reconstruct the archive and make it publicly accessible as a virtual record treasury for Irish history.

Given the massive amounts of data presently being produced, often only a sample are retained and stored rather than a full set. For example, rather than record every measurement in a sound sensor network, to save on data transfer costs via a mobile phone network and extend battery life, the data might be sampled every five minutes (see Chapter 2). Given the storage volume required to retain real-time CCTV footage from one, or more usually several cameras, every tenth frame might be kept. In the case of the Dublin traffic control room, they retain none of the footage from the 380 cameras at junctions across the city. They are simply used to monitor and react in real time. In part, this is because these data have little tactical use for controllers other than in the moment. In part, it saves on storage costs, which would be significant over the course of a year. It is also because the local authority does not want the overhead of dealing with freedom of information requests from the public seeking access to the images (for purposes such as insurance claims for theft). When I asked staff about the potential surveillance and policing uses of the data, they pointed out that they were residents of the city as well and they had no desire to create a surveillance state.[9] All they were interested in was keeping the traffic flowing. In contrast, I once had a conversation with the head of traffic data for Moscow, who told me that one of his biggest headaches was storing camera feeds for 140,000 high-definition cameras for either 30 days or a year, and using the footage to issue around 40,000 fines a day for traffic violations. Even here though, the data life cycle came to an end, with the footage deleted after a set period of time. The derived data – the database of violations – however, will probably persist for much longer than a year.

Indeed, the data we store in archives and repositories is often derived data. Derived data has greater utility and value given they have been deliberately transformed to perform additional work. Part of the transformation is often a reduction in data volume through generalization, abstraction, consolidation, aggregation and calculation, also making the data easier to store. In the case of data brokers, producing derived data is also a means to bypass the fair information practice principle of data minimization which states that data should only be used for the purpose for which it was intended – derived data being created by the broker for their ends.[10] Similarly, metadata – factual information about data – is often retained rather than the data themselves. For example, telecoms companies do not record and store the content of phone calls, but do retain the associated metadata. This metadata contains a lot of useful information, such as the call recipient's phone number, time/date, duration and cost.

Derived data and metadata are also likely to have defined lifecycles that determines when the data will be deleted. The end of the lifecycle might be legally mandated. For example, GDPR in the European Union stipulates that data must be stored for the shortest time possible and not be hoarded for some future, undefined purpose. What defines the maximum time for retention relates to the intended purpose of generating data, as well as any legal obligations to keep data for a fixed period of time. For example, the records of telecom providers (telephony, mobile telephony, internet access, email and VoIP) are mandated to be retained for between six months and two years, and banks financial records for seven years, after which they must be deleted.[11] Retention is to enable certain government bodies, such as the police, security services and tax authorities, to access the data for the purpose of investigating, detecting and prosecuting serious crimes.[12] What this means is that organizations and companies must establish time limits to erase or review stored data. Exceptions can be made for data that might be archived in the public interest, or for reasons of academic research, as long as suitable technical and organizational measures are put in place to ensure data protection (such as access controls, anonymization and encryption).[13] The nature of the exceptions should be documented in the metadata accompanying a dataset.

A good example of an organization that sets out the data lifecycle for its various datasets is Transport for London (TfL). TfL is the local government body that oversees and part delivers public transport in London, with responsibility for overground and underground rail, buses, water services, cycling, taxis and private hire cars, and dial-a-ride services. It is a large, data-driven organization, with over 25,000 staff, that coordinate and regulate the daily travel of millions of passengers. Its operations generate and use a massive amount of data from a variety of sources, including streams of real-time data: websites and smartphone apps, CCTV in stations and on trains and buses, contactless and credit card payments, Oyster cards, congestion charging (including ANPR), shared bike usage, lost luggage requests, taxi licencing, job applicants, personnel records, finance and accounting, and so on. As well as electronic records, they also have a number of physical records that have to be managed.

For all of these data, TfL set out the lifecycle and justify why data are retained.[14] The duration of retention varies from 24 hours to seven years. Following good practice, they retain data for the shortest time possible to ensure a business process can function properly, legislative compliance standards are met, and any disputes with customers, staff and service providers (including appeals, customer grievances, complaints to the Ombudsman, or legal proceedings) are resolved. In addition, they recognize the disposing of data is important for data management (reducing multiple sets of identical records and data, and removing obsolete or inaccurate information) and for improving the efficiency of business processes by destroying data whose value has expired.

The concern for many is that large swathes of useful data are not being deleted in the shortest time possible, but are instead persisting as a permanent data shadow within the databanks of data brokers and some government agencies (especially national security services). This is particularly the case with derived data and metadata, rather than original records. Rather than these data completing a lifecycle they form part of a lifelog, joining an ever-expanding data shadow that follows, and often precedes, a person over the course of their life. The extended life of these data is a key concern for many civil rights groups such as Privacy International,[15] Liberty,[16] American Civil Liberties Union,[17] and the Electronic Frontier Foundation,[18] as well as regulatory bodies such as the European Commission which has a responsibility for ensuring data protection. Nonetheless, agencies and companies continue to gather and retain data over extended periods due to their value.

Curiosity with respect to my doctoral data and code highlighted that, unlike TfL, I had not formulated and implemented a data management plan. Instead, like some agencies and companies,

I had retained the data indefinitely. Admittedly, the data contained very little personal and sensitive information and were generated two decades before GDPR and data management plans became standard practice for every research project. Moreover, the study did use an information and consent form that said that the raw data would remain confidential and the analysis would be used only for the thesis and subsequent publication. However, there was no data lifecycle plan and no strategy for archiving the data in a scientific data repository. Instead, I compressed the digital files for electronic storage on my hard disk and backup media, and placed the paper tests and surveys in a cardboard box which I stored on top of a bookcase. The data should be deleted, completing its lifecycle, or archived for re-use. I still haven't done either. Instead, they remain locked on my hard disk and confined to a box.

PART III

Living with Data

14

Traces and Shadows

Growing up in the 1970s and 1980s, I lived in a fairly analogue and small data world. All of our household appliances were electro-mechanical. My homework was paper-based and marked by hand. If I wanted to discover information, I went to the library and searched through hard copy books. Our car was purely mechanical, with no digital components or network links. I listened to music via the radio or by playing vinyl records or tape cassettes, and television consisted of three then four channels. Communication was by written letter and a landline phone. Undoubtedly, I appeared in a few key government databases, but most of my education, health and welfare records were stored in paper files.

There were some hints of the digital world to come. In the late 1970s, my parents bought a clone games machine that enabled the video game *Pong* to be played on the television,[1] and in 1981 I received a ZX81 personal computer as a Christmas present. It had 1K of memory (16K with a booster block).[2] To play games I first had to type in the programs then save them onto a tape cassette. A couple of years later, my parents bought a Spectrum computer for the family, which had slightly more local memory (16K, expandable to 128K), colour graphics, and you could buy pre-made games on cassette.[3] In the mid-1980s, my father had a satellite phone installed in his company car so he could be contacted when he was driving around the country to visit work sites.[4] I left home for university in 1988. The library catalogue was still mostly card based, but it was possible to do some electronic search for items. My essays were handwritten or typed, and communication with staff and departments was via letters and noticeboards. In 1989, I first accessed the internet, still in the pre-web era, and had my first email account in the same year, though I barely used it as few other people I knew had an address.

In the 1990s, everything seemed to change. When I started my Master's degree in GIS in 1991, my parents bought me my first personal computer. For £900 I got a 286 IBM clone with 1Mb of internal memory and 16Mb hard drive. It was painfully slow to use, and if I set it to run a program that would rotate a small, basic array (for example a portion of a remote sensing image) 90 degrees it would take hours (an operation that is now complete before I've fully removed my finger from the mouse button). My lecturers, nearly all of whom were computer-savvy, communicated with the class using email, and I would use the chat facility to real-time talk with other students on the campus network (but not off-site). In 1992, I had my first encounter with a computer virus, which corrupted my thesis files (though thankfully I had week-old versions backed up). My digital data footprint at this time was still tiny. I had a bank card which I used in ATMs, I barely explored the internet, and most communication and record-keeping was still paper based. I was certainly identified by a suite of indexical codes[5] (for example, national insurance number, bank account, credit card, passport, loyalty cards, permanent address, postcode), but the digital data shadow attached to these was relatively circumscribed and added to sporadically.

The World Wide Web (WWW) started to change things by making information accessible across the internet through an easy-to-use, intuitive graphical interface. I first accessed the WWW using the Mosaic browser in 1993/94. In the same period, I invested in a home internet connection through a modem attached to the phone line. In 1995, I published my first article about the internet that detailed the geographical resources and data becoming available online.[6] I also made my first online purchase. Using the internet, I started to leave digital traces in my wake – locations, interests and movements (websites, hypertext links), interactions (email, chat) and transactions (purchases). In everyday life, my digital data shadow was also growing through the use of debit, credit and store loyalty cards, and captured in government databases which were increasingly digital. By the late 1990s, mobile phones using 2G cellular networks were starting to become commonplace, though I didn't own one until the mid-2000s. I started to become fascinated with the transformation occurring, and my first book, *Cyberspace*, published in 1998, discussed the ways in which the culture, politics, administration and economy of everyday life were rapidly becoming mediated by internet technologies.

The speed at which digital technologies became embedded into the fabric of our homes, work and public spaces, and started to thoroughly augment and mediate everyday life – labour, travel, communication, consumption, play and leisure – is quite startling. In 2005, Martin Dodge and myself had two articles published that charted the extent of the changes. The first plotted day-in-the-life vignettes of three people's everyday encounters with digital technology from when they woke up to when they went to sleep at night.[7] Despite having very different backgrounds, lifestyles and jobs, each person encountered digitally mediated objects, systems, processes, interactions and transactions throughout their day and in different environments. In fact, we concluded that it was all but impossible to live a digitally free life and not leave data footprints[8] and cast data shadows.[9]

Running tandem to the creation of digital lifestyles was the datafication[10] of everyday life. In the space of 15 years, I'd gone from creating very narrow, selective data traces, to producing streams of varied and rich data. This was evident in the second paper which examined the various ways in which digital data was being generated and tracked using indexical codes about people, but also objects (using barcodes, RFID chips, manufacturer serial numbers, vehicle licence plates and so on), transactions (order numbers, shipping numbers), interactions (email ID, message ID) and territories (postcodes, grid references, latitude and longitude coordinates), and how these data were being used to govern people and manage organizations. To illustrate our argument we examined the data traces held within a typical wallet (which was actually Martin's wallet on 14 July 2003).[11] In the wallet was a variety of plastic cards, most with magnetic strips and/or RFID chips that stored key data, and pieces of paper. The cards included three library cards, a British rail card, a bank ATM/debit card,

a credit card, staff card, door access card and a donor card, each
with its own unique ID code, and in a couple of cases a photo.
The printed paper were mostly receipts, each of which included
a merchant code, authorization code, till receipt number, and a
portion of the credit card number used for purchase, some with
printed barcodes on them. There was also a business card (that
detailed work address, phone number, email and web address),
a bus ticket and train ticket (transaction ID), Post-it notes with
pin and telephone numbers written on them, and cash (each
note having unique ID number). Each of us and our activities
were being captured in data traces.

As the 2000s progressed, this datafication intensified through
the continued application of networked digital technologies to
every aspect of life. Systems and processes that were reliant on
mechanical or electro-mechanical systems were augmented or
replaced with digital counterparts.[12] Cars, for example, started
to be fitted with sensors and digital controllers, using real-time
data to mediate the driving experience.[13] Objects and systems
became 'smart', using data and algorithms to anticipate and be
reactive to use. They also started to log their own use, and if
networked, share that log with developers, manufacturers and
service providers.[14] The transition to Web 2.0, the introduction
of the smartphone, online purchasing, and e-governance, in
particular, deepened personal datafication.

Up until around 2003, the WWW was largely a broadcast
media. Companies and those technically savvy enough created
websites through which internet users could access a vast
collection of information and purchase goods and services.
The emphasis was on consumption rather than participation.
In the early 2000s, however, a transition to what was termed
Web 2.0 took place in which the production of web content
was diversified.[15] A new suite of media tools enabled internet
users to easily author and share their own content and to interact
with one another. These included social networking sites such
as Facebook, blogs, synchronous microblogs such as Twitter,
shared gaming spaces and multiuser virtual worlds, mash-ups,
media and code distribution services such as YouTube, Flickr,
and SourceForge, peer-to-peer file sharing via protocols like
BitTorrent, and social tagging and bookmarking. The internet

became a read+write media, in which people added value to sites as they used them.[16] In the process, users of these services shared their thoughts, opinions and values, as well as revealing their social networks.

Smartphones started to appear in the early 2000s, with the launch of the iPhone in 2007 creating a tipping point into mass use. Merging the functions of a personal computer with mobile phone, a smartphone provides powerful, networked computation. On the move, a user has access to the internet, email, a camera and a diverse range of apps. Along with the data gathered by the phone itself through its range of sensors, the data transmitted through its use mean that a smartphone constitutes a spy in our pockets, generating granular and detailed sets of data about us. Purchases and other transactions, such as online banking, are routinely conducted using smartphones, as well other personal computers, providing detailed traces of consumption patterns and lifestyle. The shift to using digital systems and e-governance at all levels of government mean that we often interface with public agencies through the internet, sharing required information by filling out forms. Key personal data are piped directly into state databases, with algorithms working on these data to ensure we are compliant with legal responsibilities and receive appropriate benefits and services. Other personal data are generated by mass surveillance via cameras, phone and Wi-Fi tracking, travel cards, and networks of transponders and sensors.

We now live in a world of continuous data production, since smart systems generate data in real time. Data streams off your smartphone, smart TV, smart car, laptop and tablet, and any other networked computational device, even when you are not directly using them. As well as seeking permission to use the camera, microphone and other sensors, Android apps can look to access a range of data stored on the phone[17] including device information, email, phone and message logs, photos and sound recordings, internet traffic and clickstreams, Wi-Fi connections, app activity and data usage, battery details,[18] GPS logs[19] and telephony information. Data are being harvested by the device manufacturer, operating system provider and app companies.

If you want to get a sense of how much data is being captured about you it is instructive to look at the data holdings of Google and Facebook. Both companies provide options to let you look at and delete all the data they hold about you.[20] Through their various services and subsidiary companies (for example, Facebook also own WhatsApp and Instagram, plus many others), these two companies generate an enormous volume of data about their users. For example, Google has a record of every search conducted across various devices and every app used on an Android phone, along with interactions made, and location and movement of the phone. If the Chrome browser is used then it knows a user's web history; Gmail, all the emails sent; Calendar, the diary of events; Google Drive, all the files stored; Play, what was bought; YouTube, what was watched; Blogger, what was blogged; and so on. Similarly, Facebook captures a date and time stamped record of every interaction with the platform, including location and device used. It logs every post made, along with edits, comments, likes, and shares; every message made; every photo and video posted; every friend and interaction; movement across websites that have a Facebook 'like' button; information about other apps on the device and any apps connected to a Facebook account. Between them, an enormous amount of detailed personal data is being captured daily for billions of people. By 2017, the Chrome browser has been downloaded over 5 billion times.[21] There were 1.5 billion Gmail accounts[22] and 1.5 billion WhatsApp users in 2018.[23] In 2019, there were 2.5 billion active Android-powered smartphones in use,[24] 2 billion monthly users of YouTube,[25] 1 billion Instagram users[26] and 2.45 billion active Facebook users.[27] That's billions and billions of data points and associated metadata being generated daily.

Much of my life used to be private. My activities, behaviours, thoughts, interests, communications, consumption, work were known to myself, some family and friends, and in a limited way by others such as my bank, employer and government department. What mass datafication means is the creation of rich and detailed data shadows. Consider location and movement. Generally, my position and travel were only known to those I was with or who'd been told of my plans. Now, they are streamed continually via my smartphone, tracked via the GPS sensor and connections to cell masts and Wi-Fi points. My network provider is updated on my location every couple of minutes, as are any apps that have location tracking enabled. My movement is also tracked via the onboard GPS of my car, the vehicle's automatic passage through tolls facilitated by a transponder, and the scanning of its number plate by ANPR cameras. Passage on public transport is captured by my use of a travel card. Movement on foot can be captured via CCTV, which is increasingly using facial recognition, and by using a MAC-address sensor to track my phone.[28] Many buildings use smart card tracking to monitor and control movement through their spaces. Smart cards are also used to access and pay for public transport.

These location and movement data are not in the public domain, visible to others, as with much social media content. However, they can circulate within data markets. The same is true for other personal data traces. For more than a century, there has been a suite of companies that specialize in gathering together data sets to extract insight and create data products and services. In the digital era, data brokers have grown enormously in number and scale forming a multibillion-dollar industry. As well as large consolidators that purchase, collate and link together data from many different sources, there are more niche brokers specializing in particular data forms, services and markets, such as consumer behaviour, search and background checks, micro-targeted advertising, and credit worthiness. In 2012, Acxiom was reputed to have constructed a databank on 500 million active consumers worldwide, with on average c.1,500 data points per person.[29] By 2018, this had grown to 2.2 billion consumers.[30] By meshing together offline, online and mobile data they claimed to be able to provide a '360-degree view' on consumers with respect to their demographics, financial and purchase history and patterns, political views and values, health, education, address history, criminal and civil case records and so on.

Brokers add and extract value from the data through linking, sorting, matching, analyzing and creating profiles. In other words, they practise dataveillance, monitoring people through their data traces.[31] In turn, they lease/sell the derived data and their data services to a range of clients including public sector bodies, banks and financial services, insurance companies, media conglomerates, retail chains, healthcare providers, telecommunications industries and others. These services are designed to help clients assess, socially sort,[32] predictively model and profile, micro-target, nudge, and deliver personalized treatment and recommendations for their customers and citizens in various ways. The aim is to minimize risky transactions by identifying which people to marginalize and exclude (for example denying credit and loans, blocking tenancy, not shortlisting for job hires) and to build customer loyalty by identifying who to value and reward (for example through special offers and personalized services). Such decisions might be based on making inferences about how likely it is a person will make their payments or how reliable a worker they might be, or their projected lifetime value if they remain a loyal custom or employee, or how likely they are to move their custom or labour. In this sense, datafication and dataveillance are key processes underpinning the rise of what has been termed 'surveillance capitalism,'[33] in which extracting value from data is a key driver of profit.

For government departments and public sector bodies datafication and dataveillance have shifted the nature of their work and the mode of governance they enact. Since the birth of the digital age in the 1950s, governments have used computers and databases to manage populations and deliver services. Cybernetic thinking in the 1960s underpinned initial attempts to plan infrastructure and services using computer models. In the 1980s and 1990s, personal computers started to become commonplace in central and local government, used for administration and operational delivery, and technologies designed to regulate behaviour, such as traffic management systems, were deployed. The rise of the internet in the 1990 and 2000s, led to large investments in e-government (the delivery of services and interfacing with the public via digital channels) and e-governance (managing citizen activity using digital tools). Our data were captured by governments intent on effectively and efficiently regulating, policing and planning for society, making sure those that deserve and qualify receive payments and services, and countering fraud. The use of digital technologies to mediate governance has deepened in the 2010s with the rise of big data systems. Data brokers provide some of these data and data services. Indeed, a key driver of government becoming data-driven has been a move to make government act more like a business, and to work more closely with businesses through outsourcing and public-private partnerships. In many cases, this has included privatizing services, and in doing so privatizing publicly owned data, which can then be monetized in various ways (which also exempt them from being released as open data).

Whether the data was intended for the purpose, or whether we like it or not, our data are corralled and combined, value extracted, and used by businesses and government to make all kinds of decisions about our lives. In this way, data are not just left in our wake, but also precede us by influencing how we are treated in subsequent transactions. One of the prices of enjoying the benefits of living digital lives – increased choice, better products and services, improved productivity, efficiency, safety, security, interaction, convenience and so on – is mass datafication and dataveillance. Presently, almost every activity seems to produce data, even many that seem to still be pretty dumb (as opposed to smart). For example, turning on a water tap appears to be an analogue activity, but in the background the utility is digitally networked and the infrastructure and its users monitored and controlled by sensors, transponders, actuators and meters that feedback digital data concerning consumption, pressure, water quality and supply levels to centralized control rooms and databases. When I was growing up we lived small data lives, leaving minor data traces across the public sector and business. Now, we lead lives saturated and thoroughly shaped by data. And we are still coming to terms with this transition and its implications. Living data lives is a work in progress.

15

Recommended Life

'So, what are we going to watch?' Arthur asked, dropping into an armchair. He was fed up of watching an endless stream of superhero nonsense with his other grandchildren. Joe was 20 and attending university; surely he'd be past the superhero phase.

'How about *The Irishman*?' Joe looked across at his grandfather.

'What's his super-power?'

'What?'

'I take it he's not a Marvel character then? Green suit, red hair, his power is luck?'

'What? No! And what's with the stereotype clichés? He's a gangster.'

'An Irish gangster; I bet there's no stereotype clichés in it at all.'

'Whatever. It says it's a 96 per cent match.'

'Match to what?'

'To my tastes. You know, based on what I like.'

'On what you like?' Arthur tried to imagine what Joe would like. Unless it was sport he wasn't sure they'd have much in common. Depending on what movie was chosen, it could turn into a long evening. And he needed distraction given his daughter was spending her third night at the local hospital. Maybe they'd be better off going to the pub, but then what would they talk about? Half the time his grandson's generation seemed to speak a different language.

'Yeah, it's Netflix,' Joe said. 'It tracks what I watch and whether I like something, then suggests other programmes it thinks I might like.'

'So, you basically watch what it wants you to watch?'

'No. Well, kind of. It suggests shows and movies, but I do the picking. Do you want to watch this or not?'

'I don't know. Do you have good taste?'

'I've impeccable taste! It's about this hitman, right, who's looking back on his life working for the Mob and the secrets he's kept. It has a load of big names in it – Robert De Niro, Al Pacino, Joe Pesci, Harvey Keitel, Ray Romano. And it's directed by Martin Scorsese.'

'So, it's like *The Godfather* then.'

'I guess,' Joe hazarded.

'That hasn't been recommended to you?' He claims to have impeccable taste, Arthur thought, but he's never watched *The Godfather*. How could that be?

'Not yet. It's probably not available. There's a decent selection, but it's limited.'

'So, you see a selection of a selection?'

'I see things I'm more likely to enjoy. What's the point of watching stuff I'm unlikely to like?'

'I don't know. Maybe so you push your boundaries?' Arthur suggested. 'Get exposed to new stories, ideas, genres. Learn stuff. Cultivate new tastes. When was the last time you watched the news?'

Joe shrugged. 'Last week? Mum had it on.' He paused. 'Before, you know ... the accident.'

'But you've not watched it since?' Arthur thought it was best not to dwell on his daughter's condition. The doctors had said she would be fine. Eventually. Serious but stable was how they'd described her condition. This evening was meant to be a break from hanging around hospital and worrying; an attempt to do something normal. 'So, you've basically no clue what's going on the world?'

'I probably know more than you,' Joe countered. 'My timelines are full of bloody news. Trump this, Johnson that. Brexit and the EU. Syria. Russia. Storm Harry and Typhoon Meghan.'

'Timelines?'

'Twitter. Facebook.'

'Oh, Facebook. Another thing that only shows you what it wants you to see. It drives me crazy; posts by the same ten people all the time. That and the trolls. And the so-called targeted ads.

Its algorithms must be rubbish if they think I'm interested in golf accessories or voting for those idiots in government.'

If it wasn't for the fact that he stayed up to date with family news via the platform, Arthur would have quite gladly left it long ago.

'You must be writing some related posts,' Joe said, 'or sharing particular stories, or visiting golf websites.'

'Why would I be visiting golf sites? I barely like the game, let alone play it. And how does it know what I've been looking at?'

'It can track you across any page with Facebook 'like' button on. Probably any website.'

'Really?' Maybe he did need to get rid of Facebook after all, Arthur reflected. Why did these companies always have to spy on people? 'So, not only does it know what nonsense I'm looking at on Facebook, it knows what other rubbish I'm seeing online?'

'And using it to recommend stuff and direct adverts. I'm not the only one living in a filter bubble, Grandad.'

'At least I still have a bit of serendipity in my life, son. Your whole life is filtered and channelled. I choose my music. Or I get a random selection via the radio. You listen to whatever Spotify wants you to listen to.'

'Hardly random. The radio station has selected it for you. Its choices are guided by market influence, consumer surveys, and analytics on its streaming services. You hear what they and music companies want you to hear. At least I guide my recommendations and I listen to things I actually like. And Nan has a Spotify account.'

'And all we do is listen to same stuff from the 1960s and 1970s. The Beatles. The Stones. The Grateful Dead. David Bowie. T-Rex. What else is there other than a gangster movie?'

'We could try the latest *X-Men* or *Transformers*.'

Arthur groaned. So, Joe hadn't passed the superhero phase. And as for impeccable taste that was now firmly debunked. 'Not a chance. How about a comedy? Something funny. A decent romcom.'

'I'm not watching a romcom with you!'

'I bet you watch them with your girlfriend between all the violence and blood; they'll be half a dozen in your recommended list.'

'We watch dramas. Mysteries. Thrillers. Independent productions.'

'Sounds very romantic. But then she was a recommendation as well, wasn't she?'

'What?'

'You met via a dating site, right? Tinder or Match, or one of them.'

'How do you know about them?'

'I'm old, but I'm not dead or stupid, son. You think only young people know what's going on in the world? You think we don't read, or watch documentaries, or use the internet? That we don't use smartphones and apps? That folks my age don't date?'

'No, I …'

'My generation invented the internet. We sent men to the moon. We started the sexual revolution.'

'I …' Joe really didn't want to think about his grandfather and the sexual revolution. He just wanted to watch a decent movie and forget about the ventilator machine keeping his mother alive. Still, he was enjoying the banter. The old man still gave as good as he got.

'An algorithm picked your girlfriend for you,' Arthur teased. 'I let serendipity find mine.'

'You met Nan at a nightclub,' Joe countered. 'And you knew her a little already. Hardly serendipity. It was just a different kind of algorithm – glances across the floor, asking for a dance, buying her a drink. You crossed a room, I swiped right.'

'We hardly followed an algorithm.' When he was courting Sheila he'd probably never even heard of the word, Arthur thought. Now the whole bloody world was guided by them.

'But it wasn't really serendipity either. Yours was a leap of faith, I had profiles and a bunch of information. I made an informed choice. And it worked. Lana's great.'

'I never said she wasn't. I'm just saying you're the recommendation generation. Most of the crap you buy online is probably suggested to you or a promotion – books, clothes, gadgets. Most of it you don't need, or actually want.'

'And it was the same for you when you were my age, except you used a paper catalogue, or selected from the narrow range in a store, all curated for you. You're the original consumer generation. And your desires and choices were guided by coupons, vouchers and adverts, they just weren't so individually targeted. Your news was curated by media moguls through a handful of channels and newspapers.'

'Okay, fine, I guess we've always been living in filter bubbles,' Arthur granted, though he wasn't really sure he believed it. When he was his grandson's age there were three channels on the television and you watched what was on, or you didn't. End of story.

'And now,' Joe said, 'you're as much a part of any recommendation generation as I am. Nan chooses books based on suggestions and reviews. You went to Italy last year because you were sent a special deal.'

'Well, at least it seems we agree that we've all been hoodwinked by the capitalists.'

'Hoodwinked? I get to watch great TV, listen to the best music, read good books, wear clothes I like, date great girls. What's not to like?'

'I just don't think it's all it's cracked up to be. We're missing what's filtered out.'

'And maybe that's a good thing. Now, are we watching *The Irishman*, or not?'

'Sure,' Arthur conceded. 'Anything but another superhero movie, or a hospital drama.' They should have gone to the pub instead, he thought. They'd be free from the gaze of algorithms, and he didn't need a recommender system to know he'd be drinking Guinness. And if they'd run out of things to say they could have at least watched the football on the big screens as they supped their pints and tried to put Anne's plight out of mind for a while. Not that she would have thought that was a good idea. She'd have probably recommended they play a board game instead.

16

The Quantified Self

The first day of the workshop is over and most of the invited guests have joined The Programmable City team for pre-dinner drinks at a restaurant close to Maynooth Castle. For once, it's not raining and we're sitting outside. The professor opposite me is twirling her wrist. Ten minutes later, she's still rotating her arm, though a little less enthusiastically. Curiosity eventually wins out.

'Is there something wrong?' I ask.

'No, why?'

'You seem a little agitated.' I point to her arm.

'Oh, that. I'm doing my steps.'

'What?'

'I'm fooling my Fitbit into thinking I'm doing my steps.'

'Why?'

'So I don't ruin my stats.'

'Why don't you just go for a walk? It's still half an hour until dinner. You could do a loop round the campus, or go along the canal.'

She shrugs her shoulders. 'I wanted to come for drinks.'

'You could always go for a walk afterwards. It'll still be light.'

'I'll be too tired then. Anyway, 15 more minutes and I should reach my quota.'

'But you'll know that you've juked your stats.'

'Yes, but there won't be a blip in them.'

'Are you part of the quantified-self movement then?' I ask, thinking she wants to maintain good stats for when she compares them with others.

'No, no. I'm just trying to get myself in shape. Walk 10,000 steps a day.'

'So you're not sharing your data with anyone?'

'God, no.' She laughs. 'I'm the only person who looks at it.'

'So why are you creating false data?' I'm genuinely perplexed. If you're the only person who's going to see your self-created data, why would you juke your own stats? It makes little sense to me.

'Because I don't want to mess up my data. I've hit the target every day for the past three weeks.'

'Except you won't have done today. And even if your data says you did, you know that you didn't. What difference does it make?'

She shrugs. 'The blip will be annoying.'

'And Fitbit will know as well. Once you upload your data they'll know your step rate is too fast and that you were stationary.'

'Yes, but that's fine. It'll just be an anomaly in my data. And I don't really care what they think. Anyway, I could be on a treadmill.'

'And you're okay that they're tracking you, as well as you tracking yourself?'

'It's no different to what your phone provider collects.' She shrugs again. 'At least I'm making use of my own data. Even if I have gamed some of it.'

She continues to twirl her wrist as we carry on the conversation, the person next to her joining in.

In the following days, I kept revisiting this exchange as there were a few themes I found fascinating: organizing daily life to fulfil a self-imposed data quota, the juking of personal stats, the ambivalence to sharing personal data with a company, and the observation that my phone was de facto generating the same data and probably sharing it with the phone manufacturer and app companies.

I'd been wary of the quantified self since the mid-2000s when I started to research what data were being generated about us by states and companies as our lives became evermore digitally mediated. In 2006, along with long-term collaborator, Martin Dodge,[1] I became interested in a counterpoint to mass surveillance, sousveillance – the personal monitoring and management of one's life through self-generated data.[2]

Sousveillance was cast as empowering, inverting surveillance practices so they are generated from an interior (first person) perspective and controlled by an individual for their personal benefit. Continuously tracking personal data via sensors and cameras, and recording and analyzing them, would allow a person to manage and memorialize everyday life. This might be supplemented by enabling access to personal (for example, CCTV, financial) and other contextual data (for example, news, weather) generated by others. The key technological idea that research teams, companies and artists were exploring at the time was lifelogs.

A lifelog was conceived as a comprehensive, unified, digital record of an individual's experiences stored permanently as a personal multimedia archive. As a person went about their daily life, wearable computing would collect continuous streams of data, including images, sounds, movement and location. A person would record everything seen, heard, said and done, organizing the data into a searchable, recallable record. The ultimate aim is the simultaneous digitization of all cognitive inputs experienced by the brain via all five human senses to create a digital parallel memory of the lived experiences of a person. Want to know what you did, where you were, who you met, what was said, how you felt, what the physiological conditions inside your body (blood pressure and heart rate) and external conditions (orientation, temperature, and levels of pollution) on a particular date, at a particular time, you would be able to retrieve this data from your personal lifelog.[3] Beyond preserving memories, their advocates argued that lifelogs would reduce the need for photo albums, diaries, scrapbooks and material media (CDs, DVDs). Losing things would become a thing of the past as the lifelog would know where they were last used. Health conditions, stress levels, diet and fitness would be continuously self-monitored and used to spot, prevent and treat illnesses.[4]

While we could see some of the attractions of creating a lifelog, to us it also seemed to constitute something of a prison – you could never escape your data and thus your past. Bad luck, mistakes, scheming, duplicity, white lies, stupidity: these would all be preserved for evermore. They could never be forgotten, or moved past, or re-made by any party involved.[5] One could never start again – even by changing names and moving locations. A resilient record would make compromise, forgiveness and reconciliation harder to negotiate. Lifelogs would make an authoritarian, Big Brother society easier to put in place and more difficult to overthrow. At the same time, the accumulation of facts would be shorn of emotion, context and meaning; one would be left with thin not thick memories. The past would be recalled not remembered.[6]

Our memory is fallible. People forget. They misremember. It's a core part of what makes us human. Daniel Schacter, a psychologist, identifies six forms of forgetting, divided into two types.[7] Loss-based forgetting consists of transience (the loss of memory over time), absent-mindedness (the loss of memory due to distractedness) and blocking (the temporary inability to remember). Error-based forgetting consists of misattribution (assigning a memory to the wrong source), suggestibility (memories that are implanted either by accident or surreptitiously) and bias (the unknowing or unconscious editing or rewriting of experiences). Each of these is important in our daily lives, actively shaping our personal interactions and activities. An openness and fuzziness in our memories and historic record is essential to how our society works; they enable us to negotiate, debate, reconcile and find common ground. We need to be able to forget, misremember and edit the past.

For Martin and myself, lifelogs also raised a series of ethical and legal questions that were largely being bypassed. There were, for example, issues concerning access and control. Who would have the right to access the lifelog, other than the individual (for example, the tech provider, family members, the police or security services, employers, researchers)? To what extent could the material be sequestered for legal cases? What would the legal status of such material be, and would access be restrictive (for example, only selected records bounded by time/ dates or recording medium) or non-restrictive? What would happen to the lifelog at death? What would the inheritance rights be? To what extent should a lifelog be editable? Should there be an option to suspend recording if desired, and are there events and actions that should be excluded from capture? Could a lifelog be stolen and used in nefarious ways, or false data (memories) inserted into them, and what would be the consequences?[8]

In addition, lifelogs also create ethical questions concerning individuals caught in other people's lifelogs. This was amply illustrated when a lifelogging researcher visited The Programmable City team and presented some of his work. The professor was wearing a camera around his neck that took a picture every few seconds. At no point did he ask us for permission to take pictures of us or to use them as data in his personal lifelog or in his research. When questioned by the team, it was clear that ethical issues had never been a major concern in his thinking or implementation. He was much more interested in the technical challenges of creating a working system and exploring how to make sense of the data. At the time, he'd been wearing the camera for a few years and had an archive of several million geo-located photos that included tens of thousands of people (even just walking down the street would lead to dozens of people being captured), none of whom he'd sought permission from.

At the same time as we became interested in sousveillance and lifelogs, a set of intersecting digital technologies and practices took off that provided components of, and pathways towards, lifelogging. So-called 'intimate technologies'[9] – that is, digital tech that are in service to the individual, such as smartphones and wearable computing – started to grow enormously in popularity. Smartphones included apps that generated personal data which were presented back to the user. All kinds of activities could be tracked, including health, finance, game play, reading and so on. In the early 2010s, wearables such as fitness trackers and smartwatches helped start a quantified-self movement, in which people tracked their behaviour, using the data to improve their health, sometimes sharing and comparing data with each other. Gamified elements were often included that sought to incentivize personal improvements and continued interaction with the tech.

These were complemented, and supported, what might be termed 'scopophilic technologies',[10] that is, digital tech that enable pleasure in looking and being looked at. These included social media, such as blogs, through which a person could share their personal views and news, and social networking sites like Facebook and Twitter, and later Instagram and Snapchat, where users could share thoughts, photos and videos, and discuss them with friends and others. As the 2000s ended and the 2010s started, there was an explosion in self-creation, self-presentation and promotion, and active curation of digital lives.

It seemed we were no longer content with having our data harvested by others, sharing freely data we once kept private, such as family photographs and videos (via Flickr, Instagram and YouTube), personal and family stories (via Facebook and blogs), personal thoughts (via Twitter, chat rooms and online reviews), health and fitness (via social media updates, or quantified-self sites), and resumes (via LinkedIn or personal/work websites). What we might have shared with a handful of people (family, close friends, employers, health professionals) in limited forums (the home, a local bar, a human resources department, a surgery) was being globally broadcast for anyone to view.[11] To offset the loss of privacy, people often sought to carefully curate the material shared in order to construct a particular view of themselves. However, as many of us have found, it is difficult to shape how readers react to posted material, and impossible to control what others post about us and how that circulates. Moreover, once our data is publicly exposed they can be taken by others and used in ways for which they were never intended – scraped for research, monetized for targeted advertising, repackaged and sold to data brokers, folded into data profiles used to make decisions with respect to us.

While I was cautious about intimate technologies, joining the quantified-self movement, and practising sousveillance, I began to use social media at this time. I started my own blog in July 2009 – *The View From The Blue House*[12] – almost exclusively publishing book reviews of crime fiction and popular history and science books. In November of the same year, I commenced writing for a collective academic blog (*Ireland After NAMA*;[13] see also Chapter 22). In November 2010 I joined Goodreads,[14] using the platform to share book reviews. In January 2012 I joined Facebook and Twitter,[15] using the former to connect with family and friends and sharing more personal events and observations, and the latter to connect with work colleagues and other academics and sharing links and observations related to my research interests. In 2013, I started another work-related blog – *The Programmable City*[16] – and a Scoop.it[17] page for sharing news stories related to our research interests. I kept these channels reasonably separate, rather than posting the same content across them.

I did not escape quantifying some of my life, however, and that shaped my behaviour to some degree. For example, Goodreads provides reading (for example, books and pages read) and reviewing (for example, average ratings, reviewer rankings) stats. Blogger provides details of number of visitors and pages visited (and Google Analytics provides all kinds of data about where visitors are from, their time spent on each page, their route through the blog and so on). Twitter details the number of followers, impressions, mentions and profile visits over time,[18] and Facebook the number of friends. I had created a Google Scholar[19] profile for a research grant application and it provides the number of citations to my work and a h-index score,[20] both of which are becoming standard academic key performance indicators (see Chapter 18). Inevitably, I started to chase readers and followers: after all, what is the point of sharing if there's no audience to consume the material produced? A certain portion of my day disappeared into commodifying a hobby (reading fiction), sharing useful links and producing public scholarship.

I had shied away from quantifying my health and fitness, however.[21] The conversation in the restaurant made me ponder what it meant to live a quantified-self life. Would I gain anything positive from the experience? Would I become a slave to my data? Would I end up juking my own stats? I've always believed that one of the best ways to come to understand something is to practise it. To that end, I started to investigate which fitness tracker to purchase. After scouring review websites, my initial conclusion was that I didn't need to buy a dedicated tracker with an associated data service. My iPhone had the same sensors a fitness tracker uses – accelerometer/motion, three-axis gyroscope, compass, GPS, barometer/altitude (as well as others).[22] If I installed some apps and carried it at all times, it would function as a fitness tracker. In fact, it had been for some time, as I discovered when I first opened the Apple Health app and saw a history of my daily step count.

After a bit of searching and research I installed three apps on my iPhone. Walkmeter supports a walking and cycling fitness regime. It records and presents in real time walk time, distance, pace, cadence, steps, elevation, and estimates heart rate and calories burned. It records the route taken and presents it on a map. All the data is stored on the iPhone or iCloud, though data can be exported and imported in a variety of data formats and shared via email and social media. Times can be compared with previous laps or completions. By leaving the phone on the mattress, Sleep Cycle measures the quality of sleep throughout the night, keeping a record of time gone to bed, restless activity while asleep, patterns of snoring (even recording it so you can listen back), and estimates the best time to wake you depending on sleep cycle. Cardiio calculates pulse rate by using the light on the iPhone. Since blood absorbs light, as it is pumped through the end of a finger the reflected light from the phone denotes the peaks and troughs of a beat. The app records this data, presenting it back to the user, and by recording at rest and after activity a general picture of heart rate and fitness can be tracked.

What became quickly apparent was the richness of the data generated. Between the three apps I was producing highly granular, indexically linked, real-time data about activity, fitness, rest and health. Through visualizations and infographics I could track performance over time in micro-detail. Being a bit of data geek, the patterns in the data were fascinating. And I did start to change my behaviour in relation to what I was seeing. I was walking for longer and at a higher pace and seeing the effect on pulse. I was regulating when I was going to bed and trying to learn from my sleep stats. I did not share the data publicly, however. And I didn't try to find ways to juke my stats. It didn't take long though before I became bored with the regime. I learned something about my bodily behaviour, but ultimately I was not that interested in what the data told me. I was also giving a lot of detailed information to Apple and the app developers.

Within six months, I had abandoned my experiment. I'd confirmed to myself that I was still deeply uncomfortable with the idea that a lifelog would contain all these data and much more for an entire lifetime. Masses and masses of details that others might find some way of monetizing, but I would almost certainly never revisit. As my initial thoughts had foretold, forgetting is useful. That's not to say that you should follow suit. You might get great insight and value from self-tracking data about aspects of your life. Indeed, while I make little use of intimate technologies, I continue to use social media, getting value from sharing my work and interactions with others. It is to say though, that it is worth reflecting on the amount of data we self-generate and openly share beyond what is externally harvested, how it reshapes the ways in which we live our lives, and the potential personal and societal implications. And to recognize that we have only begun to grapple with the social, political, ethical and legal consequences and formulate adequate responses to issues arising. In the meantime, we are sharing highly personal data and creating partial lifelogs, often with undue care.

17

Fighting Fires

Kyle was too tired to leap to anger, but he could sense that it might erupt in him shortly. He leant forward in his chair. 'So, what you're saying is my benefits have been suspended because I haven't applied for enough jobs.'

'You haven't applied for any jobs,' Mrs Costello replied, trying to hide her embarrassment. The young man was clearly exhausted, his clothes were filthy and he smelled of sweat and smoke.

'Yes, because if it hadn't escaped your notice, the country is on fire. I'm a volunteer firefighter with the Rural Fire Service.' He hadn't showered before coming to the welfare office. He'd found the letter on the mat after 14 hours of battling flames through the night and early morning and got straight back in his car.

'You still need to apply for the requisite number of jobs per week if you want to continue receiving benefits, Mr Kelly.'

'Are you serious?' Kyle closed his eyes. He was having difficulty getting his head around the situation: you bust a gut trying to help tackle a major disaster and the state screws you for your efforts. 'I've been fighting fires almost full-time since September. Every day for the past six weeks. I've barely slept.'

'I'm sorry, Mr Kelly, but there are rules that have to be followed.'

'Surely you can make an exception given the circumstances?'

'I'm afraid not. The system doesn't accept fighting fires as a valid exception.' More often than she would admit, Mrs Costello hated her work. She was left to explain the indefensible to people who deserved better. As far as she was concerned the system was failing Kyle Kelly. Not that she could tell him that. Instead, she had to parrot the institutional line.

'But that's crazy!' Kyle snapped. 'A state of emergency has been declared. Twelve million acres have burnt since July.[1] Hundreds of houses have been destroyed, millions of wildlife killed. People have been evacuated and rescued. Two dozen people have lost their lives. Most of the time day seems like night because of the thick smoke. We've been trying to fight dozens of firestorms in 40-degree temperatures, hotter with the flames.'

'I know, and personally I'm extremely grateful, but there's nothing I can do.' She stared out the window, avoiding eye contact. 'The system reacts automatically to the data and applies the rules. You have no applications, and no other credits, therefore your benefits are suspended.'

'What am I meant to live on? I have bills. Rent. Responsibilities.'

'I'm sorry, Mr Kelly, I don't make the rules, I just …'

'I'm not leaving here until this is sorted out,' Kyle said, calmly. 'I've put my life at risk to fight these bloody fires and this is how the state repays me, by cutting off my benefits? Maybe I should burn this damn place down?'

'Mr Kelly, please,' Mrs Costello said, trying to keep her voice even. 'There's no need for threats.'

'Isn't there?' Kyle said. 'It seems like it might be the only thing that'll work.'

'The only thing it'll do is make the situation worse.'

'Worse than being homeless? At least in prison I'd have a roof over my head, three meals a day.'

'Look,' Mrs Costello said, trying to move the conversation on, 'I believe there's a compensation package for those who've been tackling the fires for over ten days? But it's not administered by this office.'

Kyle snorted. 'I'm not falling for that so you can get rid of me. It only applies to those who were missing work to volunteer, not unemployed volunteers. It compensates for lost pay – at a rate well below what they would have earned otherwise. I'm working full-time.'

Kyle tapped his chest.

'More than full-time. For the state. But not only am I not getting paid, my unemployment's been suspended. I'm being doubly screwed. And no, I can't live on savings that I don't have.'

'I'm sorry, Mr Kelly, but the solution is to fulfil the application quota or get a job.'

'I had a job. I was a paralegal. Got laid off because a bloody app could do the work faster and more efficiently. Just like your damn system.'

'There must be other work for someone with your qualification and skill set.'

'You mean besides saving lives and property?' Kyle said sarcastically, his ire starting to wane. 'I doubt I'll work in the legal profession again. It's all becoming automated and data-driven: contract review and due diligence, discovery, billing, IP infringements, legal research and expertise. Algorithms now provide the trusted advice. You'd be better off with an IT background than a law degree.'

'I'm sure that's not the …'

'I read a report that said that about 50 per cent of current work activities can be automated using existing technologies.[2] Any job that is rote or rule-based is screwed: law, medicine, pharmacy, education, administration. They'll be replacing you soon,' he said, with a note of glee in his voice.

'Me?' Mrs Costello exclaimed, placing her hand on her chest.

'It was a machine that decided to suspend my payments. You're just someone to soften the blow and provide advice. Pastoral care will go out the window and the rest is rule-based. Easier to send an email, or use an automated phone service.'

'I don't think …'

'What?' Kyle said, becoming animated again. 'You think you're immune because you work for the government? We're in this together!'

'Well …'

'They'll downsize the workforce to save costs as soon as they can. I've a mate working as volunteer after he was let go from garbage collection. The street bins now measure how full they are with a sensor and an algorithm routes the trucks to only those that need emptying. Instead of going round all of them twice a day, they visit less than half of them. Reduced the staff by the same amount, saving salary and future pensions, as well as truck and fuel costs. Data-driven efficiency. Lovely.'

'I'm sure there'll be new jobs created,' Mrs Costello said, trying to inject a bit of optimism, though the tone of her voice failed her. 'As the economy changes, different jobs come and go. All the agricultural jobs were replaced by industrial ones, which were replaced by manufacturing, which were replaced by services. It goes in cycles. Now it all appears to be digital.'

'Which is great, except if you're not in IT,' Kyle said.

'There's always the gig economy,' Mrs Costello suggested, clutching at straws. 'You know, Uber, Deliveroo, Fiverr, that kind of thing.'

'Seriously, as a career? Running around as a slave to a bloody app. Another job chasing data. No, thanks. Is that what you plan to do when they replace you with a bot?'

'I …'

'It was bad enough when you forced me to work in that bloody warehouse. Ten hours a day collecting orders against a countdown clock. Up and down rows and stairs. Two items a minute. Timed toilet breaks. A supervisor monitoring your progress and berating you for missing quotas. Not so much digital leash as digital noose. My phone showed I was walking 12 to 15 miles a day for minimum wage. Could you walk 12 miles a day on a timer?'

'At least it was a job,' Mrs Costello said weakly, knowing that she'd hate a gig job, especially one that involved walking all day.

'Some job! The only reason they had employees was it was cheaper than robots – they don't need fixing and they're easier to replace. And they treated you like you were one.'

'A job has to be better than no job.'

'No, I don't buy that. And I've been doing a job. Fighting fires. Maybe I need to start making them?' He took a lighter from his pocket and flicked the wheel. A flame appeared briefly, then vanished.

'Mr Kelly, please.' Mrs Costello glanced at the door behind him, judging her chances of escape. The young man was clearly teetering on the edge, exhausted from fighting the fires on two fronts. 'Be reasonable.'

'Like you, you mean?'

'Look, I appreciate why you're upset, but I don't make the rules. I don't even enforce them. I'm just an advisor. Put away the lighter and we can fill out the forms together and start the process of applying for some jobs.'

'That'll restore my benefits?'

'It'll start the procedure for restoring them.' She turned to the computer monitor on her desk. 'I'll just …'

Kyle plucked the welfare letter from his shirt pocket and clicked the lighter wheel again. 'I want them restored now.'

'Please, Mr Kelly. Don't do anything rash.'

'All I'm asking for is a bit of sense. The state would prefer to see millions in damage done to property and industry than cover my benefits, while I try to save them a fortune in compensation and lost revenue. You must see that's a false economy.'

'I agree, but you said it yourself: it's all algorithms and data. I can help you start the process but there's little I can do otherwise. The system is designed to make it difficult to be on welfare. As far as it's concerned, you are your data. The rules are the rules.'

'And this lighter starts fires. Maybe you should go and see if you can find someone who can help. Perhaps they can "tweak",' Kyle mimicked air quotes, 'the algorithms.'

'You won't do anything silly while I'm gone?' Mrs Costello said, standing up.

'Me? I'm not the one causing the problem here.'

The welfare officer fled the room saying that she would be back shortly.

Kyle put the lighter back in his trouser pocket. He tipped back his head to stare at the ceiling wondering how he'd managed to let the situation develop as it had. It was as if the conversation had had a life of its own, like a bush fire fuelled by a brisk wind.

Three minutes later and most of his fight had evaporated, leaving him feeling like a patch of scorched earth. All he wanted now was a shower and his bed.

The door behind him opened. He glanced back and sighed. Two security guards entered the office, followed by Mrs Costello.

'Now, don't do anything stupid, son,' the older guard said. 'The police have been called.'

'Seriously? All I was asking for was a bit of humanity. Is that too much to ask?'

Mrs Costello looked sheepish but didn't answer. She felt sorry for the young man and his plight, but not for seeking help. Her job might be pretty crummy but that was no excuse for intimidation.

'You threatened one of our staff,' the guard said.

'So, it's okay for you to threaten my livelihood, but not the other way round?'

'Look, son, none of us make the rules round here. Let's just wait peacefully for the police to show up.'

'And let's hope your house isn't in the way of a wall of fire while I'm cooling my heels, or filling out your pointless applications, or, God forbid, driving a bloody Uber. It would be a shame if we all lost our homes because of an app; especially as it'll be placing you on this side of the desk as well before long.'

18

Management Through
Metrics

'So, you're opposed to using KPIs to track how well we're doing?'

'I just don't think they're a good means of comparing performance across disciplines. What's valued and expected in terms of research, teaching and service vary. There are different opportunities to land big grants or work with industry and government. The gold standard for publication differs. Some subjects are more popular with students than others, meaning higher teaching and admin demands.'

The University Research Committee are discussing a proposal to use a set of key performance indicators to measure departmental performance. A colleague from the Science faculty is arguing in favour of an indicative set of KPIs that senior management is recommending be adopted. I am pushing back. In part because I think that managing through KPIs will fail to produce the outcomes intended. But also because I think the measures chosen are inherently biased and will make some departments appear as if they are over-performing and others as if they are failing, as well as creating other counterproductive effects such as internal competition and overwork leading to loss of morale and stress-related ill-health.

The science professor continues: 'We have to have some way of measuring how well staff and departments are doing and what progress they're making. The government want us to use KPIs and we have to supply them with data. And every other country is using KPIs.'

'Okay, if we have to use KPIs I want them standardized,' I say, changing tack. I'm unlikely to win an argument about whether we'll use them if the mandate is coming from outside the university. However, if they're letting us determine our own KPIs, I can try to influence their form.

'Standardized? How?'

'Well, a lot of the ones you're proposing are actually flat counts and inputs – how much grant income earned, how many students enrolled, how many publications produced. If you're going to use KPIs they should be standardized against base resources, and performance tracked by outputs and impact. So, rather than simply counting how much research income was gained, we measure what was produced with that funding.'

'I'm not sure …'

'Okay, how about we adopt a KPI that measures return on investment for research funding by standardizing outputs by income. So, what we'd do is divide the value of a grant by the number of articles to give us the cost per output.'

'But the cost per output in science would be huge.' From the change in tone of his voice, my colleague has realized where I might be going with my argument. 'From a two-million-euro grant in bioscience you might only get six to ten good articles.'

'Whereas a historian might produce five good articles from a fifty-thousand-euro grant. So €200,000 per article versus €10,000 per article. Which one is giving us more bang for their buck in terms of investment?'

'But you can't measure research value in that way. Doing science research costs a lot of money. You need expensive labs, equipment, research assistants.'

'Yes, good point. We'd also need to standardize the outputs by staffing,' I say, labouring my argument. 'The history grant probably just had two people working on it – the PI and a postdoc – for five articles, the bioscience one might have had five or six. So not only is each output better value in monetary terms, they're better value in terms of people effort. If we invested two million euros in the humanities, we'd actually be much better off in terms of research impact – we'd have way more outputs – than spending big money in science. The return on investment would be enormous.'

'I don't think this is a sensible way to look at this.' My colleague's getting flustered. 'We ...'

'Any statistician will tell you that KPIs should be standardized. And inputs shouldn't be treated as if they are outputs. It's what you do with a resource that matters if you're measuring performance. If we don't standardize them, then we're practising poor science.'

'Other universities and countries are using these KPIs.'

'That doesn't make them good practice. We all moan about university rankings and the fact that they're completely flawed, but you seem happy to use the same measures when it suits you. The only reason you like KPIs such as flat research income is because it makes your department look great. If we're going to use them, then I propose that we at least try to use them sensibly.'

At this point, the chair of the meeting intervenes in our exchange and invites others present to comment. Not unsurprisingly, members from the humanities and social science faculties are in favour of other means of measuring performance such as external peer review. If the university is going to progress with KPIs then they would like them standardized. They also propose other KPIs that would work more favourably for them. Members from the sciences and engineering, while sympathetic to the counter-arguments, favour the non-standardized KPIs being proposed by management.

Anyone working in a university will be familiar with management through metrics and the arguments surrounding them. If you work in the public or private sector, you'll probably also be familiar with an increasing number of measures being generated to monitor, reward and punish performance and guide decision-making. You might have taken part in similar conversations about the pros and cons of such workplace governance, or been a beneficial recipient of playing the metrics game, or a victim, losing one's job or being limited to casualized contracts.

Since the 1980s and the introduction of new public management (NPM) – an approach to running public sector institutions in a more businesslike way – various kinds of assessment (for example, KPIs, ratings and rankings) have been introduced to measure and track performance. Usually these measures are institutionalized through formalized assessment schemes designed to improve efficiency, productivity and quality. Rather than trying to influence outcomes through input controls and bureaucratic oversight, NPM shifts the emphasis to output controls. Those institutions who perform well are rewarded through additional resources, whereas those who are deemed to be failing are subject to remedial interventions designed to improve outcomes.[1]

Assessment schemes are usually run across a sector, encouraging institutions to compete with each other to achieve higher scores and associated rewards. The external assessment scheme is often mirrored by an in-house scheme created to reform internal practices in order to make an institution more competitive. Critically, to be effective the mode of assessment has to be clear and transparent with respect to intent, goals, methods, indicators of progression, and rewards in order to encourage the desired reforms and outcomes. Typically, this means creating and tracking quantitative measures, with the whole process being highly data-driven.

The result with respect to universities has been a datafication of the entire third-level sector, institutionalizing measures to track performance and impact by individuals (for example, citations, h-index, invited talks, income, teaching feedback), department and faculty (for example, staff/student ratios, collective research income and outputs, teaching evaluations) and the university as a whole, across all elements of work (research, teaching, administrations, service and outreach). An entire bureaucracy has developed to oversee this datafication, and the management of institutions has transformed to become more instrumental and technocratic, guided by metrics. Decisions concerning individual promotion, departmental staffing and budgets, strategic investments are informed by KPIs and rankings. In places like the UK and Australia, management through metrics has become deeply ingrained into the working lives of academics and the management of institutions, and it is common across OECD countries that adopted NPM practices.

While Ireland has managed to avoid the worst excesses of management through metrics it has not been totally immune, as the opening conversation highlights. KPIs are now a part of the management regime and are used to guide decision-making, but they are used alongside other forms of information rather than narrowly determining outcomes. At a sectoral level, institutional KPIs are used to report to the HEA, and also supply data for the global university rankings.

These global rankings seem to have become an obsession for many university leaders, as well as being used by politicians and civil servants to shape education policy, and seized on by the media as a means to report on how institutions are performing. Every year in Ireland the global rankings generate headlines, especially since Irish institutions have been slipping down the rankings and no Irish university is now in the top 100. In 2013, I had a conversation with an RTE[2] reporter the day one set of rankings were released. They were bemoaning the lowly rankings of Irish universities and were preparing to run a story critiquing institutional performance. I tried to persuade them that Ireland was actually doing quite well, with all seven universities in the top 450 (out of 9,000 higher education institutions globally),[3] meaning that all of them are in the top 5 per cent.[4] If the scores were standardized by resourcing and staff-student ratios they would be even higher. I was told that spinning the story positively would reduce its impact. I then ran through all the critiques of the methodology employed – the use of proxy measures, the lack of site visits, biases and skewing in samples, legacy effects, not comparing like-with-like, and lack of standardization by resourcing.[5] The negative story ran. After all, how are academics and universities to improve if they are not striving to meet targets and avoid critique?

Those promoting management through metrics point to productivity and performance gains in the public sector as proof that the approach works. They argue that the system creates a meritocracy, with those performing the best rewarded for their efforts. Nigel Thrift, who finished his career as Vice Chancellor of Warwick University, expressed this opinion to me once in a conversation in which he defended the Research Excellence Framework (REF) in the UK as being profoundly meritocratic. For him, the REF's predecessor, the Research Assessment Exercise (RAE), had broken the Old Boys Network that had been dominant when he was a PhD student. He argued that up until the 1990s, around 60 per cent of all Geography appointments in the UK had gained their doctorate in just four institutions: Cambridge, Oxford, Bristol and Edinburgh. The RAE rewarded performance and enabled him to rise up through the ranks without the benefit of the network (though ironically he became a professor in Bristol and pro-vice chancellor in Oxford). Similarly, it enabled the best of the New Universities (former polytechnics and colleges of further education) to progress up the rankings and corral additional resources.

Those opposed to management through metrics also want well-run institutions, ones that are efficient, productive and deliver high-quality services, but do not believe that the highly instrumental and technocratic approach of NPM is the best way to achieve this. They argue that there are number of fundamental flaws in how the approach is constituted and works. Metrics, they contend, are overly narrow and functional, are inherently biased towards those that already have the characteristics desired, and can be gamed. Metrics are underpinned by normative assumptions about what should be measured, for what reasons, and what they should tell us.[6] They are inherently political in constitution, selection and deployment. As my opening conversation illustrates, which KPIs are selected and how they are formulated can produce significantly different impressions and outcomes. My proposed changes would have flipped the research performance ratings of the Biology and History departments.[7] If data are combined to create compound metrics, slight alterations in weightings and formula can lead to different scores and rankings.[8]

At a system level, management through metrics is typically a zero-sum game with winners and losers. Someone is always going to be ranked last, even if they actually are performing above a desired threshold. The system consolidates and reinforces reputation and reward, giving additional benefits to those who do not need them, in turn making them even stronger and more difficult to catch up to, and penalizes those that need investment. This can create some perverse effects. For example, a British primary school that my brother used to work in was deemed to be failing. English was not the primary spoken language at home for over 90 per cent of the children attending. While the school did a fantastic job at accelerating their learning, they would get limited help at home and performed poorly in tests compared to children from other backgrounds in other schools. The solution was to close the school and distribute the children into three other nearby schools, who then also became 'failing schools' with 'failing teachers' simply by absorbing 'failing students'. In reality, given the context and resources the school was not failing, except with respect to a narrow set of metrics; in fact, the school was doing very well given the circumstances.

These perverse effects arise because the performance metrics approach treats all institutions in a system as if they are trying to achieve the same ends and have the same resources. Oxford University and Bournemouth University are trying to perform very different roles and mandates. They serve different constituencies of students. They have different kinds of rosters of staff. They have significantly different resources and funding. They should be judged and rewarded based on how well they are performing in terms of meeting their objectives, not benchmarked against each other. We should expect Harvard to be ranked seventh globally[9] given it has a multibillion-dollar endowment fund, it attracts star academics and its students pay tens of thousands a year in fees. But one could make a case that my own institution, Maynooth University, is actually performing better given its resourcing base. It is ranked at 323. Of course, the global rankings are not standardized.

Critics argue that inside of institutions, NPM has created too many negative consequences that are counterproductive. Productivity gains are often created through staff self-exploiting their own unwaged labour to try and get ahead, working evenings and weekends to meet and exceed targets. This has certainly been the case in academia, with scholars spending their supposedly free time researching and writing papers, preparing lectures and marking, and undertaking admin. The typical working week now extends well beyond 40 hours[10] and the fabled 'long holidays' of the summer remain wishful thinking. Such additional work soon becomes normalized, and the outputs produced become the new expected targets. In addition, the use of metrics creates internal competition for resources at the expense of collaboration and collegiality. Workplace relations and culture can be transformed, encouraging institutions to casualize staffing in order to be flexible in relation to fluctuating resourcing and to identify high achievers for more permanent positions. The stress created by the new working conditions can alienate and demoralize staff leading to employee churn as workers seek better circumstances elsewhere. At the same time, metrics allow senior staff to manage at a distance, providing evidence to justify hard decisions and alleviating them from taking full responsibility for the actions they make. Metrics then do not simply act as a camera reflecting the world as it is, but rather act as an engine re-shaping the world they measure.[11] They not only represent academic work, but actively redefine academic labour.

Metrics can also have unanticipated effects, for example, enacting Campbell's Law: 'The more any quantitative social indicator is used for social decision-making, the more subject it will be to corruption pressures and the more apt it will be to distort and corrupt the social processes it is intended to monitor.'[12] In other words, once introduced, managers and workers start to game the system in rational, self-interested but often unpredictable ways to influence their metrics. As Steve Jobs put it: 'Incentive structures work. So you have to be very careful of what you incent people to do.' Leighton Evans discovered such an unanticipated effect in a study we undertook on data-driven workplaces.[13] In the case of a retail store, staff were being measured with regards to work rate and concentrated on meeting targets, such as number of items stocked onto shelves or scan rate at the checkout till per minute, ignoring other vital tasks such as helping customers, which were not measured. The result was an efficient store, but one which had poor customer service and satisfaction. Similarly, if you measure police performance by the number of arrests made, the police will target every infraction regardless of whether the committer is likely to be charged or successfully prosecuted. If the metric is successful prosecutions, then police behaviour around arrests changes. Similarly, if police performance is measured by crime statistics, then they will seek to avoid recording some crimes to suppress numbers.[14] Here, Goodhart's law appears to be in effect, expressed by Marilyn Strathern as: 'When a measure becomes a target, it ceases to be a good measure.'[15]

Those who critique management through metrics argue that we need to adopt less instrumental, technocratic means of achieving efficient and productive workplaces. Instead, we need a more engaged, inclusive, nuanced form of management that prioritizes collegiality and cooperation, and which minimizes counterproductive effects. There is plenty of evidence that less stressed and better rested employees working in less structured and pressured environments have fewer lost days and lower employee churn and are more innovative, prolific and profitable.[16] This is the reason that some German companies such as Allianz, Bayer, Daimler-Benz, Henkel, Telekom and Volkswagen have implemented a right to disconnect, with workers not obligated to reply to emails or calls outside of designated work hours.[17] If we are to persist with output control measures, then we need to adopt more broadly defined and nuanced ways of assessing performance that avoids a zero-sum game and supports rather than punishes staff and institutions by recognizing context and uses different kinds of incentives. Given the embeddedness of NPM and the dominance of neoliberal government regimes, realizing such an alternative means of management will be difficult to achieve in the short term. In the meantime, it is important to challenge and resist metrics and metric-driven management, especially when they are working against the best interests of ourselves, our institutions and a sector.

19

Guinea Pigs

'So if this is a testbed district,' said Mrs Gregory, a middle-aged member of the local community, 'does that make us guinea pigs?'

The small group were seated round a conference table in an office building in the heart of the city's docklands.

'No, no,' Gavin said, flustered. He'd had high hopes for this meeting but five minutes in and he already felt he was on the back foot. Recently hired as the community liaison officer for the city's smart docklands team, it had been made clear to him that the key expected outcome was to convince local residents that there was nothing to fear from the trialling of new technologies in their area and to get their buy-in. The last thing the local government or the companies involved needed now the initiative was well underway was community opposition or negative media coverage.

As with many new posts, he'd been hired on a rolling contract with continued employment dependent on performance. If he couldn't pacify these community leaders and turn their scepticism into support, he could soon be looking for another job. Which would be disastrous given the cost of his rent and his student loans and credit card debts. 'You're definitely not guinea pigs.'

'So, what are we then?' Mrs Gregory asked.

'You're nothing. I mean, not nothing, obviously.' Gavin glanced nervously at the other five attendees. 'You're community stakeholders.'

'Stakeholders?'

'In the area.'

'But not in this so-called smart district?'

'No, I mean, yes, in the smart city district.'

'And the purpose of this district is?' Ms Farrell, a woman in her late twenties, asked.

'To trial new technologies. It's a place where companies and local government can test technologies designed to improve city life. It's all about creating new products and jobs, and enhancing how the city is managed.'

'What kind of technologies? Nobody asked us about trialling new technologies.'

'And if this a testbed, then we must be guinea pigs given we live here,' Mr Logan, an older man, said.

'Well ...' Gavin started to answer.

'How long has the area been a testbed?' Mrs Gregory asked.

'Well ... about three years,' Gavin said reluctantly, aware of how his answer undermined his mission.

'Three years?' Ms Farrell said, her eyebrows shooting up.

'And you're only talking to the community now?' Mrs Gregory said. 'That doesn't sound much like being a stakeholder!'

'We've been concentrating on setting it up. Working with the companies and universities. Putting in place some of the necessary infrastructure. We've never hidden what we have been doing: there's been workshops, media coverage. We ...'

'But nobody thought to invite us? To ask our opinion, or whether we wanted to be involved? I guess we only live here; we weren't necessary stakeholders until now.'

'Yes. No. Look ...' He'd been just as surprised when he'd taken up the role to find that there'd been very little interaction with the local community. It had clearly been a secondary concern to those establishing initiative. They'd been much more focused on the technical and business aspects of building the testbed and securing investment than how it related to those that lived and worked there. It had been a mistake in his view, but one that he was now responsible for fixing.

'The website says it's all sensors and cameras,' said Mr Martin, a man in his thirties who looked like a world-weary schoolteacher. 'No doubt spying on us.'

'And is it?' Mrs Gregory asked. 'Spying on us?'

'No. They're new smart technologies designed to enable us to manage the city more effectively.'

'By collecting data about us?' Ms Farrell asked.

'No, no. They don't collect any personal data about people in the area.'

'What about the CCTV cameras?' Mr Martin said. 'And people trackers. They record the movement of our smartphones.'

'We've discontinued the people trackers.' Gavin immediately regretted admitting that they'd facilitated a company in trialling the recording of routes taken across the neighbourhood using sensors that pinged a smartphone's MAC address. 'They were only used over a couple of weekends to monitor movement around two large events. And they produced anonymized data. The company didn't know who was moving through the area,' he tried to reassure.

'They tracked our phones. They had to know who we were. And cameras capture our faces, our car number plates.'

'I can assure you that the company didn't know who owns each phone, and the tracking ID data is automatically hashed so we can never know. The CCTV footage isn't recorded and isn't equipped with facial recognition. It's just to ensure safety. And the number plate data is aggregated and deleted every 24 hours and is used only for traffic models and management.'

'Automatically hashed? Speak English, will you,' Mrs Gregory said.

'Sorry. When the data is recorded the phone ID is automatically assigned a new anonymous ID. There's no way of knowing the original ID.'

'And that's meant to reassure us, is it?' Mr Martin said. 'You didn't even tell us it was happening. Or ask us for permission. Your whole strategy seems to be to install the systems and then ask for forgiveness.'

'Honestly, we're not trying to spy on people,' Gavin re-stated. 'We're trialling new technologies that will benefit us all. It's a living laboratory.'

'So, we're lab rats now, are we?' Mrs Gregory said. 'Not guinea pigs?'

'No, no. Look, these technologies are being trialled where the companies and their workers are located; they're not going to make themselves lab rats, are they?'

'They've either exempted themselves or don't care what their workers want,' Mr Logan said. 'We're just meant to trust you and your companies, are we?'

'They're all well-known companies – Google, Facebook, Softbank, Huawei, Vodafone, Accenture. The start-ups are all local.'

'Who cares if the start-ups are local?' Mrs Gregory said. 'You think we're all saints? And as for the others, they're hardly whiter than white. Facebook has a scandal every week.'

Gavin massaged his temples. Not only was he losing the battle to convince them of the virtues of the testbed, he seemed to be making it worse. Maybe, he thought, if he could show them the tech in the wild it would make a difference. What had he left to lose? Other than his job?

'Look, how about a quick walking tour?' he offered. 'I'll point out all the hardware installed and tell you what it does.'

'Now?'

'If that suits.'

Mrs Gregory quickly glanced round at her five fellow community leaders. 'Okay.'

The group reassembled outside the building.

'Before we set off,' Gavin said, sensing that the walk might turn sentiment around, 'I can show you a few things from here. You see that box up near the top of that lamp post, that's a 5G receiver unit. It provides high-capacity, high-speed mobile internet.'

'That none of us can afford,' Ms Farrell said. 'Plus they are suspected of causing health issues.'

'Nothing's been proven on that,' Gavin replied, his newfound hope evaporating. 'We think it's quite safe. The building across the road is trialling 5G for all their comms. The place is full of data-hungry start-ups. The rig on the front of the building is a sound sensor array. It's monitoring real-time noise levels. The seat of the bench here is a solar panel and you can plug your phone in to charge it.'

'I read that it can suck the data off your phone if you plug it in,' Mr Martin said.

'We've had that feature disabled. We can configure the tech to meet our requirements.'

'But it does it elsewhere? That doesn't sound very community-friendly; data being stolen for a bit of power. Do people even know it's happening?'

Gavin decided to ignore the question, setting off along the quayside. 'Under the bridge here we have river level sensors that generate a stream of real-time data that help us predict flood events. We've also got sensors in the drains to tell us when they need cleaning out; also to help us prevent flooding. On the lamp post over there, there's a pollution sensor array so we can monitor air quality.

'On the other side of the river is a set of smart lamp posts. Each bulb can be controlled as to how bright it is and the type of light it shines. Because the post has a power source we can also add an electric vehicle charging point, electronic display boards, CCTV cameras, Wi-Fi points and other sensors.

'And you probably all know about the compactor bins. They're also solar powered. There's a sensor inside that measures how full it is. We used to empty all 108 bins in the district twice a day. Now we just go to those that are 80 per cent full. That's cut down traffic and emissions. You can also fit a sensor on them to measure environmental factors – light, noise, pollution, weather.'

'And people trackers,' Ms Farrell said.

'But we have that feature disabled,' Gavin said. 'All this tech is an opportunity for the community. All the data it produces can be used to improve quality of life. It can help us better manage the area. It provides job opportunities.'

'Jobs for one part of the community,' Mr Martin said. 'The rich blow-ins in their fancy apartments. Not much for the working-class communities who used to work the docks.'

'But that can change with training,' Gavin said, holding out the one olive branch he had the power to suggest. 'With community education programmes. With investment in community development projects. In school IT equipment and infrastructure and after-school coding clubs. The companies want to help the local community through their corporate social responsibility initiatives.'

'So now you're trying to buy us off,' Mrs Gregory said. 'Community uplift for Big Brother and corporate profits.'

Gavin inwardly groaned. He was now regretting having offered to give a guided tour. The group were an impossible audience, approached way too late in the district's development. He was going to need a better olive branch if he was to persuade them to embrace the initiative. Or someone more skilled to offer it.

He'd be lucky at this stage if they managed to avoid headlines in the local, then national, newspapers.

'Nobody is trying to buy anyone off,' he said, with as much patience as he could muster. 'I'm just saying that it would be good to use the opportunity of the testbed to help local communities beyond providing better services. And I know you think that we're really interested in personal data, but really, we're not. We're even trying to move away from cameras. Do you see what look like cameras on the pole there?' Gavin pointed to a traffic island at the intersection they were approaching. 'They're actually radar units. We're using them to replace our traffic cameras. All they do is a sense the movement and shape of a vehicle; they don't show us a picture of it. So, we have no way of identifying the make, colour or registration of a car. We just know a car went over the bridge at 30 miles an hour.'

'But you still have the ordinary cameras,' Mr Martin said.

'Yes, but if the trial goes well, we might look to phase them out. This is one of the smart lights.' He stopped next to the post. 'Over there is one of our new secure bike stations that you can reserve using an app. And on that buoy in the river is a real-time weather station. The next buoy out towards the sea also measures wave height, swell and tides.

'All around us are smart buildings, full of sensors that collect data about the building and activities within and which react accordingly. That building there,' he pointed down the quayside, 'the one that's all glass. It's got over 10,000 sensors in it controlling the heat, light, blinds, windows, energy use, security and so on. It's reputed to be one of the most connected, smart and sustainable buildings on the planet.'

'Except with respect to producing all the materials and tech; running the servers,' Ms Farrell said. 'They're made with metals mined in war zones. I bet its stats don't include the number of people whose lives are made a misery creating all their gizmos.'

'Probably not,' Gavin conceded. He'd now resigned himself to the fact that whatever he said it wasn't going to mollify his audience. With good reason. There'd been nothing smart about the initiative's approach towards citizens to date.

'How could you not think to ask the local community about all of this before doing it?' Mrs Gregory asked as if reading his thoughts. 'You're not so much asking whether we want to live in a testbed, or getting us involved in its development, more telling us that we are, whether we like it or not.'

'But it's all for your benefit,' Gavin lamented, not believing it himself. He'd no idea what he was going to say to his boss about this meeting. He'd have to try and spin it somehow or he'd be back on the job market; a data point in the unemployment statistics.

'It seems more for the benefit of the companies using us as guinea pigs,' Mrs Gregory said. 'Personally, I'd sooner whatever it is costing the state to be invested in community development projects, more police on the streets, training and education programmes, better amenities. We don't need data and sensors for those; we need political action.'

Gavin was starting to think that maybe she was right. Maybe a data-driven city wasn't all it was cracked up to be. Maybe a smart city was one that started with its citizens not the tech.

Big Brother is Watching and Controlling You

'You should take a blank.'

'What?'

'When you go to Hong Kong you should take a blank phone. Or wipe your present one.'

'I'm sure it'll be fine.'

'Well, you're the one who's been writing about pervasive surveillance and social credit scoring in China, and how the protestors in Hong Kong are trying to protect their data traces.'

So begins a conversation with one of my colleagues about a trip to Hong Kong and Taiwan to present a set of talks about smart cities, ethics and social justice. I think he's being somewhat paranoid. He's quite serious, however.

My smartphone, he rightly points out, is a lifelog of my recent past. It provides a detailed itinerary of my movements. The apps reveal interests, activities and purchases, and the web browser the information I've searched for and browsed. The device gives access to several years' worth of email, text and social media posts, and thus my thoughts, values and opinions. These communications, plus my address book, provide my network of contacts, including family, friends, colleagues, students and journalists.

My network does not include the details of those taking part in anti-government protests in Hong Kong or subversives in China, with whom I have had no contact. Nonetheless, my colleague was worried I might be considered a 'person of interest', particularly to security police in Hong Kong given that I write critically about what states do with citizen data, and issues of equity, citizenship, justice, civil rights and democracy. And I had recently been researching the Chinese state's policies.

The conversation unnerves me. Expressing opinions and values, especially those that question the state, can get you in trouble in China; not that I'm going to China proper. Since 1997, when Britain gave up its lease on the territory, Hong Kong has been a special administrative region of the People's Republic of China. Under the principle of 'one country, two systems' this special status means that there are separate governing and economic systems in Hong Kong to those in China, with devolved executive, legislative and judicial powers and local elections. China claims it is the rightful territorial sovereign of Taiwan, though the island's democratically elected government rejects this, and there is an ongoing political dispute. China is seeking reunification, preferably by peaceful means, though there is the potential for military conflict should Taiwan declare *de jure* independence. Given its territorial claims, China refuses to have diplomatic relations with countries that recognize Taiwan as a sovereign state.

In both territories, millions of people are worried about China's political regime and its implications to their lives. And they are worried about China's domestic politics concerning mass surveillance and control of its population through data-driven systems of mass surveillance and social credit scoring. With good reason.

Over the last decade, China has put in place a state-sponsored system of mass automated surveillance. The Chinese government estimate that by the end of 2020 there will be 626 million CCTV cameras in operation, many of them capable of performing facial recognition.[1] It has successfully managed to limit the internet to state-approved websites, apps and social media, corralling users into a monitored, non-anonymous environment and preventing access to overseas media and information. From December 2019, all mobile phone users registering new SIM cards must agree to a facial recognition scan to prove their identity,[2] with an expectation that facial recognition will become the de facto means of gaining access to the internet (thus definitively linking identity with online behaviour). The state has facilitated the transition from anonymous cash to traceable digital transactions, with the vast majority of payments now made using the virtual wallets of WeChat or Aliplay via a smartphone.[3]

Most significantly, the state has created a social credit scoring system that pulls together various forms of data (transactional, educational, medical, legal, financial, recreational and consumer)[4] into a historical archive and uses it to assign each citizen and company a set of scores that affects their lifestyles and ability to trade.[5] The social credit scoring system, developed as the National Credit Information Sharing Platform (NCISP), is designed to increase integrity and mutual trust in society and business.[6] Under development since 2014 it is due to be fully deployed by 2020.[7] While state-directed, much of the architecture and data are supplied by large companies (including online platforms, financial institutions, retailers). The system pulls together 400 datasets from 42 central agencies, 32 local governments and 50 market actors related to four different domains: public administration (central and local government services), judicial affairs (law enforcement and security), social activities (including social media and travel) and commercial activities.[8]

These data are used to assess trust, reputation and creditworthiness, which in turn are used to enact social management, create a fairer society and increase public safety and market security.[9] In large part, this is achieved by creating incentives that ensure that those organizations and people who are deemed most deserving receive appropriate services and tax deductions, and those with low scores are penalized and denied access to some services.[10] Scores can influence access to: government supports and services; market permits; public procurement; economic and financial sectors; housing provision; schooling and university; and what modes of public transport one can travel on.[11] In addition, credit evaluations become a vital aspect of living daily life, used in assessing financial transactions and hiring practices, for example.

An interesting feature of China's social credit system is the social part of the system. On the one hand, this is about making the credit information publicly accessible, so that those who are deemed untrustworthy are publicly shamed and lose their reputation.[12] On the other, it is about guilt-by-association and administering collective punishment. China has a long history of collectivizing penalties stretching back to the Qin dynasty (221 to 206 BC).[13] As applied to social credit scoring, what this means is that the scores of family, friends and neighbours can affect a person's scores, thus incentivizing them to manage the behaviour and activities of their social network. This sociality works to minimize protest and unrest and reinforce the logic of the system.[14]

Not only are the state's powers strengthened by the data architecture of social credit scoring, but so too is the ruling Communist Party. With the NCISP, governance is mediated by data and algorithms rather than public officials, courts or the police (thus reducing corruption, bias and variance in treatment). Centralized control of the data enhances the authority of the central state over subnational governments and companies. At the same time, the ability of citizens and civil society to hold the state, and its commercial allies, to account is diminished.[15] This strengthening of centralized power has led to accusations that social credit scoring is leading to 'IT-backed',[16] or 'data-driven',[17] or 'gamified'[18] authoritarianism.

A few weeks before I travelled to Hong Kong I met a Chinese professor in London at a social event. We chatted about social credit scores and their implications. It was a matter-of-fact conversation and it was clear that, for him, the issues we discussed had become normalized. In fact, at times he seemed quite enthusiastic about the credit score system and at one point he showed me his score on his smartphone (though this was most likely his Sesame Credit score[19]). He was quite proud of his high value, noting that this provided him with some privileges, for example being able to get quick approval for a loan. His view was as long as you did what the party expected, and acted as a good citizen, maintaining a good score and increasing it was straightforward.

This chimes with claims by some researchers that many Chinese people find social credit scoring appealing because they see it as a means to tackle distrust, antisocial behaviour and local corruption, and foster corporate social responsibility and force companies to comply with rules and standards (for example, related to pollution and work safety).[20] And for most people, the system will work quietly in the background, gently nudging and reprogramming behaviour; it is only once a score drops below a threshold that more punitive measures will apply, and even then they might have to be court-sanctioned.[21] After all, a system designed to instil and perform trust should not prompt a moral panic and mass resistance; the majority of people need to be seduced by its logic. It's no surprise then that the system is accompanied by a programme of moral education that spells out why it will help society.[22]

The professor did, however, acknowledge that there were some downsides to mass surveillance and social credit scoring. He went on to talk about the fact that there are now two sets of cameras in his classrooms: one set directed at the teacher to record what was being taught, the other set pointed at the students to make sure they were paying attention. His lessons were being monitored, and if the reviewers were unhappy with an aspect of what he was teaching they would send him a report asking him to modify the future lesson plan and content. He knew that if his lessons continued to contravene acceptable bounds he would be questioned in person and there might be negative implications. For example, he had some colleagues who were forbidden from travelling on high-speed trains and could not travel overseas. He had one colleague who had simply disappeared, presumably to be re-educated. He told me that he had recently published a book, but the state censor had cut a whole chapter from the text.

He also noted that facial recognition cameras tracked him leaving and returning to his apartment, but he was reasonably certain that there were no cameras inside his apartment. Then, holding up his smartphone, he laughed and said, 'But this is probably watching and listening! Don't worry, they probably won't understand English, especially with your accent.'

While he was fairly blasé about China's programme of social credit scoring, my Western liberal sensibilities were clanging alarm bells. My initial reaction was one of horror and fear. Having read *1984* and *Brave New World* and dozens of spy novels set in East Germany and Russia as a teenager, and grown up with numerous dystopian SF movies about authoritarian, police states – *Brazil, Minority Report, V for Vendetta, Gattaca* – the system appears to form the technological architecture to enforce rigid systems of control. In *1984*'s terms it seems to be the nascent data infrastructure of the Ministry of Truth designed to ensure that 'Big Brother is Watching You', thus reproducing the power of the Inner Party. If you are unfamiliar with the book or film, *1984* depicts a Soviet-style totalitarian state where ubiquitous surveillance combined with brutal state policing and a strict diet of media propaganda rigidly control people's everyday lives. It would be my idea of a living hell (along with a post-apocalyptic, anarchist, survival society).

Although my account of China's surveillance machine is fairly dystopian, it is important to remember that mass surveillance and social credit scoring is not a peculiarly Chinese system of managing populations. According to a recent report, London was the sixth ranked city in the world for the most number of surveillance cameras per person (627,707 cameras; 68 per 1,000 inhabitants),[23] and cameras saturate other Western cities, including facial recognition cameras (over 25,000 in Chicago and New York).[24] Other hidden technologies monitor movement: for example, sensors that track the MAC address on your phone or the public Wi-Fi network.[25] The Snowden revelations detailed extensive monitoring and scoring of citizens by state bodies for the purposes of security. Large data-brokers manage massive data reserves for government and use these data to determine service and payment entitlements. I recently purchased mobile broadband in Ireland. On the receipt is my Experian credit check reference number. I was vetted as to my credit trustworthiness via a social credit score assigned by a private company. A score I could not see and cannot easily access. A score whose calculation I have little idea about or how to nudge upwards its value.

In fact, I have several social credit scores compiled by different data brokers and by states. But unlike the Chinese system they are all opaque in nature with respect to the data and methodology used to calculate them. These scores are used to socially sort and predictively profile all of us, assigning a value that then feeds into decisions about our lives – whether we get a loan, or tenancy, or job, or a special offer, or a service, or whether we can access high-speed mobile internet with unlimited data.

The Chinese system is clearly designed to enforce a particular political ideologically – that of a single-party communist state.

Social credit scoring in the West also performs an ideological role – that of reproducing neoliberal and surveillance capitalism in which people's rights are reduced to their ability to qualify or pay for services based on their data profile, and any data harvested can be monetized. Both are problematic, and I would prefer a different guiding ideology that is more rooted in fairness, equity, transparency and individual data sovereignty.[26] Given the choice, however, I'd favour the neoliberal option. While the neoliberal model discriminates, exploits and reinforces social divisions, the Chinese system centralizes power, locks down freedoms and subjugates citizens. This is a key concern of those living in Hong Kong, many of whom are political and economic migrants from China, or are their descendants. While the protests have been about the relationship between sovereign state and special administrative territory, and the authority of Hong Kong to make policy and act independently of China, it has also become about mass surveillance, privacy, free expression and policing.

Fearing the consequences of protest, activists have developed a sophisticated suite of tactics for trying to protect their identities, events, and their strategies of protest. Some means of protection are analogue and involve covering faces with masks, hiding behind umbrellas, wearing gloves and black clothes with no labels, spray-painting cameras, and paying for public transport with cash rather than traceable currency. In a few cases, lamp posts that host facial-recognition cameras have been cut down.[27] With respect to the digital realm, the protestors have taken to using burner, blank phones, or significantly reconfiguring their existing phones, and always using encrypted communications. For example, they will set up a SIM card PIN, disable FaceID and FingerID, lock their phones with a long PIN, remove WeChat and other Chinese apps, disable audio and location permissions of apps, disable the GPS, log out of apps when they are not in use, and delete any sensitive information from the phone (chat logs, photos, videos, browsing history, YouTube history).[28] When browsing the internet they use Tor (or Orbot for Android) and a VPN, use the Brave browser or Firefox with privacy add-ons, and use DuckDuckGo as their search engine. For communication, they will use an encrypted messenger such as Telegram, configuring it to ensure the most security and privacy,[29] and use encrypted email, setting up one-time accounts for accessing other social media which are used to try and influence international opinion. When typing into a phone or laptop, they try to avoid doing it where a camera might pick up their keystrokes.

I didn't do any of those things prior to my trip and, as I suspected, nobody in the Hong Kong's authorities seemed interested in my visit or the data accessible via my phone. I was approached, however, by university researchers who regularly work with government officials as to whether I would be a co-investigator or advisor on a research funding bid to the regional government for a project to investigate the ethics, standards and regulation of urban big data. Rather than seeing me as a threat, these stakeholders saw me as a potential ally in creating regional data infrastructure for the government, but one guided by a different set of values.

As to whether I would take a blank phone if visiting China, it's something I would consider depending on circumstance. As it stands, I am not contributing to or leading a campaign against China's social credit scoring or its use of data. My analysis has little wider traction and is not being used as political capital in the media or by states to critique China's government. I have not had any contact with subversives in China or protestors in Hong Kong, so do not have the personal details of others to give away. If the status of any of these were to change, then I'd have to take them into account when making travel plans.

Security Theatre

The TSA official has a hang-dog face.[1] Several hours repeating the same phrases, performing the same tasks, and dealing with hassled passengers for barely above minimum wage had taken its toll.

He passed the boarding card back to the woman and waved her to the left and a new queue. He gestured for Harry to step forward.

'Your boarding card please, Sir.'

Harry handed it over.

'Look into the camera here. Look up a bit. That's it. Can you proceed to that queue over there please, Sir.' The official held out the boarding card and gestured right.

'Over there,' Harry confirmed, pointing.

'That's the one.'

This was the second time in a row that he'd been selected for a special security check. Two months ago it had taken him over an hour to clear through to departures. He glanced at his watch. An hour this time would see him missing his flight. There wasn't another until the following day, which would totally mess up his schedule. And since it wasn't an 'act of God' the company would expect him to pay if a new ticket was needed.

'Is there a reason I keep getting picked?' he asked the official.

'I've no idea. I just follow what it says when the barcode's scanned. 4Ss. Secondary Security Screening Selectee.'

'You think I'm a security risk?' How could he be a risk, Harry mused. He hadn't even had a parking fine, let alone done anything to warrant special attention when flying.

'Not me personally,' the agent said, looking over Harry's shoulder at the next passenger. 'The system. Probably something odd in your data. Or a glitch. If you don't mind, Sir, you're holding up the queue.'

'But I might miss my flight.'

'We tell everyone to arrive at the airport in good time. Please, sir, that way.'

Reluctantly Harry headed as directed joining the back of a short queue of ten people. At its head were two agents that were quizzing passengers before directing them to the hand luggage screening behind them. He hoped the queue would move quickly. He glanced at his watch again; he should make it. Fingers crossed.

His mind wandered, pondering what would happen if couldn't fly at all – he'd probably lose his job, which involved travelling to meet key suppliers. Which would be a disaster. He was mortgaged up to the hilt and the alimony was already killing him. Plus his daughter was heading to college next year. He tried to suppress his anxiety. Wasn't nerves a key tell for potential criminals?

Five minutes later, the queue was still stationary. He was definitely worried now. Surely, they'd let him jump the queue if his gate was closing?

He was startled back into his surroundings by the raised voice of a woman at the head of the line.

'I've had enough of this!' She dropped her skirt to the floor and pulled her blouse over her head so she was standing in her underwear.[2] 'There! Does that help?'

'Ma'am, can you please put your clothes back on,' a TSA agent said. 'Ma'am.'

A nervous ripple coursed through the queue, everyone aware that this could further delay their progress.

'I've probably missed my flight because of this stupid charade!' the woman screeched.

'Ma'am, please. Calm down and put your clothes back on.'

'Do I look like a terrorist to you? Do I? Is that what your stupid database is telling you? Well?'

'I'm sorry, Ma'am, but we'll need to ask you some further questions.'

'She shouldn't have said terrorist,' the man in front said, turning so his head was side-on to Harry. 'You can't say that word here without triggering a reaction.'

'But she ...' Harry started.

'Further questions! This is ridiculous! I pay my taxes. For this?'

'Doesn't matter,' the man continued. 'You can't use it in jest, can't use it to deny. Can't use it at all. Ever.'

Three security guards had surrounded the woman and were moving her to one side.

'You can't do this to me! I'm an American citizen. Get your hands off me.'

'She'll get the full grilling now; also a full body search. The best policy is nod, smile, answer all their questions and do whatever they ask.'

'Sounds like you're talking from experience.'

The man nods. 'Yeah, I've been suffering this drama for four years. I've been pulled out of line. Had the full works. I've been trying to find a way to get off their damned list, but they genuinely don't seem to know why you're on it, unless they're consistent with their lies. And there's no process to get off it. Querying it probably makes it worse. It's all black-boxed pattern recognition algorithms and profiling data. One guy told me that not even the folks that programmed it know why a person's selected. They don't know what the critical data points are. The system self-learns.'

'So it's impossible to get this straightened out?'

'It's like something dreamt up by Kafka, isn't it?'

'But ...'

'Sorry, we need to stop.' The man nodded towards a pair of staff watching them. 'They don't like us talking. Looks like collusion. We might get extra scrutiny now.'

Harry nodded his head, that's all he needed. At the same time, he had a dozen more questions he'd like to ask, the chief one being, could he jump the queue?

Once the woman's clothes and suitcase had been removed, the queue shuffled forward under the shouted instructions of an agent. The outburst had unsettled the atmosphere, adding a nervy vibe.

Twenty minutes later he finally reached the head of the line. A female agent asked for his boarding card and scanned it. The photo taken when he entered the security area popped up on her screen. She started to run through a set of security questions.

'Did you pack your bag today yourself, Sir?'

'Yes.'

'Has it been left unattended?'

'No.'

'Does it contain any battery-controlled or electronic devices.'

'No.'

She rattled on through a series of other questions: 'Where did you start your journey this morning? What line of business are you in? What is the purpose of your trip? Can you prove that's the case? Where will you be staying at your destination? Who will you be meeting? What is your relationship to them? Do you have a criminal record?' Occasionally she glanced at the screen, seemingly checking his answers.

She paused and looked him up and down. He couldn't help glancing to his left and the route through to his flight, then down to his watch.

She then started on the questions again, varying the order. He wondered if maybe there'd been something in his body language, disposition, or tone of voice that triggered the re-run. Or maybe it was the penalty for talking to a fellow passenger when in line. He just hoped he was giving the same answers. It was definitely going to be touch-and-go as to whether he made his flight. The key thing now was to avoid getting pulled out of line for additional attention.

Eventually she handed back his boarding card and directed him to the screening area. 'Have a nice flight, Sir.'

Assuming I make my flight, Harry thought. Or I'll no doubt see you again tomorrow morning. At my expense.

At least there was no waiting now. He removed his coat, jumper, belt, shoes and watch. He fished everything from his pockets, placing them in a tray. His backpack went into another, and into a third his laptop and bathroom kit. An agent pushed them towards the scanning machine, and he was directed into one for people.

He formed a star shape, his hands above his head. The door closed and he was blasted with air. After his last passage through enhanced security he'd googled the machine, discovering it was a GE EntryScan that used an ion trap mobility spectrometer to test for traces of explosives and drugs. He'd also be screened for foreign objects and body shape (that gives an indication of gender).

After a few moments an agent motioned him forward.

'Can you step this way, please, Sir. Can you raise your arms and spread your legs.'

'Is there a problem?'

'The machine's created a couple of flags.'

Harry looked at the screen. There's a dot on his hip, another on his chest.

Gloved hands traversed his shoulders, swept down both arms, tracked down his torso, rotated round the waist of his trousers, and then patted down his legs.

'You're good to go,' the man said, standing to one side. 'Please take a seat.'

At least that was relatively painless, he thought. At the same time he couldn't shake the feeling that he was on trial and at any moment a vital piece of evidence would emerge that would derail his passage.

From his hard-plastic chair he could see half of the X-ray scanner's screen. The operative was studying a sequence of neon slices through a bag. She zoomed in on something, quickly jumping through scans of the bag again. Eventually, his first tray popped out of the machine, closely followed by the second. The third followed 30 seconds later.

Another agent carried the first tray to a machine off to one side. Laboriously, he swabbed each individual item in turn, placing the swabs in the machine. Another test for explosives and narcotics. Eventually he passed the tray to Harry, taking the second tray to the machine and removing everything from Harry's bag for swabbing.

Harry retrieved his watch from the tray. He felt his shoulders lift. He might still make it. He wouldn't need to reschedule his meetings or rebook his flight. He threaded his belt through his trousers' hoops and bent over to put on his shoes.

'Excuse me, Sir?'

He looked up.

The agent was holding his laptop cover. 'I'm going to have to take this to be scanned again.'

'What? Why?'

'It's giving a funny reading. I want to get it checked.'

'How long will that take?' Harry asked, his heart sinking. 'Can I just leave it here? Bin it?'

'I'm afraid not. If there's a problem then we'll need to interview you.'

'Interview me? I've a plane to catch.' This was the last thing he needed.

'I'll just be five minutes, Sir. I'm going to use a machine over there.' The agent pointed to the adjacent security area and headed off.

Harry placed his head in his hands. This was all theatre; the script driven by data – answers, observation, X-rays, scans, interactions, test results, databases – acted out by agents and passengers in choreographed scenes. But somehow his script had been corrupted; rewritten by Kafka as his fellow passenger had put it. He shouldn't have even been in this queue. No wonder the woman had freaked out earlier. The whole thing felt ridiculous. Did they really catch terrorists this way? Or was it really about deterrent not apprehension?

Almost exactly five minutes to the second, the agent reappeared and pushed the remaining two trays across the metal table.

'Thanks for your patience, Sir. You're free to go now. Enjoy your flight.'

'That's it?' Harry said, starting to repack his bag quickly.

'Everything came out clear.'

'But I'll have to do this again next time I fly?'

'That's up to the data and algorithms, Sir. I'm just a cog in the machine.'

Aren't we all, Harry thought, as he dashed into the departures area. Next time he was going to give himself at least a two-hour window to pass through security.

On the tannoy a woman's voice announced that his flight was closing. He rounded a bend at a trot. Up ahead he could see the door at his gate starting to close. He upped his speed; he might still make it yet.

22

When a Country Ignores Its Own Data

'Are you trying to destroy the country?'

'I'm just quoting your data back to you.'

'To what end? To halt development and crash the housing market!'

I hadn't anticipated that a data story might cause so much venting of anger. Especially when development had already halted and house prices were 30 per cent lower than they had been 18 months previously. The woman shouting at me worked for a county council. Earlier that day, I'd published a blog post in which I estimated how long it would take to clear the housing oversupply in each local authority. The press was now hounding her so she was passing on the grief.

In the previous couple of days, I'd had similar exchanges with people working in banking, property development and real estate about earlier posts. Some of them had been pretty hairy, with abusive language and threats. The following day, after a caller hadn't waited to be transferred but simply hurled insults at one of the Institute administrators, my phone was diverted to the university press office. It remained re-routed for two more weeks.

I had thought my posts about the state of property in the country were providing some much-needed insight. Journalists seemed to think so, or at least saw an opportunity to use my analysis to heap more scorn on the government, and I'd done a number of interviews for newspapers, radio and TV. And that was, no doubt, the problem. The last thing vested interests wanted was some clarity about the scale of the problem they'd created and this to be broadcast to the general public. Ireland was in deep trouble and my analysis was identifying causes and predicting that the situation was going to get worse.

At the start of 2006, Ireland's Celtic Tiger economy was booming. The country was at full employment, jobs were continuing to be created and wages were growing steadily. Cranes dominated the skyline in Dublin and other cities as office complexes, shopping centres and apartment blocks multiplied. House building was on course for a record year of units completed. The new stock was needed. Given the growing economy, returning Irish emigrants and new immigrants, plus natural increase, were expanding the population. Between April 1991 and April 2006, Ireland increased by 704,129 persons (20 per cent) and the number of households grew by 440,437 (43 per cent). This new wealth and people had transformed the country from a conservative nation on the periphery of Europe to a global, cosmopolitan hub. While other developed countries were stagnating, Ireland seemed to offer a blueprint for success.

However, by mid-2006, as the first signs of a global recession started to bite, it was clear that the Irish rocket ride was slowing down. House prices, that had been rising at a phenomenal rate since 1991 (over 550 per cent for second-hand homes in Dublin),[1] were levelling off. By early 2007, it looked as if the rocket might plummet to the ground, despite reassurances from the government and Central Bank that there would be a soft landing. By the end of the year, as the extent of the sub-prime mortgage crisis in the US started to become clear, the hopes of a soft landing were receding. House prices started to fall in November 2007 and liquidity in the Irish banks dried up. On 29 September 2008, shortly after Fannie Mae and Freddie Mac were taken over by the US federal government and Lehman Brothers collapsed, to avoid a run on Irish domestic banks, the Irish government issued a €64bn state guarantee for six banks.

Like the rest of the world, Ireland was now experiencing a severe financial crisis. This in turn was creating a set of related crises. Fiscally, the tax in-take was falling, meaning the government needed to borrow to cover costs and also to cut services. The property sector was imploding, with building work halting and house prices tumbling. Unemployment was rising quickly as the economy contracted. By mid-2009, the situation for the country was serious and on 10 September the government signed into law the establishment of the National Assets Management Agency (NAMA) to further bail out the banks and attempt to provide stability in the property sector. NAMA's role was to acquire all loans valued at over €5m related to land and property from six Irish financial institutions (four banks and two building societies) and to manage these assets on behalf of the state. Assets that had been valued at €74b were transferred to NAMA for a cost of €32b.[2]

A couple of months later, on 23 November 2009, I was a co-convenor of an event titled 'Geography After NAMA'. The workshop sought to examine how the crisis was playing out across the country, but also to consider what those attending could do to respond in productive ways. A decision was taken to start a collective blog – *Ireland After NAMA*[3] – that would provide geographical and sociological analysis as a counterpoint to a public discourse that was dominated by economists. The blog was created that evening and all the participants were provided with the username and password and invited to contribute.

The principle aim of the blog was to provide empirically rich, non-academic analysis of key decisions, actions, events and processes.[4] We wanted to be able to use a range of official data sources to explain what was happening, not just in relation to the macro-economy and finance, but as experienced by ordinary people with respect to work, housing, migration, government services, policy and other issues. Rather than simply present analysis and interpretation, we would also provide data through tables, graphs and maps. In essence, we wanted to practise public scholarship by producing data stories.

Almost immediately one of our data stories had an impact. In the months prior to the formation of the blog I had been drafting a crime novel centred on planning corruption, the collapse of the property sector and the murder of an estate agent. As a result, I'd become interested in 'ghost estates': half-built, mostly empty residential developments that were visible in every county in the country. They were symbolic of the crash, but nobody knew how many there were, or how many people were trapped living on them. In addition, the size of the housing oversupply was unknown. Ireland's population had grown rapidly, but it was apparent that more homes had been built than additional households formed.

I decided it would be useful to try to estimate the number of ghost estates and housing oversupply as it would provide some sense of the scale of the property crisis. The institute I was running was well used to analyzing spatial data related to planning and development. We'd done extensive analysis for the formulation of the National Spatial Strategy (which was now defunct given the crisis) and for cross-border planning in the wake of the Peace Process, as well as a range of work for other stakeholders, and we'd recently started to trawl through databanks with a view to creating an annual all-island housing report. We therefore had a good sense of what data existed and what we might be able to do with it.[5]

Working with two colleagues, Peter Foley and Justin Gleeson, I helped to create procedures for producing two sets of derived data. The first of these sought to calculate the number of ghost estates using Geodirectory data (a national address database), the second the level of oversupply nationally, and subsequently within each local authority, using data from the 2006 Census, the DEHLG, Geodirectory and market sources. We published our first post in early January 2010. It was picked up by the *Sunday Times* in a story titled 'Residents stranded on ghost estates', but travelled no further.

On 18 January 2010 we published a blog post that estimated the number of empty residential units in the country (for whatever reason: they were unoccupied, for sale or rent, abandoned, or holiday homes). We calculated that just over 300,000 units were vacant, about one in six nationwide. By late afternoon, I found myself standing outside of government buildings giving a TV interview to the national broadcaster, RTE. The following day, 'Over 300,000 homes empty' was the headline in all the national broadsheet newspapers and I did more radio interviews. We received several queries and challenges regarding our methodology and data, and in the next few days we provided clarification and refined our analysis to include estimates for each local authority. To be transparent, we provided the workings of the housing model we'd constructed and spreadsheets of the data we had used and our calculations. As well as providing journalists and the public with insight as to how we'd performed our analysis, we did this to enable any detractors the opportunity to find flaws in our model, or our choice of data, and to challenge them to try and make the data say something else. We also provided links to the work of others exploring the same issues in Ireland or elsewhere.

The Construction Industry Federation were particularly excised by our analysis, claiming that there were only 23,000 vacant units (though rather disingenuously their calculation only included unsold properties), and I did a particularly feisty radio debate with one of their senior staff. The owners of one of the key datasets we used were also annoyed, threatening to discontinue our academic licence to use their data (for which we had paid €30,000 over the previous five years) and insisting that any future analysis using their database had to be vetted by them. Their argument was that the data were used inappropriately, though it was clear that their main worry was upsetting their key sales market – the property sector. Losing access to this dataset would make some of our other research work almost impossible, so this was a tricky issue to deal with. In addition, at the time, we were conducting some contracted research for the DEHLG, and the public criticism they were receiving placed a strain on our working relationship. Although privately the civil servants mainly agreed with our analysis, they did not appreciate the lack of a heads-up or the media exposure.

One evening, to escape the media blitz and de-stress, I went to one of the pubs in my village. For what will probably the only time in my career, I heard my research being discussed at different tables. '300,000 empty houses' had become a meme, one that had traction for a few years. Thankfully, the CSO confirmed our estimate with the release of the 2011 census. It reported that there were 289,541 vacant units (including holiday homes). By this stage, Ireland's fortunes had slipped even further, with the country receiving an €85b bailout in November 2010 from the International Monetary Fund (IMF), European Union (EU), and European Central Bank (ECB). Ireland was now one of the so-called PIIGS,[6] whose economy could not function without external support.

Dealing with the media storm around our research and the fraught conversations with angry stakeholders was an unsettling experience. Our work and reputation were being challenged. We were being asked for our full research report, but all we had were blog posts. For the first week that our phones were on redirect to the university press office we stopped blogging as we tried to decide what to do. I spoke to a senior colleague who had a lot of media experience. He explained that the attacks were a deliberate strategy designed to make us stop posting and withdraw from the media debate. His advice was to ride it out and I would then become accepted as another media commentator. That proved to be the case and, despite creating other data stories unpopular with vested interests, we received few further difficult communications.

Continuing to post,[7] we started work on a full report – *A Haunted Landscape* – pulling together as much housing and planning data as we could find. We published this in July 2010,[8] accompanied by a spreadsheet that contained all the data we had used and our calculations. Somewhat unusually, we had several media outlets seeking exclusive first coverage. We decided to go with RTE Primetime, an investigative news programme, mainly because they offered us the opportunity to produce our own short documentary, followed by an in-studio debate. Following the programme, we did another round of media work. In the subsequent months, we started to help a couple of the Irish broadsheets with data journalism, producing interactive data graphics to embed in the online versions of their stories.[9]

One of my conclusions from working with housing and planning data is that evidence-informed policy matters. Irish policy makers and politicians had been ignoring the data. The census data showed that all the way through the boom vacancy rates were increasing, housing completions were running way ahead of household increase, more land was being zoned than could realistically be developed, and land and property prices were overheating. Worse, policy makers had been implementing interventions, such as Section 23 tax breaks and the Upper Shannon Rural Renewal Scheme, that were actively making the situation worse by encouraging unnecessary development.

Those in power and vested interests had convinced themselves and a large section of the electorate that the property boom was benefitting everyone. Central and local government were flush with additional direct and indirect tax; each household's primary asset was gaining value; the property sector was creating employment and paying decent salaries; and there were significant spillover effects into the wider economy through increased wealth and consumption and better services and infrastructure. It seemed to be in very few people's interest to put the brakes on development. There was also a sense that Ireland was a special case. The patterns of housing boom and busts in other countries were dismissed. Ireland was simply catching up after decades of stagnation and decline; when the boom came to its end, construction would simply level out to a needed baseline level and prices stabilize. Masses of international data were ignored, and those that tried to sound alarm bells were ridiculed.[10]

When the crash happened, the market collapsed and it affected everybody. House prices dropped by over 50 per cent, apartments by over 60 per cent. Up to 50 per cent of homes went into negative equity. Over 18 per cent of mortgages went into arrears. Unemployment rose to over 15 per cent. Salaries were cut in both the public and private sector.[11] Business suffered and companies closed or relocated. Banks went bust and had little to invest. Government spending declined and services were cut. Domestic policy was shaped by outside interests, particularly the EU, IMF and ECB.

If politicians, policy makers, local government, the banks and property developers had paid proper attention to the data, the crash may not have happened (in the Irish case, the collapse was related to Irish property loans not exposure to the sub-prime mortgage scandal), or at least might have had a softer landing. Instead, the data were ignored. As a consequence, Ireland was still paying the price and continuing to experience a housing crisis at the time of writing. While some oversupply still existed in parts of the country, over a decade of suppressed construction activity and rising population had led to a shortage of housing in the cities and their commuter belts. Rents were back above pre-crash levels and house prices had risen, both being largely unaffordable given wage levels. There were still home owners in negative equity and in mortgage arrears. There was a national homelessness crisis, with over 10,000 people living in emergency accommodation and hotels.[12] There were over 71,000 households on the social housing waiting list.[13] Housing construction activity remained weak.

And Ireland still has an issue with property data, with some datasets being discontinued, some having quality issues, some released in non-open formats and some still non-existent. With respect to the latter, the Irish government still does not generate any non-residential property data concerning offices, retail units and industrial buildings. It makes planning decisions on commercial developments almost entirely blind to existing stock and occupancy rates. Here, it is not so much ignoring data as actively seeking to remain ignorant. If you're worried about destroying your country's economy through another property crash, this approach to state-level data is a flawed strategy.

Data Theft

Jason knocked on the open door. 'Todd, we have a problem.'

'Yeah?' Todd said, without looking up from his screen.

'Yeah,' Cynthia said from the corridor. 'A massive one.'

Todd shifted his gaze to the doorway. 'And you are?'

'Cynthia Jones.' The young, black woman pushed past Jason, entering the office. 'And you should be glad I wear a white hat not a black one.'

'You're not wearing any hat.'

'You really are clueless, aren't you?' Cynthia said, examining Todd's bookcases. 'You've no frigging idea the shit you're in.'

'I'm sorry, who *are* you exactly? And what's the shit you think we're in.'

'I'm the person that discovered that you have my personal details stored in an unencrypted database on an insecure server located somewhere in Idaho.[1] And that some enterprising hacker has put up the entire database for sale on the dark web for $320,000. Or $35,000 for a 10 per cent sample.'

'What?'

'Are you slow?' Cynthia plucked a glass paperweight from a shelf. 'You are the Chief Operations Officer for this company, right?'

'What the … How did you get to my office? Jason, get security.'

'Get security! You're hilarious. You're way too late for that.' Cynthia laughed, placing the paperweight back. 'About six months too late.'[2]

'We've had a major data breach, Todd,' Jason said. Cynthia was right, his boss was often slow on the uptake, though never hilarious. 'She showed me the server and the files and the data auction.'

'You're saying someone has stolen our data?'

'Ding, ding!' Cynthia crowed. 'The penny has finally dropped. Yes, genius, someone has stolen your data. But not the shitty data in your app, but the personal data of your customers. Which they're selling for one cent a record. One cent! Which is a total frigging bargain, except it's free if folks know where to look. But even if you pay, the buyer is laughing all the way to the bank given they get everything they need to steal an identity and go on a spending spree. You didn't even hash the frigging credit card details! What kind of amateur operation are you running?'

'And it's definitely our data?' Todd asked, looking at Jason.

'Yes, it's your frigging data!' Cynthia said.

Jason nodded.

'But it can't be.'

'But it is. Your cybersecurity isn't worth a damn if you lock everything up except the door to the crown jewels. An open, unencrypted database. Duh!' Cynthia slapped her forehead with an open palm.

'Wait a second. You're saying we have open files on an open server? That isn't possible; we take our cybersecurity seriously here.'

'Except it is possible, isn't it, Jason? For the last six months.'

Jason nodded.

'But that can't be right. We have a full cybersecurity plan. We had it externally validated.'

'You want to ask for your money back. Which is precisely what your customers and Visa and Mastercard are going to request.'

'But how? Our entire system is encrypted. We have a full suite of access controls and cybersecurity checks.'

'My guess is somebody probably fell for a phishing attack. Gave their username and password away. Probably still doesn't realize they were stung. Then someone got in and dismantled your security from the inside.'

'Like that damn ransomware attack when some idiot in HR fell for a scam.' Todd got to his feet and started to pace behind his desk.

'So this isn't the first time!'

'It's almost impossible to protect yourself from idiots. We're not the only ones to be caught, you know. Other companies, governments, city administrations have all been victims.[3] The city was reduced to providing services manually for a few days last summer.[4] Same with Baltimore, Atlanta, New Orleans. At least we didn't have to pay the ransom to get our back-end services running again. Just wiped everything clean and reinstalled the backed-up data.'

'Which itself might have been compromised.'

'Jesus.'

'Jesus, is right. This could cost you millions.'

'Millions?' The colour had drained from Todd's face.

'I believe the average cost to a company for each record stolen is about $200. You're talking 32 million records. What's that, $6.4 million? $64 million? $640 million? Six four something.'

'$640 million! We'll go bankrupt. $6.4 million might finish us. $200 a record. For what?'

'Compensation to customers and credit card companies, class-action lawsuits by customers and shareholders, loss in share price, fixing the problem. It cost Sony more than $1 billion when PlayStation was hacked, and that was nine years ago.'[5]

'Jesus. We need to plug that hole. Jason, I want Gavin up here. Right away. What are you waiting for?'

Jason scurried from the room.

'He's the head of our cybersecurity team,' Todd explained.

'Too late for that. You're not going to be able to get it off the dark net.'

'Shit!'

'All the way up to your eyeballs. And wait till your customers find out and start suing your ass for identity theft.[6] Have you any idea how difficult and stressful it is to have your identity taken over by someone else? It's almost impossible to clear your name. You'll provide the evidence and the compensation.'

'I need to talk to our CEO, the media relations team.'

'You need a miracle and to tell your customers that you've been breached.'

'I'm not telling anyone anything until we've done a full evaluation of the damage.'

'If you don't, I will. They need to know.'

'One or two more days won't make a difference if this did take place six months ago. There's no point causing panic. And how the hell did you discover this breach when we didn't?'

'Because I'm a hacking genius! And I protect myself. Someone tried an unauthorized use of my credit card. Except I have two-stage authentication enabled. They also tried to access my account with you, but encountered the same problem. So, I went looking. It wasn't hard to find given it's up for auction.'

'And what's in this for you? You're looking for a reward?'

'Sorry?'

'What are you doing here?'

'I'm trying to do you a favour, you ungrateful bastard. I'm a white hat. I hack for good. And I don't want a reward; I want it fixed. You've put millions of customers at risk without a notion that you've done so. Someone had to tell you.'

'Yeah, well, thanks.'

'Say it like you mean it, why don't you.'

A flustered middle-aged man entered the room, followed by Jason.

'Ah, Gavin,' Todd said. 'Meet … what was your name again?'

'Cynthia Jones. If this dufus has got any gumption,' she pointed at Todd while looking at Gavin, 'I'll be taking over your job.' She waited a beat then said, 'Only joking, dead guy. There's no way I want to be in your shoes.'

24

Data for the People,
by the People

The occupants of the room are gathered in small groups at circular tables. The place is buzzing with chat and laughter. The tables are a mess of laptops, cables, brightly coloured stick-it notes, and paper cups and mugs. Off to one side is an open-plan kitchen with help-yourself drinks and snacks. Boxes of pizza will arrive later.

The attendees are taking part in a Code for Ireland[1] meet-up. Participants gather once a month in the offices of different tech companies – this evening it is one of the lower floors of Google's European headquarters in Dublin's Docklands – to catch up and work on community-focused, tech-based, data-driven projects. Code for Ireland's vision is to 'Improve society and the lives of people in Ireland using technology.' Their mission to 'Develop innovative and sustainable solutions to real-world problems faced by communities across Ireland, by fostering collaboration with civic-minded individuals, businesses and public sector organisations.'

Most of those attending the meetups work in the tech-sector, and Code for Ireland enables them to apply their coding and data analytics skills to solve civic issues for the public good. Most of the issues being tackled relate to fixing something experienced by the participants. Interested stakeholders, such as local authority staff, have suggested others. The focus is specifically community and public services, and there is a transparency and open science ethos to the endeavour, with projects making their code freely available for others to use rather than seeking to make commercial products. The projects being worked on this evening all involve creating apps that provide useful information to members of the public.

I'm at the event for a couple of reasons. Given my work with AIRO and DRI, knowledge of open datasets, and working with public bodies on data issues, I am advising the attendees on possible sources of data, or how they might go about building a data relationship with those that hold relevant data. In addition, two of my colleagues, Sung-Yueh Perng and Sophia Maalsen regularly attend the meetings, as well as other citizen-led data and code initiatives, and I'm interested in what they are doing.[2] While Sophia has yet to attach herself to a specific project, Sung-Yueh has become involved in a venture to build a queuing app for Irish immigration offices.

Many of those attending Code for Ireland events are immigrants, attracted to Dublin by the vibrant and booming tech sector. The meetups provide an opportunity to make new friends and contacts, but also contribute to the local community. The idea of the 'Myq.ie' project,[3] being worked on by Sung-Yueh, was to tackle an issue that many participants, and thousands working in the tech sector, had to deal with at least once a year: queuing for hours at the Garda National Immigration Bureau (GNIB) office where immigration registration and renewal takes place. Visiting the GNIB office in Dublin requires pre-registration to be assigned a day to attend, then on that day arriving to collect a ticket number and waiting to be called. Those attending cannot book a time slot and have no way of knowing when a ticket number is likely to be called. Queues form outside the office well before it opens to try and secure an early slot. To make matters worse, people can wait in the queue only to discover that the daily quota for the kind of visa they require has been reached, so they have to take another day off work to visit again. The only way to find out if there is still a visa available is by staying and waiting in the queue to receive the verdict.

Like a lot of bureaucracy related to immigration it is a system that seems to purposefully frustrate and annoy immigrants (without whom the Irish economy would be much worse off). The aim of the Myq.ie project was to manage the pain of queuing at the GNIB office by providing an estimate of queuing time, so applicants could better use their time instead of waiting for hours without a sense of when they would be seen. Some of the team were Irish, or from EU countries that do not require visas, motivated to try to improve the situation for friends, work colleagues and immigrants in general, and by the possibility of creating a solution that might scale up or move across to other government agencies that require queue management. The team tried to engage with GNIB to create a workable solution, but due to a lack of response they turned to using crowdsourcing instead. The plan was to ask people to publicly share the time a ticket was received, when they were seen and whether the process was successful, and to then use that information to create a model that would predict wait time and outcome. The crowdsourcing would use data harvested from social media or uploaded by GNIB users via a Google form.

The 'Myq.ie' project, and the other Code for Ireland projects, are an example of civic hacking: citizens linking together practices of civic innovation with computer hacking to address local issues.[4] Members of a local community collaborate to develop a technical solution to a problem. In the case of Code for Ireland, creating their own data-driven apps using accessible datasets, and in some cases producing their own data as well, for other citizens to use. The work is altruistic, performed for the good of the community rather than to create a paid service, and is often undertaken over a number of months or years.

Closely related to civic hacking is the practice of citizen science. Here, members of the public generate data and undertake analysis on an ongoing basis to better understand a local phenomenon, or to contribute to a wider scientific study.[5] For example, a group of citizens might create their own sound sensors to monitor noise pollution from a nearby airport or major road, or make their own air sensor to measure local pollution levels, in order to campaign for state inventions that will improve their quality of life. Or they might use a local weather station or their own telescope to contribute data to projects run by professional scientists. Citizen contributions can be highly valuable to science projects because they are distributed widely geographically and embedded in a locale over time, whereas using professional research assistants to gather field measurements is costly and time limited. While some citizen science projects are led by citizens, or the project is co-created with professional scientists, in many cases citizens merely contribute to the project which is designed and led by professionals.[6] Nonetheless, the work is driven by an open science agenda and the findings from these initiatives benefit humankind in general.

Hackathons and data dives usually take place over the course of a weekend, rather than being longer-term endeavours. Like civic hacking, they seek to harness the ideas and skills of citizens to solve problems, rather than create data under the direction of others. Instead of a broadly collaborative approach, in which everyone intent on solving an issue works together, hackathons are set up as competitions, with several teams competing to create workable solutions, with the most effective or promising solution being declared the winner. Moreover, hackathons are not necessarily altruistic in nature. In fact, they often have the aim of creating solutions that might be commercialized, with prizes including business advice and places on start-up incubator programmes for the winning team.

I've attended a few hackathons, either as a participant, observer or mentor providing advice to teams. Members of my research team have also participated in a number of them and shared their experiences.[7] While there is often a lot of goodwill and enthusiasm in the room, and teams can produce some interesting tech solutions, there are some unsettling disjunctures as well. The event is bottom-up, with local participants taking part and devising solutions that will aid other local people. However, the motivation for participating is often more about making new friends, seeking new work contacts, gaining new skills or winning a prize than creating something that will make a difference to people's lives. For those sponsoring the event it is an opportunity to promote their own work and technologies, foster innovation, support entrepreneurship and the start-up economy, spot talent and gain ideas.

More troubling is that most of solutions are fairly mundane and mostly reinvent the wheel. This is because participants often possess little domain knowledge. At a smart city hackathon I attended, hosted at the NDRC[8] in Dublin, this became abundantly clear. For almost every idea that teams forwarded I could point them to an existing university project or commercial product. Team members had limited background knowledge of the specifics of urban problems, what smart city initiatives already existed, or the history of other approaches used to try to solve these issues. While this meant their thinking was not pre-conditioned, potentially making it easier to think outside the box and find novel solutions, it also meant a lack of deep knowledge about an issue, making it more likely that the proposed solution would fail (or had already been tried). Moreover, none had reflected on or taken account of any ethical concerns arising from their proposed solution, nor had they considered that the optimum solution might not be an app but rather policy, investment or community development. For example, homelessness is not going to be solved by an app devised by citizens; it is an issue rooted in structural inequalities and requires access to affordable housing, social welfare policy and mental health interventions to address. Instead, the participants practised what Evgeny Morozov terms 'technological solutionism': a belief that all problems can be effectively tackled through technological interventions.[9] Ultimately, their aim was to make an app or gizmo that functioned and had the potential in their view to win a prize, with the kinds of issues I was raising placed to one side. Little surprise then that very few projects devised at hackathons continue afterwards, and only a handful of those make it to market.

This might sound like an overly harsh critique of hackathons. However, I think they do have a useful role to play in encouraging and enabling citizens to take an active part in engaging with local issues. In our data-driven world, data work is most often executed on us rather than by us, and in the interests of companies and states rather than citizens. This structuring and performance of data power is strongly evident in smart city initiatives. One of the initial criticisms of smart city systems was that they are top-down and technocratic, more about generating profit and enacting governance than improving quality of life. In response, companies and states re-branded their initiatives as 'citizen-centric' or 'citizen engaged'. Paolo Cardullo and myself have argued that this was little more than a rhetorical move, designed to give the impression that citizens' lives were the focal point of systems deployed, and that citizens took an active role in their conception and design.[10] In reality, citizens continue to be the target of technological interventions but have little say or control with respect to them.

This lack of citizen involvement in the design and deployment of technologies that shape our everyday lives became especially evident when we applied Sherry Arnstein's ladder of citizen participation to smart city initiatives being used in Dublin. Arnstein's ladder has been enormously influential in the planning profession since it was published in 1969, used to assess the extent to which citizens are involved in the planning of the places in which they live. The bottom rungs of the ladder denote little to no involvement in an initiative: people are data points or users and their involvement is to be steered, nudged and controlled. On the next rungs up, people are consumers and recipients who browse, consume and act. Higher up the ladder, citizens might be participants or testers who provide feedback and suggestions. At the top of the ladder, citizens are co-creators, decision makers, leaders who produce, own and control initiatives. Residents of a city occupy the bottom rungs with respect to most smart city initiatives. They have little say or involvement in whether they happen in the first place, and if they do, what form they constitute (see Chapter 19). In those cases where there are high levels of citizen participation, it is usually by a handful of people who are not necessarily representative of the broader population. Civic hackers, citizen scientists and hackathon attendees are usually young, male, tech-savvy, well-educated and reasonably well-off. In the case of Dublin, they consist of a couple of hundred people in a city of 1.2 million.

A key question for the data-driven age then is how do we ensure that the deployment of digital technologies is truly citizen-centric? That they are created and used in the best interests of citizens? That citizens are actively involved in decision-making concerning their design and deployment? And that the citizens involved are representative of the wider population and their interests? These questions are not easy to answer, especially given that there are dominant vested interests that will seek to protect their data power. Civic hacking, citizen science and hackathons are useful starting points, but will be difficult to scale up given the approach and skill set required. What is really needed is an ideological shift in how society approaches the creation and use of technology.[11] There are a couple of places which have been actively exploring alternatives with respect to smart city technologies which provide some ideas worth exploring.

Prior to 2015, Barcelona used to have a top-down, technocratic approach to data-driven urbanism, partnering with multinationals such as CISCO, to drive forward its smart city agenda.[12] Following a change of local government it shifted direction quite radically to become much more citizen-centric and participatory. At the core of the new approach to using data-driven technologies to manage the city is the concept of 'technological sovereignty': the notion that technology should be orientated to and serve local residents, and be owned as a commons.[13] Here, there is a commitment to using open source technologies and to retaining ownership and control of data infrastructure while guaranteeing access for its citizens.[14] A new set of experiments with open data, control of personal data, civic apps and crowdsourced sensors is connecting citizens to technology without curtailing their rights and entitlements.[15] The aim has been to shift the creation and control of smart city technologies away from private interests and the state towards citizens and communities, civic movements and social innovation.

In Medellín in Colombia, the city has sought to enact what it terms 'urbanismo social' (social urbanism), promoting the idea of social inclusion in a shared public realm. From the mid-1990s the Medellín city government has focused on empowering citizens, beginning in the poorest neighbourhoods, through a series of initiatives relating to access to ICT, education, cultural activities, infrastructure and economic development, as well as using participatory budgeting and community planning, to create an urban commons of public services and spaces.[16] In recent years, this has extended to its smart city initiatives, seeking to enrol public and private actors to build consensus on how the city should be organized politically and economically. One aim is to enact data-driven urbanism that serves existing local residents and prevents gentrification that would displace them. As its critics have noted, the approach struggles to work in practice,[17] but there is at least an attempt to imagine and create a different form of smart urbanism.

There are limited signs that such shifts in approach to data power are being adopted in other cities. And as discussed in other chapters, in many cases data power is being centralized and consolidated, not shifted to citizens. As a consequence, rather than pursuing civic hacking and citizens producing their own technological solutions to local issues, a more politically focused approach to data power is being pursued by some. In effect, they are practising data activism. This data activism on the one hand seeks to enact data justice through campaigns focused on data policies, standards and laws, and on the other seeks to use data to tackle social injustices and improve the conditions of citizens, including increasing data literacy so that people can pursue data justice for themselves.

Data justice concerns the fair treatment of people with respect to their data. Richard Heeks and Jaco Renken contend that data justice exists when 'people have the right to decide, choose and use data that assists them in leading the kind of life they value, without compromising the ability of others and future generations to do the same.'[18] They continue, 'The goal of data justice demands universal access to the data and data services needed for a reasonable quality of life. It also demands that consumers and developers of data systems consider their impact on other people, on the planet, and on our future, to guide more just innovation and use of data.' They divide data justice into three aspects: instrumental data justice concerning the fair use of data; procedural data justice that ensures the fair handling of data; and distributive data justice and the fair distribution of data. Data justice draws much of its moral argument from the ideas of social justice. Just as social justice is underpinned by moral rights that set out what people can expect as members of a society (for example, in most of the Global North: freedom of expression, vote in elections, full recourse to the law, access to education and medical treatment and so on), data justice is underpinned by a claim to moral rights such as those set out in the Fair Information Practice Principles (for example, notice, consent, choice, security, integrity, access, minimization, accountability).

Organizations such as the American Civil Liberties Union,[19] Amnesty International,[20] Electronic Frontier Foundation,[21] Liberty,[22] and Privacy International[23] all seek to produce data justice through their political and legal campaigns, and practical interventions that member of the public can use to protect themselves, such as privacy enhancement tools. The role of the public is largely to provide funding and support, and some skilled volunteer labour. Data for Black Lives[24] similarly draws on the skills of data scientists and activists to create data tools and analysis that creates concrete and measurable change in the lives of Black people. Other organizations, such as Detroit Digital Justice Coalition (DDJC) and Detroit Community Technology Project (DCTP),[25] and Practical Action[26] work more closely with communities, seeking to co-create interventions and data tools with local residents and help develop data literacy and skills. They are motivated by the notion that 'data is power, but only if people are able to: access, understand, apply it.'[27] For example, the DDJC and DCTP have run a series of workshops to inform local communities about digital technologies and their data rights, created a 20-week training programme, Digital Stewards to train the members of three neighbourhoods to build and own their own wireless internet network, and worked with local people to produce guidelines for equitable and ethical open data.

The danger in a data-driven world is that data power is centralized and used to subjugate us. We need to find ways to take charge of data and ensure that it works for and not against us; to maximize the benefits of data-rich digital technologies and minimize any perils. That means becoming active data citizens, producing data-driven technologies for the people, by the people, and committed data activists, ensuring that data justice prevails. Inevitably, this means challenging businesses and governments to approach data in more progressive ways. A difficult task given vested interests, sunk costs, entrenched ideologies, and shareholder demands. Nonetheless, it is only in these ways that we will create the kind of data-infused world that many of us desire.

25

Black Data Matter

Alyssa found Michael sitting at the kitchen table.

He held up a couple of letters. 'Our insurance premium has jumped by a third and they'll give us the loan we asked for, but only if we pay the top rate of interest. It seems we're too high-risk. I'd love to see the algorithms and data behind those decisions. You okay?'

'I'm fine. Tired. I've got spreadsheet eyes. And I've just had a call from Brandon. He had a visit by the police this morning. Said he'd been identified as a potential pre-criminal by some programme they've got. He's as ornery as a bag full of hornets.'

Michael put the letters down. 'Pre-criminal? What the hell is that bullshit?'

'They think he's either already a criminal and not yet been caught, or he's at risk of becoming one.'

'Brandon? He's training to be a paralegal.'

'That's what he told them. But they said that their data indicates he's related to, or is a friend or known associate of, people who do have a record.'

'So, if my brother commits a crime, or my old school friends do, I'll be flagged as a potential criminal? That constitutes warranted suspicion? No actual evidence, just a hunch based on bullshit data? And what is this so-called data? Because it sure as hell doesn't know anything useful about Brandon; the man acts like a wannabe saint.'

'He says it was his network of friends on social media linked to arrest records.'

'Seriously? If I'm friends with someone on Facebook who's been arrested I'm assumed to be a criminal as well? And the police come and hassle me? You're his sister and I follow him on Instagram, are we also in this bullshit database?'

'Look, calm down, honey. They were warning him that they're keeping an eye on him. It sucks, but …'

'Calm down? Are they also *keeping an eye* on rich white dudes? It's bullshit, Alyssa. It's racial profiling dressed up as predictive policing.'

'I know, but getting mad doesn't solve anything.'

Michael's phone started to ring. 'And nor does ignoring it. Yes, David? … What? … Channel 9.' He pointed at the television. 'Dead? What the …'

The voice of the television reporter boomed into the room: 'The man, who wasn't resisting arrest, died while being taken into custody after being pulled over by police. It seems that he asphyxiated as a result of a chokehold …'

'Another one,' Michael said, over the top of the commentary. 'And I bet he wasn't even labelled a pre-criminal! He was probably just driving while black.'

'Michael,' Alyssa said.

'David, get over here. And bring Madison. We need to start planning and plotting.' Michael ended the call.

'Honey, you're not going to do something stupid, are you?'

'I'm a computer programmer not a vigilante. I'm going to write some code. They want data, they're going to get data! Data about the murder of black lives. Data about systemic, institutional racism. Data that demands justice. Black data.'

★ ★ ★

'Are you sure we're not wasting our time?' David said.

'Just give me a moment,' Michael replied, his eyes glued to the screen. 'I just need to tweak the code.'

'I mean this whole thing. Even if we get it working, it's not going to change anything.'

'It would be out there for whoever wanted to use it. Knowledge is power.'

'They'd still be killing us. And it ain't going to stop the racism.'

'But it will help show things as they really are; what needs to change. Okay, this should work now.' Michael clicked the mouse and leant back. 'Deaths of people killed by the police by district. Twenty-three. Twenty-three since 2013.'

David leant forward and studied the graph.

'Most of them in black neighbourhoods.'

'And those in white ones were probably black as well. Or Hispanic. Nationally we're three times more likely to die at their hands than white folks. Hispanics one and half. And we're more likely to be unarmed when murdered.'

'And there's no sign it's going to stop.'

'Not without radical change in how the police are policed. They're killing with impunity; not one of them here has been charged with a crime.[1] And this is only deaths from the Mapping Police Violence[2] database, though that pulls together data from three others.[3] I'm still writing a script to search back through online news stories to extend the archive historically.'

'This might be a waste of time, but you're killing this.'

David put up his hand for a high-five and they slapped palms.

'To killing, killing,' Michael said. 'So, that's me. How've you been getting on?'

'I found some crime data for the city at district level that goes back to 1994. I also got the census data and some housing and welfare data.'

'Cool.'

'Michael?' Madison shouted from the front door.

'In the den.'

A few moments later Madison entered the room, trailed by a tall woman with dreadlocks, wearing a flowery summer dress.

'Where's Alyssa?'

Michael glanced at his watch. 'She had to work late; she should be home soon.'

'Okay, great. This is Lisa. She's a professor and community activist.'

'Professor?' David said, rising to his feet.

'Roll up your tongue and close your mouth,' Madison quipped.

'I hope you don't mind me intruding,' Lisa said. 'Madison told me what you're working on. Showed me a few of your mock-ups. It looks fascinating.'

'It's just a small project,' Michael said, casting a WTF glance at Madison. 'Please, take a seat.' He pointed to a futon covered in a throw.

'Madison said it's a black atlas of the city.'

'Well, more a bunch of graphs and tables. Though we're planning on making some maps. We're just trying to pull some useful data together to show the city as it really is – the segregation, inequalities, injustices. That kind of thing.'

'You're citizen scientists doing your own analysis of the city.'

'More like interested amateurs. I'm a programmer. David's a web developer and Madison's a designer. Alyssa works in an accountants and she's good at database stuff.'

'Sounds like you're professionals to me. And doing important work. What are you planning to do with it?'

'We thought we'd put it all up on a website,' David said. 'And make the data openly available for others to use. Assuming it works or is any good.'

'I'm sure it'll be great.' She motioned at the screen. 'Then what?'

'David shrugged. 'That's it. If others want to do anything with the visuals or data they're welcome. We just want to let people know how things are.'

'Hmmm,' Lisa said, nodding her head.

'You don't think it's a good plan?'

'No, no, it's fine. But it could be a lot more.'

'How? We don't ...' David and Michael said together.

'Well, in the immortal words of Killer Mike, to change things we need to work as a community to plot, plan, strategize, organize and mobilize.[4] It seems to me that you're missing the last three of those. You've made a start, which is often the hardest part, and you're building something that could be very useful. Possibly transformative. Data matter. Statistics and maps matter. They can change narratives and actions. And understanding them and how they shape our lives matter. But for them to make a difference we have to strategize, organize and mobilize around them. You're leaving it for others to do that.'

'You're saying we need to do more than make a website?' David asked.

'Duh,' Madison said, rolling her eyes.

'Have you heard of the Detroit Digital Justice Coalition,[5] Lisa said. 'Or Our Data Bodies,[6] or Data for Black Lives?'[7]

The two men shook their heads.

'They're all about doing more with the data than just making them available or displaying them. They're about making them actionable. About working with local communities to empower them to be able to use the data, rather than just being the data, or being affected by them. I've a small philanthropy grant to do something similar here. The initiative's called Black Data Matter. I'm working with two local communities and some other local citizen scientists. Maybe you could get involved?'

'If you don't say yes, Michael, you'll be sleeping on that futon,' Alyssa said from the doorway.

★ ★ ★

'Are you sure this is a good idea?' David asked, nervously eyeing the assembled crowd. 'We're not qualified for this. We're just four people that built a website.'

'That made the third page of the city paper and got covered by local radio,' Lisa said. 'That's had tens of thousands of hits.'

'Because you spread the word.'

'I just started a rumour. It got media interest and hits because it's useful. And this is peer-to-peer learning; everyone in the room is qualified to talk about their own experiences. Everyone wants to be here; they're thirsty for knowledge.'

'Uh-huh. I don't feel well.'

Lisa clapped her hands, ignoring him. 'Okay, everyone, let's get started.'

She waited for people to settle.

'Welcome everyone to the third of our "data days". I'm delighted to be able to introduce you to Alyssa, Madison, David and Michael who developed the black atlas website. They're here today for four reasons.

'First, there're going to run us through the website, give us an overview of the content and show us how to interpret the graphs and maps. Then either side of lunch they're going to demonstrate how to access the data and teach us how to make our own graphs and maps. In the final session they're going to outline their idea for a crowdsourcing initiative. They want help filling out their historical archive of police violence and for the whole community to help record data about ongoing issues and events.

'Lastly, they're here to learn themselves. They want your feedback and suggestions. They want your ideas. If you've got access to data or contacts that might be useful, they want to hear them. If you've skills that might help, especially with interactive mapping – I'm looking at you Malik – or building crowdsourcing tools then volunteer them. We're all here to learn from each other, to find ways to make data about the city work for us, to make black data matter.'

'Amen, sister,' a man at the back of the room shouted.

The room burst into laughter.

'How the hell am I meant to follow that?' Michael whispered to Alyssa. 'It's like I'm next on stage after Rosa Parks.'

'Just be yourself. Remember to make it as fun and interactive as possible. The sessions are meant to be hands-on and practical. Show, tell and do.'

'Fun? How did we end up here? David's right, we're out of our depth.'

'We're here because you got mad about Brandon and police brutality and the need for things to change. That led to something useful. Together we can do a lot more. That's your cue.' Alyssa nodded towards Lisa.

'What?'

'You're up, honey. Go break a leg.'

★ ★ ★

'Well, this is exciting,' Lisa said, glancing round the meeting room.

'What are we doing at the mayor's office?' David asked.

'Duh! You know why,' Madison said. 'We're meeting the mayor!'

'But why?' Malik said. 'Do you think she wants us to take down the website, or some of the content?'

'I knew this whole thing was asking for trouble,' David said.

'She might want to thank you for what you've been doing in person,' Lisa suggested.

'For what? Making the city look bad?'

'For showing …' She trailed off as the door was opened and the mayor entered, followed by four of her staff and a tall man in a police uniform.

'I knew it,' David whispered to Michael as they rose to their feet. 'I knew we'd pay a price at some point.'

'No need to stand, folks,' the mayor said. 'Please, sit. Sorry I'm a few minutes late; a budget meeting overran.'

She worked her way round the table and greeted each visiting guest individually, then took her seat.

'I think we should start with a quick circuit of introductions. As you know, I'm the mayor of this great city. I'm one year into my second term and I'm determined that when I leave office it'll be a stronger, better place than when I entered. Martha, do you want to start?'

Each person briefly introduced themselves, the mayor's team consisting of the Chief Information Officer, the head of the open data team, and two senior members of the data analytics team. The policeman was the deputy commissioner.

'Well, you're probably wondering why I invited you here today. I've been taking a look at your atlas website and Leila's attended some of the Black Data Matter "data days" and we're very interested in the work you've been doing. We think they're both wonderful initiatives.'

'What?' David blurted out.

'You sound surprised.'

'Well, you know, I just ...' he said, his voice trailing off.

'We want to embrace both initiatives. As a city I want to ensure that black data *do* matter. As an organization we're going to show how we're performing with respect to race and ethnicity in terms of the staff we employ, the services we run and the dollars we spend. We going to do this across all of our departments and agencies – education, health, emergency services, housing, planning. We want to help improve the data literacy and skills of our communities. And we want you to be involved.'

'Us?' Michael said. 'The professor, I understand. She's the real deal. And the Black Data Matter initiative, that's cool. But we're just a group of friends that built a website. We did it because we were angry. Frustrated. We're not experts.'

'The website and your work with the community says different. I plan to form a new unit within the Office of Innovation and Technology that specializes in civic data and apps and works with the community on citizen-focused projects. We're interested in sponsoring your atlas, we'd like one of you to serve on our advisory board, and I want to encourage you to bid for our tenders.'

'And we'd like you to advise our data team as well,' the deputy commissioner said. 'We know we have issues with some of our policing practices. We want to try and drive reform through effective data and tracking.'

'But that's … that's just wild,' David said.

'We have no official status,' Alyssa said. 'We're not an organization or company. We're just citizens.'

'Then form one,' the mayor suggested. 'You could probably make a reasonable living. Or run it as a non-profit. That's up to you. The main thing is to realize that your efforts are making a difference. And they'll help change things. And from small acorns great oaks can grow.'

'I'm not working with the police unless they stop their pre-criminal programme,' Michael said.

'It's already halted, pending review,' the deputy commissioner said. 'The data days workshops had an influence on that decision.'

'And the institutional racism and police violence? I'm not being used to blackwash the police.'

'You won't be. We know we have problems and we're working on them.'

'So, what do you think,' the mayor asked.

'Mind … blown,' David said. 'I mean, what the …'

'I kept telling you we weren't wasting our time,' Madison said.

'The proof will be in the outcomes, and it'll be a long road, but this is what happens when people work together,' Lisa said, smiling. 'It's what happens when people realize that black lives and black data matter.'

PART IV

Conclusion

26

A Matter of Life and Death

I submitted a first draft of *Data Lives* to Bristol University Press at the start of February 2020. At the time, the coronavirus pandemic was in its initial phases. News media were highlighting the number of cases and deaths in China and other East Asian countries, and reporting on the delay and containment measures being put in place to try and limit the spread of the virus. While there was uncertainty and complacency in the West, there was also a sense that the virus might sweep around the world in a fashion more akin to Spanish Flu in 1918–20, than SARS in 2002–04 or MERS in 2012–13. The first case had been recorded in the United States on 21 January and in Europe on 24 January, and the World Health Organization had declared a global health emergency on 30 January.[1] While I followed the news stories and viewed the numbers, graphs and maps with interest, the virus and its effects still seemed somewhat distant and otherworldly. I chatted with colleagues about what effect the pandemic might have if the virus got established in Europe and what might be done to prevent this, but it was in passing over coffee and mostly speculative and uninformed. There was little sense that the virus, and data about its circulation and effects, would come to saturate national discourses and everyday conversation within a few short weeks and be *the* key driver of public policy and determinant of the bounds of everyday life.

And yet, in May as I write this chapter, the lives of the majority of people on the planet are being thoroughly shaped by data about the virus. In particular, the number of new cases and deaths and the reproduction rate, which are fed into predictive models of disease, are driving public health policy, which is dictating wider sectoral policies, and are informing public and political debate. These data are literally about life and death and they are underpinning decisions of enormous consequence – shutting down all but essential services, limiting movement to only vital trips, cocooning the elderly, supporting the healthcare system, laying off millions of workers, government borrowing to support families and businesses, and shaping the timeline and composition of how restrictions will be lifted. In addition, a variety of data-driven systems have been quickly developed and deployed to try to limit any further spread and ward off potential second and third waves of infection, including smartphone apps, facial recognition and thermal cameras, biometric wearables, smart helmets, drones, and predictive analytics to perform quarantine enforcement, movement permission, contact tracing, pattern and flow modelling, social distancing and movement monitoring, and symptom tracking.

Data about the same phenomena matter in very real and tangible ways across scales from the local to the global. And the politics and life of data, and how we live with data, have been laid bare, becoming part of everyday conversations at home, debates on social media, and commentary in local and national media. Indeed, the coronavirus pandemic illustrates perfectly the cooked and contingent nature of the data lifecycle and its inter-relationship with how data shapes our everyday lives. Here, I examine this contingency and connectedness – drawing the two parts of the book together – through a brief discussion of infection and death rates and the use of surveillance technologies designed to trace contacts, monitor movement and regulate people's behaviour.

Being a bit of a data geek from the beginning of March I started to track the Irish coronavirus data, entering the daily new cases and deaths into an Excel spreadsheet and calculating the percentage growth in daily rates. I did this until mid-April, at which point I just kept a watching brief on the government's own COVID-19 dashboard,[2] built by my colleague Justin Gleeson (from Chapter 5) in collaboration with others.[3] Occasionally I'd compare the Irish data to other countries to get a sense of how we were faring internationally, in particular viewing the data visualizations prepared by the *Financial Times*[4] using data from a variety of sources.

What the comparative data started to reveal by mid-to-late April was that Ireland was not performing particularly well, which ran contrary to popular belief. According the Worldometer's dataset, Ireland ranked ninth globally at the time for deaths per capita (141.5 per million).[5] A Twitter thread by 'Danny Boy'[6] caught my attention because, he argued, while the Irish data were reasonably accurate the ranking was misleading and the statistic was being politically weaponized by some. After reviewing policies concerning the recording of deaths to COVID-19,[7] he noted that deaths were being recorded in different ways across Europe (an issue that was also noted in mainstream media).[8] Ireland was following the World Health Organization's (WHO) guidelines for certification and classification of COVID-19 as the cause of death. The WHO advised that all deaths resulting from COVID-19 regardless of other pre-existing conditions should be recorded as COVID-19 deaths and not attributed solely to the existing condition.[9] This should include clinically epidemiologically diagnosed suspected and probable cases. However, other countries at the time, such as the UK, were only measuring deaths that occurred in hospital, omitting those that died in nursing and residential settings and at home. Others still, such as Austria, were only including those who had tested positive and omitting suspected and probable cases and those that died with comorbidities (along with another condition). 'Danny Boy' calculated that Ireland was ranked sixteenth for deaths per capita using the UK method (43.94 per million) and forty-first (7.91 per million) using the Austrian method. While his workings were not presented, his thread did make it clear that understanding the Irish COVID-19 death rate with respect to other countries was not straightforward.

Indeed, undertaking a direct comparison of deaths per capita was a flawed and often misleading exercise. Put simply, some countries were following WHO guidelines and others were suppressing the true rates, either intentionally or due to difficulties in ramping up recording and reporting procedures. In addition, there are other factors such as demographics, population distribution and health systems that affect death rates that need to be taken into account.[10] When comparing Ireland with the UK, the fact that Ireland has a much smaller percentage of people over the age of 65 (a key risk group) and a much lower population density (that would affect transmission rates) needs to be considered. Similarly, when comparing European and African countries it needs to be remembered that the latter are much more youthful, they might have different levels of comorbidities, and their health systems are less extensive meaning that fewer people will be tested and treated.[11] Similarly, infection rates are highly dependent on the extensiveness of the testing regime, with some countries hugely undercounting those who have been infected by limiting who is eligible to be tested. While Ireland was seemingly scrupulous at counting deaths, it struggled to ramp up its testing regime, and access to a test was curtailed by criteria that kept altering over the initial months of the pandemic.

Disquiet with respect to the data being published by governments started to be expressed in some countries, with a sense that the numbers were, at best, misleading and, at worst, deliberately manipulated for political purposes. In the UK, for example, the government was accused of performing 'number theatre', with the figures for testing, infection rate and deaths being deliberately counted and presented in a misleading, rather than transparent and accurate way.[12] The testing figures were being manipulated by counting the number of samples collected but not yet analyzed and kits posted out but not yet used, rather than counting the number of people tests were administered to and analyzed. On 9 May, it was reported that 92,837 tests were undertaken.[13] In reality, 92,387 samples were collected from 64,362 people (some people needed more than one sample collected);[14] the number of test results reported for that day was not stated. When more than one test kit is used per person and tests can take days to be processed and results returned, reporting in the manner chosen is disingenuous. The infection rate, commentators argued, was being curbed due to an inadequate testing regime. The death rate was being significantly undercounted because all those dying outside of hospitals were initially excluded from the figures and there were significant delays in the recording and reporting of fatalities. These suppressed figures suited a government under pressure due to its handling of the crisis as they suggested that the situation was not as bad as feared. However, contrary evidence soon started to appear. In particular, the Office of National Statistics (ONS) mortality figures revealed far higher levels of COVID-19 related deaths because they also captured those occurring in community settings.[15]

In addition, an analysis of excess deaths – the number of fatalities in a given time period above the number expected based on historical trends – suggested that the rate in the UK was higher again than the ONS estimates. For example, all deaths for the week of 17 April 2020 in England and Wales totalled 22,351, 113 per cent above the five-year average of 10,497.[16] While 8,758 of these excess fatalities had death certificates mentioning COVID-19, 3,096 did not.[17] However, the consensus of analysts was that the majority of the excess deaths that do not mention COVID-19 were in fact related and are absent from official figures. When accumulated across several weeks, these excess deaths would suggest the true number of deaths in England and Wales was underestimated by roughly a third. As the analysis of EuroMOMO (the European mortality monitoring activity[18]) and the *Financial Times*[19] makes clear, the same pattern of excess deaths occurred in many countries, though to varying degrees. In addition, by reporting the deaths at an aggregate level, internal variances between groups is hidden. As Gary Younge argues, the COVID-19 pandemic revealed racial inequalities in workplaces, access to protective equipment, and overcrowding and poverty,[20] with the ONS reporting that BAME (Black, Asian and Minority Ethnic) were much more likely to die from COVID-19 than white people (Black four times more likely, Pakistanis and Bangladeshis three times, and Indians, twice).[21] In the care sector, one in five nursing and support staff were BAME, but they constituted two thirds of COVID-19 deaths.[22]

The life of data – how it was produced, processed, analyzed, presented and interpreted – was not a neat, neutral, objective endeavour. The data were cooked in various ways across their stages of production and use. Some of this cooking might have been undertaken in good faith, trying to follow scientific principles, and presented to enact a public good; however, a sizeable proportion of the cooking was highly political, designed to produce a carefully crafted, misleading impression. The latter created a second front in the battle with the disease: one that focused on the use of gamed data, misinformation and fake news by some stakeholders, and those trying to expose and refute such practices and provide a more transparent analysis and interpretation. The UK was far from alone in these practices. In Brazil, a country that similarly has also been one of the worst affected, the government stopped publishing COVID-19 data and deleted swathes of data from its official site after declaring it to be 'adapted' and 'fanciful or manipulated' by health officials.[23] In reality, the data – which revealed that over 1,000 people a day were dying – was an embarrassment and a threat to a regime that had consistently underplayed the seriousness of the pandemic. The reason this battle over COVID-19 data was important was because the infection and death data, and the models they fed into, were having direct and indirect effects on people's daily lives by shaping policy that dictated containment measures. We were living thoroughly data lives – our actions, behaviour, movement, work, social life determined by the life of data, which in turn was being shaped to perform this role.

In addition, other types of data were being generated through the rapid deployment of new surveillance technologies to try to and help limit the spread of the virus by monitoring and policing citizens' contacts, behaviour and movement.[24] For example, over 30 countries launched contact tracing apps that used Bluetooth to record details of nearby phones so that if any owners tested positive proximate contacts over the previous 14 days could be contacted.[25] In South Korea, the government utilized surveillance camera footage, smartphone location data and credit card purchase records to track positive cases and their contacts.[26] Citizens in some parts of China had to scan QR codes when accessing public spaces to verify their infection status and permission to enter.[27] Hong Kong issued electronic tracker wristbands to ensure compulsory home quarantine was observed.[28] The Polish government introduced a home quarantine app that required people in isolation to take a geo-located selfie of themselves within 20 minutes of receiving an SMS or risk a visit from the police.[29] Italy used thermal cameras mounted on drones to monitor the temperature of people in public space, as well as to police the breaking of lockdown restrictions.[30]

In addition, a number of companies actively repurposed their platforms and data as a means to help tackle the virus. For example, Apple and Google developed a contact tracing solution for iOS and Android smartphones.[31] In Germany, Deutsche Telekom provided aggregated, anonymized information to the government on people's movements; likewise Telecom Italia, Vodafone and WindTre did the same in Italy.[32] Unacast, a location-based data broker, used GPS data harvested from apps installed on smartphones to determine if social distancing was taking place, creating a social distancing scorecard for every county in the United States,[33] and partnering with individual states to help determine if implemented measures were working.[34] Palantir monitored and modelled the spread of the disease to predict the required health service response for the Center for Disease Control in the US and the National Health Service in the UK, and pitched its services to other states.[35]

The use of these technologies raised questions and active debate concerning the data life cycle and their effects on civil liberties and governmentality. By late March, these questions had become the focus of my attention and analysis, driven by a desire to discuss the issues in two courses I was teaching at the time and respond to two invitations: to write a short piece on how Ireland was using digital technologies to aid the containment measures for the Global Data Justice project; and to take part in a webinar on data, ethics and responding to COVID-19 organized by the Moore Institute at the National University of Ireland Galway.[36] These motivations inspired researching and drafting a more general working paper examining the feasibility and consequences of using surveillance technologies to tackle the spread of the virus[37] and a blog post that critically assessed the proposed CovidTracker Ireland app for contact tracing and symptom tracking.[38] In turn, this led to working with the Irish Council of Civil Liberties, Digital Rights Ireland and others to draft an open letter to the Irish government about the requirements and risks of the contact tracing app.

What my research revealed in terms of the data life cycle was that there were concerns about data veracity and whether the technologies were fit for purpose. In particular, many doubted that contact tracing apps would work as intended (at the time of writing, none did). These apps either used Bluetooth to monitor nearby phones, or GPS to track location. However, neither GPS nor Bluetooth have sufficient spatial precision to detect if people are breaching the recommended social distance of two metres. GPS can be accurate up to one metre, but more typically it is five to 20 metres, and the technology does not work indoors, works poorly in the shadow of large buildings and in bad weather.[39] Bluetooth has a range of up to 30 metres and while the Received Signal Strength Indicator (RSSI) gives some indication of closeness it lacks accuracy and varies with conditions (such as being in a bag or pocket).[40] Neither GPS nor Bluetooth can determine if there is a wall or window between people and they are sharing the same airspace. In order to exclude fleeting and seemingly meaningless encounters, the apps only record cases where two people have been near to each other for 15 minutes or more. However, this has the effect of excluding brief, but potentially significant, encounters such as a person passing in a supermarket aisle sneezing, or sitting near someone coughing on a short bus ride. There were also concerns about tracing based on self-diagnosis rather than formal testing, and the fact that the apps were open to duping and spoofing by turning off Bluetooth or the location function, or leaving the phone at home, using a secondary device, or borrowing someone else's.[41] Moreover, not everyone owns a smartphone (in the US, 19 per cent of people), with ownership rates being lower for poorer and more elderly populations.[42]

Most of the critical analysis of contact tracing apps, however, focused on its potential infringement of civil liberties, particularly privacy, since they require fine-grained knowledge about social networks and health status and, for some, location. The concern was that intimate details about a person's life would be shared with the state without sufficient data protection measures that would foreclose data re/misuse and ensure that data would be deleted after 14 days (at which point it becomes redundant) or stored indefinitely. A fairly heated debate took place in the media and on social media concerning the potential trade-off of civil liberties for public health, the necessity and proportionality of the apps, and whether a centralized (data stored on government servers, which would be protected by cybersecurity measures) or decentralized (data stored on users' phones) model should be used. A number of organizations published statements demanding that if surveillance technologies were to be deployed they should comply with existing legislation, and protect civil liberties. For example, the Electronic Frontier Foundation, American Civil Liberties Union, the Ada Lovelace Institute,[43] and the European Data Protection Board[44] demanded that:

- data collection and use must be based on science and need;
- the tech must be transparent in aims, intent and workings;
- the tech and wider initiative must have an expiration date;
- a privacy-by-design approach with anonymization, strong encryption and access controls should be utilized;
- tools should ideally be opt-in and consent sought, rather than opt-out, with very clear explanations of the benefits of opting-in, operation and lifespan;
- the specification and user requirements, a data protection/ privacy impact assessment, and the source code for state-sanctioned coronavirus surveillance be published;
- data cannot be shared beyond the initiative or repurposed or monetized;
- no effort should be made to re-identify anonymous data;
- the tech and wider initiative must have proper oversight of use, be accountable for actions, have a firm legislative basis, and possess due process to challenge misuse.

The result of the critique was that several governments altered the design and functionality of their apps during development and after launch, in particular moving from centralized to decentralized models.[45]

Beyond privacy concerns there were fears about what the use of surveillance technologies would mean for governmentality and civil liberties more generally. The technologies and the data they utilized were designed to reshape and police how people behaved. The various surveillance technologies being deployed were intended to determine who can and cannot mix, and move and access spaces and services. They sought to implement disciplining (nudging people to comply with social distancing for fear of the consequence for close contacts) and control (actively prescribing spatial behaviour, where there is little choice but to comply) forms of governmentality. The power to enact close management of bodies, and their circulation and contact, and to control movement and spaces, was enabled by the creation of a state of exception[46] to respond to the pandemic, where usual rights were suspended and measures imposed without the customary checks and balances as legitimate actions of good government for collective benefit.[47] Importantly, the use of these technologies extended beyond public space to start to become a feature of workplaces (for example, temperature testing, certified status, or the use of contract tracing app to access work spaces; and monitoring a range of performance metrics including keystrokes, emails sent and status updates of those home-working).[48]

Here, existing technologies such as smartphone infrastructure were subject to control creep; that is, their original purpose was extended to perform surveillance and governance work. While optional in some cases, there were already signs that they might shift to become mandatory. For example, there were suggestions that using a state's contact tracing app might be necessary to access workspaces, or states might make its use a condition of lifting restrictions.[49] This was already occurring in India where their app, Aarogya Setu, was made mandatory for those living in containment zones and for all public and private sector employees, with failure to install the app leading to a fine or prison term.[50] The worry was that this control creep would normalize government tracking and new forms of management, potentially leading to the kind of Big Brother surveillance regime operating in China (see Chapter 20). In addition, by pursuing surveillance-based solutions in collaboration with industry, either through procurement or partnership, there were worries that the methods and logics of surveillance capitalism were being legitimated and cemented in place, undermining arguments against their practice.

To live with the coronavirus was to live in relation to data about the coronavirus – data about infection, deaths, reproduction rates, quarantine, movement, access, behaviour, work and benefits; data that were cooked in various ways; data that were used politically and as 'number theatre'; data that determined whether one had to self-isolate, or could move and work, or whether a business stayed open or closed; data that shaped feelings, moods and personal decisions and actions. Coronavirus-related data was literally a matter of life and death, and a lot more besides. Understanding and taking account of the contingent, relational, contextual nature of data lives thus mattered, and still does.

27

Data Futures

We live in a data-driven world. How we make sense of the world is increasingly mediated through data-rich technologies, not based simply on our everyday experiences, practical knowledge and learned ideas. Many of our activities produce data and are shaped by data-driven processes and systems. How society is governed and organizations managed is evermore technocratic in nature, dependent on big data streams and mass dataveillance. Our economies and practices of work are transforming through the rise in digital labour, automation, platform ecosystems and surveillance capitalism. As digital technologies come to be further embedded into the fabric of our infrastructures, environments and social systems, and actively mediate our everyday lives, our reliance on data will intensify. Our future is one saturated with and molded by data.

My aim in this book has been to shine a critical light onto the nature and life of data and to chart the rapid unfolding and impact of data-driven technologies, processes and practices on how we live our lives. To use my own professional experience of working with data, creating data infrastructures and data policy, and reflecting on data-driven technologies and their consequences, to provide data stories and analysis that reveal the praxes and politics in the life of data and how we live with data.

What those stories revealed is that up until relatively recently, we have focused little conceptual and critical attention on data themselves. Instead, we have tended to think about and treat them in quite technical terms: focusing on how to collect, handle, process, analyze, store and share them. Data were understood to be the building blocks for information and knowledge, and what critical attention were paid to them generally concerned issues such as access and data quality. In the last couple of decades, it has become apparent that data are not simply a raw material that are mined, assembled and worked upon through technical processes. Rather, data are produced within a socio-technical context, their life cycle influenced by a range of factors. Data do not pre-exist their generation and are not teleological, absolute and essential (pre-determined, natural and invariable). Data are cooked and are contingent and relational; mutable under the conditions of their production and use.

Understanding data in this way has important consequences for how we view any practice or system that is data-driven as it renders them contingent, relational and contextual, constantly in a state of unfolding. There is nothing pre-given or inevitable in science, administration and business reliant on data. That's not to say that all science is invalid, or administrative systems are flawed and perform little useful work, or business practices are questionable. But it is to say that we should have a healthy scepticism with respect to the findings and conclusions of science, we should be on guard with respect to the workings and decisions of administrative systems and we should query the motivations and processes of business. We should ask diverse (not just technical) questions about data and probe the methods of data production across the life cycle and their effects, and not just accept them at face value. We should use the answers to these questions to establish the extent to which we trust data and how it is used to produce knowledge, extract value and profit, and shape our everyday lives. And based on our levels of trust we should push back against questionable approaches and practices and seek refinements and improvements across the socio-technical elements of a data assemblage (for example, framing, methods, technologies, legal and regulatory, governmentality, resources and so on).

Similarly, there is nothing inevitable or pre-determined with how we live with data. Data-driven systems and processes are social and political in nature in terms of how they are conceived, rolled out, and perform their work. They are shaped by numerous choices and decisions that are framed by ambition and a wider personal, institutional, legal, cultural, financial, social and political context. Science isn't simply about producing new knowledge, but is also applied, seeking to shape policy, help communities, produce new inventions and industrial products. Public administration seeks to enact a political ideology and create a society and economy in that image. Business seeks to turn a profit and satisfy shareholders. Moreover, while data-driven systems are designed to produce particular outcomes, poor conception and implementation, gaps, glitches and resistance mean they work imperfectly. And yet, data-driven enterprises are becoming the norm; in fact, they have entirely replaced the old means of doing some tasks, in the process erasing tacit knowledge. For example, the only way to check in at an airport is to do so electronically to ensure that security checks and downstream automated processes work. If the check-in machines crash or go offline, not only can you not check in manually but the staff have not been trained how to perform the task. Similarly, if the checkout till in a supermarket crashes, the till operator does not know the price of goods and cannot process payments.

We are rapidly creating a data-driven world, often without sufficient attention being paid to the consequences of doing so. To be sure, digital technologies offer us many potential benefits – improved efficiency, productivity, competitiveness, safety, security, profit, choice and entertainment. But they also introduce turbulence and ethical concerns in terms of job security through automation and platform economies, less privacy through dataveillance, inequities through profiling and sorting, and less freedoms through enhanced control. The speed of the transition to a data-driven world has left policy and legal responses trailing in their wake. A new technology or app or process is rolled out and adopted by tens of thousands, or millions, of users with little public debate or putting in place a regulatory regime to mitigate the worst effects of disruption. For example, Uber and Airbnb were incredibly disruptive for taxi services and drivers, and guest accommodation businesses and local housing markets, but response to their negative consequences were slow and piecemeal across jurisdictions. As policy makers and law makers have discovered, trying to put the genie back in the bottle after it has been released and changed a situation dramatically is incredibly difficult to do.

This doesn't mean that we just have to accept our data-infused fates. At personal and collective levels we can work to produce alternative data futures. My book *Slow Computing: Why We Need Balanced Digital Lives*,[1] written with Alistair Fraser, provides a practical guide for enjoying the joys of computing while protecting oneself from the more pernicious effects of living in a data-driven world. Our argument was that we needed to enact 'a digital ethics of care', and claim and assert 'data sovereignty'.

An ethics of care promotes moral action at the personal and collective level to aid oneself and others.[2] Rather than focusing on rights and entitlements, questions such as 'what is just?', and seeking to formulate and implement generalizable standards, rules and principles, an ethics of care is more about everyday practices. Rooted in the ideas and ideals of feminism, it asks 'how best to respond?' or 'how best to treat people?' or 'in whose interest is this?'[3] It not about simply acting towards people in a way prescribed by rules or law, or driven by our own desires or aims, but about treating people with compassion, fairness and humaneness. Our actions are thus guided by the consequences for others rather than the benefits to ourselves, or the consequences of not acting as socially or legally prescribed. There are four elements of care: attentiveness – recognizing the needs of oneself and others in order to be able to respond; responsibility – taking it upon ourselves to take action; competence – having the knowledge and skill to deliver on one's responsibilities; and responsiveness – that those being cared for are able to adequately receive the care.[4] Some care is reciprocal, in that we act towards others as we expect them to act towards us, and some care is non-reciprocal, acting because we are obliged to do so (as a friend, colleague, parent or employer), or through altruism (as a volunteer).

An ethics of digital care is practising reciprocal and non-reciprocal care with respect to digital life, including data practices: that we care for ourselves and others in ways that we expect to be treated, and are supportive and promote well-being and not exploitative. This means acting in moral ways with respect to the generation and use of data. When we are designing data-driven systems we should consider the potential consequences of these for others – whether they will aid people in their lives, or be used purely to regulate or exploit them, or simply extract (additional) profit. Or how any data produced through their operation might be shared or used in unanticipated ways that may be harmful to those the data concern. When formulating projects and experiments we should consider the ethical implications of the research and eliminate or limit the potential harms arising from its implementation. We should consider whether people have sufficient knowledge and skills to be able to make informed choices and decisions as they navigate data-driven lives and seek ways to enable such insight and data literacy. We should perform reciprocal and non-reciprocal digital care.

Accompanying an ethics of digital care should be digital rights and entitlements. The world is an uneven and unequal place, full of thoughtlessness, exploitation and oppression. While we might want people to act with care, we know that people often act in their own interest and to the detriment of others. Hence, we have a system of regulations and laws to protect people and ensure they are treated with fairness, respect and dignity, and receive assistance where due. Data sovereignty is the idea that we should have some authority and control over data that relates to us and that other individuals, companies and states should recognize the legitimacy of that sovereignty. In other words, we should have a say in what data are generated about us and have an ownership stake in those data that dictates how they are treated and shared, and for what purpose they can be used.

Data sovereignty is both an individual and collective claim to dominion. We personally should be able to express sovereignty with respect to our data and what happens to it. As members of communities within society we should also be able to collectively dictate what happens to data about us as a group. Indeed, the notion of data sovereignty has its roots in the claims of indigenous peoples to control how data related to their cultural heritage, traditional knowledge and territories are generated, analyzed, documented, owned, stored, shared and used.[5] They have asserted this right, recognized by the United Nations through its Declaration on the Rights of Indigenous Peoples (UNDRIP),[6] because data has been generated about them and used to make decisions concerning them without their permission throughout colonialism. Other marginalized groups have experienced similar data politics and practices aimed at policing and controlling them, for example ethnic and religious minorities, people of colour, disabled people, women, the LGBT community and others.

The notion of data sovereignty does not reject the utility and value of producing and using data, or express the view that those that produce and add value to data or provide data-driven services should have no claims or rights given their investment. Rather it seeks some equilibrium in that relationship, shifting the balance of who controls and benefits from data while maintaining services that people want and enabling states and business to operate. In theory, we already possess some individual and collective data sovereignty rights through pieces of legislation like the GDPR of the EU, the Fair Information Practice Principles of the OECD, the privacy, data protection and data security legislation and principles of individual states, and the terms and conditions notifications of companies. In practice, however, as has been discussed, much more data are generated about us than we realize, these data circulate and are reworked across data processors and controllers, and we possess little knowledge or control over how our data are used, often in ways that are not to our benefit.

In *Slow Computing* we detailed four sets of interventions we can use to assert our individual data sovereignty, resist data extraction and data-driven harms, and practise an ethics of digital self-care. The first of these is curation. On the one hand, this means taking time to configure settings on devices and apps to minimize exposure to excessive data capture, using privacy enhancement and cybersecurity tools when online,[7] and only visiting websites of known provenance and reputation.[8] On the other, it means actively managing our data footprints by only sharing personal information (for example, thoughts, opinions, photos, video, files, diary) we really want in the public domain and will not cause us or others potential harm now or in the future. The second intervention is to use open source alternatives to mainstream, proprietary software products which practise excessive data capture and generate profit through trading on those data. Nearly all forms of proprietary software have open source alternatives: for example, Linux for Windows, LibreOffice for Microsoft Office, Firefox browser for Google Chrome, GIMP for Adobe Photoshop and so on. Open source software is created by users for the public good and do not have a commercial imperative to extract and monetize data, and their workings are transparent. The third intervention is to 'step out' of systems that do not recognize our data sovereignty on terms with which we are comfortable. This means leaving services and closing down accounts, or not using them to begin with (for example, not upgrading formerly analogue devices to digital networked ones). The key question here is, is swapping data for an enhanced service really a trade that works in your interest? Finally, there is the option of obfuscation: the deliberate use of ambiguous, confusing or misleading information to interfere with data extraction.[9] Obfuscation includes providing false answers, evasion and noncompliance in data capture and encrypting data and communications to keep them secret.[10]

Beyond individual interventions we can work together to seek collective data sovereignty. This involves us expressing our disquiet about aspects of the data-driven world being created, lobbying for the pursuit of alternative paths and holding government and business to account. We can perform such action personally, joining lobby groups and actively campaigning for change (for example, writing submissions to politicians or key institutions), or we can support organizations (such as Electronic Frontier Foundation, Privacy International, Liberty, Amnesty International, American Civil Liberties Union) that perform this work through financial donations, promoting their ideas and ideals, supporting their legal actions, and using their products (such as privacy enhancement tools). In addition, we can use our own digital and other skills to take an active role in creating alternative data-driven apps and systems that hold and practise different values. This might mean helping on open source projects and taking part in hackathons and data dives. Such help is not restricted to those who can code or have specialist technical knowledge. Open source projects need other skilled work (administration, accounts, marketing, legal services and so on) and people to create and manage content (for example, write Wikipedia entries, or generate map data for Open Street Map), and domain knowledge is important at hackathons to make sure what is produced is fit for purpose for the intended task. In addition, those of us working in business and government can try and influence how data-driven initiatives are configured and executed within those domains, promoting an institutional ethics of digital care.

Practising slow computing and creating alternative data futures is not easy. There are many vested interests – both commercial and governmental – that benefit from the data-driven world being created. Data produce value and profit and enable new forms of social control. They work to not only protect but also extend their interests, which often run counter to our desire for data sovereignty. Indeed, they might only partially recognize our desire and then only because it is enshrined in legislation and enforced through regulation. In addition, there are a number of factors that keep us tied to devices and locked into data regimes. There are social pressures to stay in data-infused loops, such as chatting and sharing stories via social media. There are pressures from bosses and colleagues to use certain technologies and platforms and to always be available to answer emails, take a call or perform digitally mediated work. There are structural imperatives to interface with government through digitally mediated systems if we want to comply with legal expectations and receive services and payments. There are real systems of power at play here: we need to maintain family and friend relationships, perform work as required and do as the state demands. And there are real penalties and potential hardship for failing to do so. Challenging the status quo in these circumstances can be difficult, though not impossible.

In addition to societal expectations, there are compelling psychological reasons that keep us ensnared in data-driven systems. Many digital technologies are designed explicitly to be compulsive and addictive,[11] refined by neurologists and behaviourists to become habit-forming, baking a 'hook cycle' into the design.[12] The hook cycle consists of four parts. The trigger is the hook that gets us to visit a site or download an app – what it promises to deliver (new interactions, friends, entertainment, free stuff and so on). Stage two is action: interacting with and through an app, preferably in a way that is intuitive and quickly becomes unconscious in nature (scroll, swipe, click). The action needs to lead to a reward: something amusing (a meme), useful (information), stimulating (a comment or prize) or profitable (a discount or change of user status). For the reward to be habit-forming it needs to be variable, thus adding a sense of uncertainty and anticipation. The action and reward then translate into the final stage: investment, such as providing content to the app, or paying for an additional service. Investment reinforces the trigger and leads to further action, and reward helps keep the cycle spinning. This hook cycle is the reason that so many of us check the apps on our smartphones dozens of times a day. We crave the hit of a new message or comment, a new high score or a prize. Breaking free of addictive technologies, even if they are hoovering up data and using these against our best interests, is difficult. Just as we know that cigarettes or drinking alcohol is bad for us, yet we continue to smoke or get drunk, we are aware that we are sharing far more data than we might be comfortable with, but the hook cycle and societal pressures compel us to continue to do so.

Pushing back against a data-driven world then can seem like hard work. Indeed, we are unlikely to be able to go back to an analogue world of small data streams. Many of us also do not want that – we get value from our digital devices and systems. What we are really seeking is some balance. It is about reconfiguring our data-driven lives and data-saturated society, not abandoning them. About claiming some data sovereignty and a modicum of control, rather than simply being swept along in the data deluge. A key element in being able to intervene in how digital life is unfolding and to assert sovereignty is to know and understand what is occurring, and to recognize that data, data systems and society's relationship with data are contingent, relational and contextual. We make our world; we do not simply live in it.

The essays and stories in *Data Lives* makes these contingencies clear. They will have also, hopefully, prompted you to reflect on the role of data in your own lives: to consider your own data stories. How your life and work might influence the life of data, and how data are being used to reshape your own life and the lives of others. My sense is we need to get better at telling and sharing these data stories as they help us reflect critically and think through what kind of data futures we desire and how they might be created. To that end, I would encourage you to produce your own data stories – through writing, art, new media, music or any other creative form – to act as fables, shining critical light on our unfolding present, to act as salutary forecasts, imagining our coming future, and to act as manifestos for producing the data-infused world we want to live in.

Notes

Chapter 1

1 Information is Beautiful (2020) World's Biggest Data Breaches & Hacks. https://informationisbeautiful.net/visualizations/worlds-biggest-data-breaches-hacks/

2 Myself and James Kneale edited a book discussing these and other ways in which science fiction provides a useful way to reflect on our present world: Kitchin, R. and Kneale, J. (eds) (2002) *Lost in Space: Geographies of Science Fiction.* Continuum, London.

3 While these stories have shaped my research interests and academic arguments over the years, most of them have not previously been committed to print before. In the main, because they are not straightforward to weave into formal academic papers and books.

4 Kitchin, R. (1995) 'Issues of validity and integrity in cognitive mapping research: investigating configurational knowledge'. Doctoral thesis, University of Wales, Swansea.

5 Kitchin, R. (1996) Methodological convergence in cognitive mapping research: Investigating configurational knowledge. *Journal of Environmental Psychology* 16(3): 163–85.

6 Kitchin, R. and Stehle, S. (in revision) Can smart city data be used to create new official statistics? *Journal of Official Statistics.*

7 http://progcity.maynoothuniversity.ie/

8 https://irelandafternama.files.wordpress.com/

Chapter 3

1 Bowker, G. (2005) *Memory Practices in the Sciences.* MIT Press, Cambridge, MA.

2 Poovey, M. (1998) *A History of the Modern Fact: Problems of Knowledge in the Sciences of Wealth and Society.* University of Chicago Press, Chicago.

3 Bowker, G. (2005); Gitelman, L. and Jackson, V. (2013) Introduction. In Gitelman, L. (ed) *'Raw Data' is an Oxymoron.* MIT Press, Cambridge, MA. pp 1–14.

4 This is the core idea at the heart of critical data studies. See Dalton, C. and Thatcher, J. (2014) What does a critical data studies look like and why do

we care? *Society & Space* blog, 19 May, https://www.societyandspace.org/articles/what-does-a-critical-data-studies-look-like-and-why-do-we-care; Iliadas, A. and Russo, F. (2016) Critical data studies: An Introduction. *Big Data and Society* 3(2): 1–7; Kitchin, R. and Lauriault, T. (2018) Towards critical data studies: Charting and unpacking data assemblages and their work. In Thatcher, J., Eckert, J. and Shears, A. (eds) *Thinking Big Data in Geography*. University of Nebraska Press, Nebraska. pp 3–20.

[5]   Kitchin, R. (2014) *The Data Revolution: Big Data, Open Data, Data Infrastructures and Their Consequences*. Sage, London.

[6]   https://en.wikipedia.org/wiki/If_a_tree_falls_in_a_forest

[7]   For my thoughts on maps lacking ontological security, see Kitchin, R. and Dodge, M. (2007) Rethinking maps. *Progress in Human Geography* 31(3): 331–44.

[8]   Rosenberg, D. (2013) Data before the fact. In Gitelman, L. (ed) *'Raw Data' is an Oxymoron*. MIT Press, Cambridge. pp 15–40; Puschmann, C. and Burgess, J. (2014) Metaphors of big data. *International Journal of Communication* 8: 1690–709.

[9]   Poovey, M. (1998); Rosenberg, D. (2013).

[10] Rosenberg, D. (2013).

[11] Puschmann, C. and Burgess, J. (2014).

[12] Floridi, L. (2008) Data. In Darity, W.A. (ed) *International Encyclopedia of the Social Sciences*, 2nd edition. Macmillan, Detroit. Vol. 2, pp 234–7.

[13] Hey, T., Tansley, S. and Tolle, K. (2009) Jim Gray on eScience: A transformed scientific method. In Hey, T., Tansley, S. and Tolle, K. (eds) *The Fourth Paradigm: Data-Intensive Scientific Discovery*. Microsoft Research; Redmond, Washington. pp xvii–xxxi.

[14] These are not applicable to the social sciences and humanities which have different philosophical traditions. They are also paint a very broad-brush caricature of the evolution of scientific approach and are used here to illustrate a point.

[15] Kelling, S., Hochachka, W., Fink, D., Riedewald, M., Caruana, R., Ballard, G. and Hooker, G. (2009) Data-intensive science: A new paradigm for biodiversity studies. *BioScience* 59(7): 613–20.

[16] Prensky (2009); Steadman (2013).

[17] Dyche (2012).

[18] Solove, D. (2013) *Nothing to Hide: The False Tradeoff Between Privacy and Security*. Yale University Press. New Have, CT.; Lane, J., Stodden, V., Bender, S. and Nissenbaum, H. (eds) (2014) *Privacy, Big Data and the Public Good*. Cambridge University Press, Cambridge; Lyon, D. (2018) *The Culture of Surveillance*. Polity Press, Cambridge.

[19] Davies, T., Walker, S.B., Rubinstein, M. and Perini, F. (eds) (2019) *The State of Open Data: Histories and Horizons*. African Minds and International Development Research Centre, Cape Town and Ottawa.

[20] Kitchin, R. (2014).

[21] Manyika, J., Chui, M., Brown, B., Bughin, J., Dobbs, R., Roxburgh, C. and Hung Byers, A. (2011) *Big Data: The Next Frontier for Innovation, Competition, and Productivity*. McKinsey Global Institute.

Chapter 5

[1] CSO (n.d.) Residential Property Price Index. https://www.cso.ie/en/statistics/prices/residentialpropertypriceindex/

[2] CSO (n.d.) New Dwelling Completions. https://www.cso.ie/en/statistics/construction/newdwellingcompletions/

[3] McCarthy, E. and Kitchin, R. (2012) Data visualizations of Residential Property Price Register. *Ireland After NAMA*, 3 Oct, https://irelandafternama.wordpress.com/2012/10/03/data-visualizations-of-residential-property-price-register/; McCarthy, E. and Kitchin, R. (2012) The Geography of Actual Sales Prices. *Ireland After NAMA*, 4 Oct, https://irelandafternama.wordpress.com/2012/10/04/the-geography-of-actual-sales-prices/

[4] See a data viz of all residential properties across all local authorities at: http://airo.maynoothuniversity.ie/external-content/resiential-property-price-register-2010-2014

[5] Lyons, R. (2012) The first house price index based on the house price register. *Ronan Lyons* blog, 16 Oct, http://www.ronanlyons.com/2012/10/16/the-first-house-price-index-based-on-the-house-price-register/; Lyons, R. (2012) Three tips for using Ireland's property price register. *Ronan Lyons* blog, 1 Oct, http://www.ronanlyons.com/2012/10/01/three-tips-for-using-irelands-property-price-register/; Daft.ie (2012) Residential Property Price Register 2012 Q3. http://www.ronanlyons.com/wp-content/uploads/2012/10/daft-ie_rppr_research.pdf

[6] In other words, to map all the properties at street level would require a huge amount of manual address matching. Not integrating Geodirectory into the database design was, in our view, a mistake. To put this in context, in other countries this would be like deliberately omitting the use of postcodes.

[7] In the subsequent days, other errors were spotted and fixed. In some cases, errors are spotted a few years later. For example, when updating the Cork Dashboard, my colleague Oliver Dawkins spotted an error in one of the tables which was investigated by the CSO and fixed.

[8] They still do not correct any errors, unless the error is corrected by The Revenue Commissioners. On their website they state: 'The Authority acknowledges that there may be errors in the data in the Register. The Register is compiled from data which is filed, for stamp duty purposes, with the Revenue Commissioners. The data is primarily filed electronically by persons doing the conveyancing of the property on behalf of the purchaser and errors may occur when the data is being filed. The PSRA does not in any way edit the data. It simply publishes, in a fully transparent manner, the data from the declarations which are filed with the Revenue Commissioners. If the data filed contained typographical errors then those errors will appear

on the Register. Where errors are reported to the Authority they will be brought to the attention of the Revenue Commissioners.'

[9] McArdle, G. and Kitchin, R. (2016) Improving the veracity of open and real-time urban data. *Built Environment* 42(3): 446–62.

[10] Place of Work Census of Anonymised Records (POWCAR) data is not publicly available and can only be used by approved researchers who have to comply with special provisions regarding data use and publication.

[11] McArdle, G. and Kitchin, R. (2016).

[12] https://www.cso.ie/en/releasesandpublications/ep/p-ndc/newdwellingcompletionsq12018/ec/

[13] Burke-Kennedy, E. (2018) New homes overstated by nearly 60%, CSO figures show. *The Irish Times*, 14 June, https://www.irishtimes.com/business/economy/new-homes-overstated-by-nearly-60-cso-figures-show-1.3530388

[14] CSO (2018) New Dwelling Completions Q1 2018. https://www.cso.ie/en/releasesandpublications/ep/p-ndc/newdwellingcompletionsq12018/bgn/

[15] Report of the Garda Siochana Inspectorate (2014) Crime Investigation. Oct, https://www.gsinsp.ie/wp-content/uploads/2019/07/Crime-Investigation-Full-Report.pdf

[16] CSO (n.d.) Resumption of the Publication of Recorded Crime Statistics as Statistics 'Under Reservation'. https://www.cso.ie/en/methods/crime/statisticsunderreservationfaqs/

[17] CSO (n.d.)

[18] Gallagher, C. (2017) Garda breath test scandal: How did we get here? *The Irish Times*, 6 Sept, https://www.irishtimes.com/news/crime-and-law/garda-breath-test-scandal-how-did-we-get-here-1.3211601

[19] Kitchin, R. and Lauriault, T. (2015) Small data in the era of big data. *GeoJournal* 80(4): 463–75.

[20] Crampton, J.W., Graham, M., Poorthius, A., Shelton, T., Stephens, M., Wilson, M.W. and Zook, M. (2013) Beyond the geotag: Situating 'big data' and leveraging the potential of the geoweb. *Cartography and Geographic Information Science* 40(2): 130–9.

[21] Batini, C., Cappiello, C., Francalanci, C. and Maurino, A. (2009) Methodologies for data quality assessment and improvement. *ACM Computing Surveys* (CSUR), 41(3). Article No. 16, doi.10.1145/1541880.1541883.

[22] Guptill, S.C. and Morrison, J.L. (eds) (1995) *Elements of Spatial Data Quality*. Elsevier, Oxford; Turner, S. (2004) Defining and measuring traffic data quality: white paper on recommended approaches. *Transportation Research Record*, No. 1870. pp 62–9.

[23] McArdle, G. and Kitchin, R. (2016).

[24] http://data.london.gov.uk/

[25] http://opendata.paris.fr/

[26] https://data.smartdublin.ie/

[27] http://open.dataforcities.org/

[28] McArdle, G. and Kitchin, R. (2016).

[29] The others were provided to us as test data.

Chapter 6

[1] This is a fictionalised account of a real data error. €3.6b euros was double counted on the Irish national accounts in 2010. As a member of the Central Statistics Office Audit Committee I took part in the internal review of the error, hearing testimony from officials involved, reading some of the documentation and making procedural recommendations. I never met with officials in the Department of Finance and the content of this story is based on what was made public via the media. See, for example: Carroll, S. (2011) State gains €3.6bn from 'error'. *The Irish Times*, 1 Nov, https://www.irishtimes.com/news/state-gains-3-6bn-from-error-1.886247; O'Brien, C. (2012) Officials knew of 'recent' €3.6bn error for a year. *The Irish Times*, 13 Feb, https://www.irishtimes.com/news/officials-knew-of-recent-3-6bn-error-for-a-year-1.462184; RTE News (2011) 'Human error' blamed for €3.6bn mistake. 21 Nov, https://www.rte.ie/news/2011/1102/308186-finance/; Reilly, G. (2012) Report on €3.6 billion accounting error may be published next week. *The Journal*, 14 May, https://www.thejournal.ie/report-on-e3-6-billion-accounting-error-may-be-published-next-week-450763-May2012/

Chapter 7

[1] Small Area Population Statistics.

[2] The CBRRO was renamed the All-Island Research Observatory (AIRO) in 2006. In 2020 it was still going strong employing a core, full-time team of four staff.

[3] The CSO does now selectively re-classify the Republic of Ireland census into the classes used by the Northern Irish census to make more comparable data. See the Appendix 1 and background notes of: CSO and NISRA (2014) *Census 2011: Ireland and Northern Ireland*. https://www.cso.ie/en/media/csoie/census/documents/north-south-spreadsheets/Census2011IrelandandNorthernIrelandwebversion1.pdf

[4] The principal investigators were Ann McGeeney from Dundalk Institute of Technology, and myself and Stewart Fotheringham from Maynooth University.

[5] Masser, I. and Plummer, S. (1990) The Regional Research Laboratory Initiative: A Progress Report. *Area* 22(4): 333–8.

[6] Nomenclature of Territorial Units for Statistics.

[7] https://ec.europa.eu/eurostat/web/nuts/background

[8] https://ec.europa.eu/eurostat/web/regions-and-cities

[9] https://en.wikipedia.org/wiki/NUTS_statistical_regions_of_Ireland

[10] Kitchin, R., Bartley, B., Gleeson, J., Cowman, M., Fotheringham, S. and Lloyd, C. (2007) Joined-up thinking across the Irish border: Making the data more compatible. *Journal of Cross Border Studies* 2: 22–33.

[11] For example, with respect to social class defined by job type in the censuses, 'semi-skilled' and 'unskilled' are separate classes in the Republic but are classified together in Northern Ireland; the closest class to 'professional workers' in the Republic is 'Higher and intermediate managerial/administrative/professional' in the North.

[12] Since we conducted the research, Ireland has introduced two new statistical geographies. The Small Area is principally used for outputting census data. There are 18,641 small areas, typically containing 80–100 households. The closest equivalent in the North are Output Areas, of which in 2006 there were 5,022 with an average population of 337. Eircodes are Irish postcodes and are unique to each household. In the North there are 56,114 postcodes averaging 20 addresses per postcode. See https://www.cso.ie/en/census/census2016reports/census2016smallareapopulationstatistics/ and Kitchin et al (2007).

[13] CSO and NISRA (2014).

[14] In the case of the Republic of Ireland, there were 774 variables published in 1981. In 1991 this had increased substantially to 1,750.

[15] Gleeson, J., Kitchin, R. Bartley, B., Driscoll, J., Foley, R., Fotheringham, S. and Lloyd, C. (2008) *The Atlas of the Island of Ireland.* AIRO/ICLRD, Naas.

[16] The book was originally to be titled '*The All-Ireland Atlas*' but the DUP (Democratic Unionist Party) objected to the title. 'Island of Ireland' was deemed geographically correct rather than being a political designation.

[17] We queried with senior management in CSO whether it was possible to disaggregate Donegal from Border region, but this was not possible and there were no plans to create sub-regional data.

[18] Many of the data were generated using different methodologies and included extrapolation from a baseline (often the census) using estimates calculated through survey samples.

[19] We also found a number of errors in the data, reporting these to the relevant data producer.

[20] Inspire (2015) EU INSPIRE Directive for Spatial Data. http://inspire.ec.europa.eu

[21] https://en.wikipedia.org/wiki/United_Nations_System

[22] https://www.dataforcities.org/

[23] For an account of the creation of ISO37120 see: White, J.M. (2019) 'Standardising the city: A material-discursive genealogy of CPA-I_001, ISO 37120 and BSI PAS 181'. PhD thesis, National University of Ireland, Maynooth. http://mural.maynoothuniversity.ie/10848/

[24] For a discussion of city benchmarking initiatives see: Kitchin, R., Lauriault, T. and McArdle, G. (2015) Knowing and governing cities through urban indicators, city benchmarking and real-time dashboards. *Regional Studies, Regional Science* 2(1): 6–28.

25 http://progcity.maynoothuniversity.ie/

26 Kitchin, R. and Moore-Cherry, N. (2020, online first) Fragmented governance, the urban data ecosystem and smart cities: the case of Metropolitan Boston. *Regional Studies*, doi: 10.1080/00343404.2020.1735627.

27 https://www.somervillema.gov/departments/mayor/somerstat

28 See Kitchin, R. and Moore-Cherry, N. (2020).

29 https://www.mass.gov/orgs/massgis-bureau-of-geographic-information

Chapter 9

1 Kitchin et al (2015).

2 http://progcity.maynoothuniversity.ie/

3 https://people.ucd.ie/gavin.mcardle

4 For a more detailed academic account of creating the Dublin Dashboard, see Kitchin, R., Maalsen, S. and McArdle, G. (2016) The praxis and politics of building urban dashboards. *Geoforum* 77: 93–101.

5 http://citydashboard.org/london/

6 https://data.london.gov.uk/ This dashboard has changed significantly in design and content since 2013.

7 The dashboard we created was launched as the Dublin Dashboard. http://www.dublindashboard.ie/. The dashboard now displayed is significantly different in design and content to the original site.

8 https://airo.maynoothuniversity.ie/

9 https://www.dataforcities.org/

10 Dublin City Council (2012) *Sustainability Report 2012: Part B Sustainability Indicators.* http://dublincity.ie/sites/default/files/content/WaterWasteEnvironment/Sustainability/Documents/SIR2012.pdf

11 One of these – water consumption – subsequently became unavailable due to privatization.

12 Henderson, L.J. (2003) The Baltimore CitiStat Program: Performance and Accountability. Managing for Results Series, IBM Endowment for The Business of Government. http://www.businessofgovernment.org/sites/default/files/CitiStat.pdf

13 For example, Baltimore: https://opi.baltimorecity.gov/citistat-reports and Buffalo: https://data.buffalony.gov/stories/s/CitiStat-Buffalo/

14 https://sydney.edu.au/architecture/about/our-people/academic-staff/sophia-maalsen.html

15 We insisted that they should be included and that deliberately excluding indicators that cast the city in a negative light would draw critique and negative media scrutiny.

16 Young, G. and Kitchin, R. (2020, online first) Creating design guidelines for city dashboards from a user's perspectives. *International Journal of Human-Computer Studies* 140: doi: 10.1016/j.ijhcs.2020.102429.

17 Young, G., Kitchin, R. and Naji, J. (2020, online first). Building city dashboards for different types of user. *Journal of Urban Technology*, doi: 10.1080/10630732.2020.1759994.

[18] The team is hierarchically structured and stakeholders control access to some resources such as data.

Chapter 10

[1] This story is not a critique of this paper, but it is an example of research that uses Twitter data to examine fertility. Mencarini, L., Hernandez-Farias, D.I., Lai, M., Patti, V., Sulis, E. and Vignoli, D. (2019) Happy parents' tweets: An exploration of Italian Twitter data using sentiment analysis. *Demographic Research* 40(25): 693–724. https://www.demographic-research.org/volumes/vol40/25/40-25.pdf

Chapter 11

[1] This is a dramatized version of a conversation that did happen. A fuller account of funding models examined can be found at: Kitchin, R., Collins, S. and Frost, D. (2015) Funding models for open access digital data repositories. *Online Information Review* 39(5): 664–81.

[2] http://www.dri.ie

[3] The Irish government department which controls a significant chunk of university research funding.

[4] The Irish government department responsible for directing and overseeing government spending.

[5] Initiated in 1998, through the donation of matching funds from Atlantic Philanthropies, the PRTLI cycles of funding, administered by the Higher Education Authority of Ireland (HEA), were designed to scale collaborative and interdisciplinary research across the Irish universities and institutes of technology by investing in sizable research initiatives, including the funding new buildings, large specialist equipment, shared research and graduate education programmes, doctoral cohorts and postdoctoral research fellows. By 2008, €835m had been spent or allocated to Cycles 1 to 4, into a number of inter-institutional research centres.

[6] https://airo.maynoothuniversity.ie/

[7] http://www.iqda.ie

[8] The SSAI Databank – now the Measurement Instrument Database for the Social Sciences (MIDSS) – contains psychometrically standardized assessment instruments for social science research and facilitates the pooling of data across centres. http://www.midss.org/

[9] Minister O'Keeffe launches €300m plan for higher education research. https://www.education.ie/en/Press-Events/Press-Releases/2009-Press-Releases/PR09-01-08D.html

[10] National College of Art and Design.

[11] Dublin City University, Queen's University Belfast, University College Cork, University of Ulster.

[12] Centre for Cross Border Studies; Chester Beatty Library; Consortium of National University Libraries; HEAnet; IBM; Intel; International Centre for Local and Regional Development; Microsoft Ireland; National Archives of

Ireland; National Economic and Social Forum; National Gallery of Ireland; National Library of Ireland; Radió na Gaeltachta, Radió Telifís Éireann; TG4; Western Development Commission.

13 A trusted digital repository (TDR) is a certified single or multi-site repository whose mission is to provide reliable, long-term, trusted access to the data it manages. It must have the following attributes: accept responsibility for the long-term maintenance of digital resources on behalf of its depositors and for the benefit of current and future users, consumers or designated communities; have an organizational system that supports not only long-term viability of the preservation system, but also the digital information for which it has responsibility; demonstrate fiscal responsibility and sustainability; design its systems in accordance with commonly accepted conventions and standards to ensure the ongoing management, access and security of materials deposited within them; establish methodologies for system evaluation that meet community expectations of trustworthiness; be dependable and carries out its long-term responsibilities to depositors and users openly and explicitly; have policies, practices and performance that can be audited and measured. RLG and OCLC. (2002) *Trusted Digital Repositories: Attributes and Responsibilities.* http://www.oclc.org/research/activities/trustedrep.html

14 Strand 1 – Management & Long-Term Planning: Work Package 1: Long-Term Planning; Work Package 2: Project Management.
    Strand 2 – Context: Work Package 3: Requirements Analysis; Work Package 4: Policies and Guidelines.
    Strand 3 – Design and Implementation: Work Package 5: Design of Software Architecture; Work Package 6: User Interface Tools; Work Package 7: Data Management Layer; Work Package 8: Storage Layer.
    Strand 4 – Roll-out: Work Package 9: User Support, Training and Advocacy; Work Package 10: Demonstration Projects.

15 DRI (2015) Minister English launches Digital Repository of Ireland. 25 June, https://dri.ie/minister-english-launches-digital-repository-ireland

Chapter 12

1 That's the Finance Minister's constituency.
2 Okay, well, he needs some allocation; we have to get a second round of funds after all.
3 But not at the cost of the Gaeltacht.
4 Except there isn't a single area in the Finance Minister's constituency.
5 We'll get to that.
6 Gerrymandering is the practice of manipulating geographic boundaries to produce unfair or unequitable outcomes that favour particular groups or parties.
7 The legislature of Ireland, consisting of The President of Ireland, Dáil Éireann (lower house) and Seanad Éireann (upper house).

Chapter 13

[1] Kitchin, R. (1993) Using bidimensional regression to analyse cognitive maps. *Swansea Geographer* 30: 33–50; Kitchin, R. (1996) Methodological convergence in cognitive mapping research: Investigating configurational knowledge. *Journal of Environmental Psychology* 16(3): 163–85.

[2] Kitchin, R. (1996) Exploring approaches to computer cartography and spatial analysis in cognitive mapping research: CMAP and MiniGASP prototype packages. *Cartographic Journal* 33(1): 51–5.

[3] DOS was the Microsoft operating system prior to Windows and it can still be used to run command line functions. Search for 'Command Prompt' from the task bar in Windows.

[4] Manyika, J., Chui, M., Brown, B., Bughin, J., Dobbs, R., Roxburgh, C. and Hung Byers, A. (2011) *Big Data: The Next Frontier for Innovation, Competition, and Productivity*. McKinsey Global Institute.

[5] Crowe, C. (2012) Ruin of Public Record Office marked loss of great archive. *The Irish Times*, 30 June, https://www.irishtimes.com/opinion/ruin-of-public-record-office-marked-loss-of-great-archive-1.1069843

[6] The first census of Ireland took place in 1821.

[7] National Archives (n.d.) History of Irish census records. http://www.census.nationalarchives.ie/help/history.html

[8] https://beyond2022.ie/

[9] They also noted that the police have their own access to the camera feeds and they did record them.

[10] OECD (1980) *OECD Guidelines on the Protection of Privacy and Transborder Flows of Personal Data*. www.oecd.org/sti/ieconomy/oecdguidelinesontheprotectionofprivacyandtransborderflowsofpersonaldata.htm

[11] European Commission (n.d.) For how long can data be kept and is it necessary to update it? https://ec.europa.eu/info/law/law-topic/data-protection/reform/rules-business-and-organisations/principles-gdpr/how-long-can-data-be-kept-and-it-necessary-update-it_en For information on data retention in the US concerning telecoms see Storm, D. (2011) How long does your mobile phone provider store data for law enforcement access? *Computer World*, 28 Sept. https://www.computerworld.com/article/2471232/how-long-does-your-mobile-phone-provider-store-data-for-law-enforcement-access.html

[12] For an overview of data retention policies in different countries see https://en.wikipedia.org/wiki/Data_retention

[13] European Commission (n.d.).

[14] Transport for London (n.d.) *Enforcement operations, Schedule 2, Appendix 24 – Data retention and information/record disposal*. http://content.tfl.gov.uk/eops-schedule2-appendix24-data-retention.pdf

[15] https://privacyinternational.org/

[16] https://www.libertyhumanrights.org.uk

[17] https://www.aclu.org/

[18] https://www.eff.org

Chapter 14

[1] https://www.ponggame.org/

[2] https://en.wikipedia.org/wiki/ZX81

[3] https://en.wikipedia.org/wiki/ZX_Spectrum

[4] My father designed pallet racking systems for warehouses and had to travel to the sites to check on installation. While his friends were envious he hated the phone and always being contactable.

[5] Identifiers that are unique to a person, object, transaction, interaction and territory.

[6] Kitchin, R. and Sykes, L. (1995) Invisible geography on the Internet. *Geographical Magazine*, Nov: 22–4.

[7] Dodge, M. and Kitchin, R. (2005) Code and the transduction of space. *Annals of the Association of American Geographers* 95(1): 162–80.

[8] Data produced deliberately by us.

[9] Data captured about us by others.

[10] van Dijck, J. (2014) Datafication, dataism and dataveillance: Big Data between scientific paradigm and ideology. *Surveillance & Society* 12(2): 197–208.

[11] Dodge, M. and Kitchin, R. (2005) Codes of life: Identification codes and the machine-readable world. *Environment and Planning D: Society and Space* 23(6): 851–81.

[12] Kitchin, R. and Dodge, M. (2011) *Code/Space: Software and Everyday Life*. MIT Press, Cambridge, MA.

[13] Dodge, M. and Kitchin, R. (2007) The automatic management of drivers and driving spaces. *Geoforum* 38(2): 264–75.

[14] Dodge, M. and Kitchin, R. (2009) Software, objects and home spaces. *Environment and Planning A: Economy and Space* 41(6): 1344–65.

[15] O'Reilly, T. (2005) What is Web 2.0: design patterns and business models for the next generation of software. http://www.oreillynet.com/pub/a/oreilly/tim/news/2005/09/30/what-is-web-20.html

[16] Kitchin, R. and Dodge, M. (2011).

[17] Hein, B. (2014) Uber's data-sucking Android app is dangerously close to malware. *Cult of Mac*, 26 Nov, http://www.cultofmac.com/304401/ubers-android-app-literally-malware/

[18] Batteries provide proxy IDs for phones as they unique characteristics. Battery information sought includes health, level, status, technology, temperature, voltage.

[19] Providing details of altitude, latitude, longitude, movement direction, speed of movement.

[20] Google: http://google.com/takeout; Facebook: https://www.facebook.com/help/1701730696756992

[21] Verma, K. (2019) Google Chrome pasts 5 billion downloads; a huge lead over Mozilla Firefox. *The Geek Herald*, 30 June, https://thegeekherald.com/p/google-chrome-pasts-5-billion-downloads-a-huge-lead-over-mozilla-firefox/

[22] Kerns, T. (2018) Gmail now has more than 1.5 billion active users. *Android Police*, 26 Oct, https://www.androidpolice.com/2018/10/26/gmail-now-1-5-billion-active-users/

[23] Constine, J. (2018) WhatsApp hits 1.5 billion monthly users. *Tech Crunch*, 31 Jan, https://techcrunch.com/2018/01/31/whatsapp-hits-1-5-billion-monthly-users-19b-not-so-bad/

[24] Protalinski, E. (2019) Android passes 2.5 billion monthly active devices. *Venture Beat*, 7 May, https://venturebeat.com/2019/05/07/android-passes-2-5-billion-monthly-active-devices/

[25] Sprangler, T. (2019) YouTube Now Has 2 Billion Monthly Users, Who Watch 250 Million Hours on TV Screens Daily. *Variety*, 3 May, https://variety.com/2019/digital/news/youtube-2-billion-users-tv-screen-watch-time-hours-1203204267/

[26] https://instagram-press.com/our-story/

[27] Statista (2020) Number of monthly active Facebook users worldwide as of 2nd quarter 2020 (in millions). https://www.statista.com/statistics/264810/number-of-monthly-active-facebook-users-worldwide/

[28] In London it is the bins that track you, in Chicago the lamp posts. The same technology is also used within malls and shops to track shoppers, sometimes linking with CCTV to capture basic demographic information such as age and gender. Vincent, J. (2013) London's bins are tracking your smartphone. *The Independent*, 9 August, https://www.independent.co.uk/life-style/gadgets-and-tech/news/updated-londons-bins-are-tracking-your-smartphone-8754924.html; Lanks, B. (2014) Chicago's new high-tech lamp posts will track everything, always. *Bloomberg*, 25 June, https://www.bloomberg.com/news/articles/2014-06-24/chicagos-new-high-tech-lamp-posts-will-track-everything-always; Kopytoff, V. (2013) Stores Sniff Out Smartphones to Follow Shoppers, *Technology Review*, 12 Nov, https://www.technologyreview.com/2013/11/12/251897/stores-sniff-out-smartphones-to-follow-shoppers/; Henry, A. (2013) How Retail Stores Track You Using Your Smartphone (and How to Stop It). *Lifehacker*, 19 July, http://lifehacker.com/how-retail-stores-track-you-using-your-smartphone-and-827512308

[29] Singer, N. (2012) F.T.C. Opens an Inquiry Into Data Brokers, *The New York Times*, 18 December, http://www.nytimes.com/2012/12/19/technology/ftc-opens-an-inquiry-into-data-brokers.html

[30] Coffee, P. (2018) IPG Confirms $2.3 Billion Deal to Acquire Data Marketing Company Acxiom. *AdWeek*, 2 July, https://www.adweek.com/agencies/ipg-confirms-2-3-billion-deal-to-acquire-data-marketing-company-acxiom/

[31] Clarke, R. (1988) Information technology and dataveillance. *Communications of the ACM* 31(5): 498–512.

[32] Social sorting consists of categorizing people into categories based on their data in order to treat them differently, with some receiving a preferential

status and others marginalized and excluded. For example, a company might socially sort customers based upon where they live, with those living in poor neighbourhoods receiving different special offers, prices or credit. Graham, S. (2005) Software-sorted geographies. *Progress in Human Geography* 29(5): 562–80.

[33] Zuboff, S. (2019).

Chapter 16

[1] Dodge, M. and Kitchin, R. (2007) 'Outlines of a world coming in existence': Pervasive computing and the ethics of forgetting. *Environment and Planning B: Planning and Design* 34(3): 431–45.

[2] Mann, S., Nolan, J. and Wellman, B. (2003) Sousveillance: Inventing and using wearable computing devices for data collection in surveillance environments. *Surveillance & Society* 1 (3): 331–55.

[3] van Dijck, J. (2005) From shoebox to performative agent: The computer as personal memory machine. *New Media & Society* 7(3): 311–32.

[4] Schuurman, N. (2004) Databases and bodies: A cyborg update. *Environment & Planning A: Economy & Space* 36(8): 1337–40.

[5] Allen, A.L. (2008) Dredging up the past: Lifelogging, memory, and surveillance. *University of Chicago Law Review* 75(1): 47–74.

[6] Dodge, M. and Kitchin, R. (2007).

[7] Schacter, D.L. (2001) *The Seven Sins of Memory: How the Mind Forgets and Remembers.* Houghton Mifflin, Boston, MA.

[8] A fuller account of our concerns is detailed in Dodge, M. and Kitchin, R. (2007).

[9] Bell, G., Brooke, T., Churchill, E. and Paulos, E. (2003) Intimate (ubiquitous) computing. In: Proceedings of Ubicomp 2003, ACM. https://citeseerx.ist.psu.edu/viewdoc/summary?doi=10.1.1.109.4953

[10] Dodge, M. and Kitchin, R. (2007).

[11] Minelli, M., Chambers, M. and Dhiraj, A. (2013) *Big Data, Big Analytics.* Wiley, Hoboken, NJ.

[12] https://theviewfromthebluehouse.blogspot.com/

[13] http://irelandafternama.wordpress.com/

[14] https://www.goodreads.com/robkitchin

[15] https://twitter.com/RobKitchin

[16] http://progcity.maynoothuniversity.ie/

[17] https://www.scoop.it/topic/the-programmable-city

[18] https://analytics.twitter.com/user/RobKitchin/home

[19] https://scholar.google.co.uk/citations?user=Y_3-GBQAAAAJ

[20] A h-index provides a measure of impact across the body of an academic's work. The score is the largest number of articles (h) where h publications have at least h citations – so a score of 15 means a person has 15 articles with 15 or more citations; a score of 30 means 30 articles with 30 or more citations.

21 For an academic discussion of the quantified self, especially relating to health, see Lupton, D. (2016) *The Quantified Self*. John Wiley, Chichester.

22 Proximity to screen surface, ambient light, moisture, thermal, touch ID, Face ID, camera, microphone, Wi-Fi and radio. See Costello, S. (2020) The Sensors That Make the iPhone so Cool. *Lifewire*, 4 Feb, https://www.lifewire.com/sensors-that-make-iphone-so-cool-2000370

Chapter 17

1   For a factual summary account of the 2019–20 fires in Australia, see McNamara, A. (2020) Australia fires: 5 questions answered. *CBS News*, 2 Jan, https://www.cbsnews.com/news/australia-fires-fire-map-5-questions-answered-how-many-hectares-have-burnt-where-are-the-fires-burning/

2   By Manyika, J., Lund, S., Chui, M., Bughin, J., Woetzel, J., Batra, P., Ko, R. and Sanghvi, S. (2017) Jobs lost, jobs gained: What the future of work will mean for jobs, skills, and wages. *McKinsey Global Institute*, 28 Nov, https://www.mckinsey.com/featured-insights/future-of-work/jobs-lost-jobs-gained-what-the-future-of-work-will-mean-for-jobs-skills-and-wages

Chapter 18

1   See Beer, D. (2016) *Metric Power*. Palgrave, London; Mau, S. (2019) *The Metric Society*. Polity Press, Cambridge; Muller, J.Z. (2019) *The Tyranny of Metrics*. Princeton University Press, Princeton, NJ.

2   The national broadcaster.

3   https://univ.cc/

4   To say I think the global rankings are dubious science would be an understatement. Anyone who believes that only two of the top 20 universities in the world are outside of the UK and USA is deluded. The metrics and algorithm are highly skewed towards Anglo-American institutions. The highest ranked German university is 32, the highest ranked French is 45 and the highest ranked Dutch is 59.

5   Kitchin, R. (2013) New EU university ranking exercise – U-Multirank. *Ireland After NAMA*, 30 Jan, https://irelandafternama.wordpress.com/2013/01/30/new-eu-university-ranking-exercise-u-multirank/

6   Kitchin et al (2015).

7   These are actually both top performing departments in my university, though a flat comparison of research metrics such as funding income and citations might not give that impression.

8   This was nicely illustrated to me on a project that sought to create a new social deprivation index that would cover both the Republic of Ireland and Northern Ireland. By tweaking the weightings of variables in the index formula we altered the scores and thus the ranking of neighbourhoods. Which in turn altered whether they would benefit from area-targeted investment. Playing with the algorithm could mean dramatically different outcomes for a place.

9   https://www.timeshighereducation.com/world-university-rankings/2020/ world-ranking#!/page/0/length/25/sort_by/rank/sort_order/asc/cols/ stats

10 Kinman, G. and Jones, F. (2008) A Life Beyond Work? Job Demands, Work-Life Balance, and Wellbeing in UK Academics. *Journal of Human Behavior in the Social Environment* 17(1–2): 41–60; Sang, K., Powell, A., Finkel, R. and Richards, J. (2015) 'Being an academic is not a 9–5 job': Long working hours and the 'ideal worker' in UK academia. *Labour and Industry* 25(3): 235–49.

11 MacKenzie, D. (2008) *An Engine, not a Camera: How Financial Models Shape Markets.* MIT Press, Cambridge, MA.

12 Campbell, D.T. (1979) Assessing the impact of planned social change. *Evaluation and Program Planning* 2(1): 67–90.

13 Evans, L. and Kitchin, R. (2018) A smart place to work? Big data systems, labour, control, and modern retail stores. *New Technology, Work and Employment,* 33(1): 44–57.

14 Goodhart's Law: How Measuring The Wrong Things Drive Immoral Behaviour. https://coffeeandjunk.com/goodharts-campbells-law/

15 Strathern, M. (1997) 'Improving Ratings': Audit in the British University system. *European Review* 5(3): 305–21.

16 Honore, C. (2005) *In Praise of Slowness: Challenging the Cult of Speed.* HarperCollins, New York.

17 Fraser, A. and Kitchin, R. (2020) *Slow Computing: Why We Need Balanced Digital Lives.* Bristol University Press, Bristol.

Chapter 20

1   Keegan, M. (2019) Big Brother is watching: Chinese city with 2.6m cameras is the world's most heavily surveilled. *The Guardian,* 2 Dec, https://www. theguardian.com/cities/2019/dec/02/big-brother-is-watching-chinese-city-with-26m-cameras-is-worlds-most-heavily-surveilled

2   Kuo, L. (2019) China brings in mandatory facial recognition for mobile phone users. *The Guardian,* 2 Dec, https://www.theguardian.com/world/2019/dec/ 02/china-brings-in-mandatory-facial-recognition-for-mobile-phone-users

3   Mozur, P. (2017) In urban China, cash is rapidly becoming obsolete. *The New York Times,* 16 July, https://www.nytimes.com/2017/07/16/business/ china-cash-smartphone-payments.html

4   Daum, J. (2017) China through a glass, darkly: What foreign media misses in China's social credit. *China Law Translate,* 24 Dec, https://www.chinalawtranslate. com/en/seeing-chinese-social-credit-through-a-glass-darkly/

5   Meissner, M. and Wubbeke, J. (2016) IT-Backed Authoritarianism: Information Technology Enhances Central Authority and Control Capacity Under Xi Jinping. *MERICS China Monitor.* https://research.vu.nl/ws/files/1512000/ MPOC_ChinasCoreExecutive.pdf

6   Daum, J. (2017).

[7] Liang, F., Das, V., Kostyuk, N. and Hussain, M.M. (2018) Constructing a data-driven society: China's Social Credit System as a state surveillance infrastructure. *Policy and Internet* 10(4): 415–53.

[8] Liang et al (2018).

[9] Daum, J. (2017); Liang et al (2018).

[10] Hoffman, S. (2017) Managing the State: Social credit, surveillance and the CCP's plan for China. *China Brief* 17(11), 17 Aug, https://jamestown.org/program/managing-the-state-social-credit-surveillance-and-the-ccps-plan-for-china/; Liang et al (2018); Daum, J. (2017).

[11] Meissner, M. and Wubbeke, J. (2016).

[12] Daum, J. (2017).

[13] Lee, C.S. (2019) Datafication, dataveillance, and the social credit system as China's new normal. *Online Information Review* 43(6): 952–70.

[14] Lee, C.S. (2019).

[15] Liang et al (2018).

[16] Meissner, M. and Wubbeke, J. (2016).

[17] Lee, C.S. (2019).

[18] Mitchell, A. and Diamond, L. (2018) China's surveillance state should scare everyone. *The Atlantic.* https://www.theatlantic.com/international/archive/2018/02/china-surveillance/552203/

[19] Sesame Credit is a product of Ant Financial, a subsidiary of Alibaba. It uses its vast trove of commercial and consumer data to create a credit score for individuals who use its services. It is partly a loyalty rewards programme and partly a credit rating, with a high score providing preferential treatment, discounts, rewards and access to loans. Daum (2017).

[20] Meissner, M. and Wubbeke, J. (2016).

[21] Daum, J. (2017).

[22] Daum, J. (2017).

[23] Keegan (2019).

[24] Wellman, T. (2015) Facial Recognition Software Moves From Overseas Wars to Local Police. *The New York Times*, 12 Aug, www.nytimes.com/2015/08/13/us/facial-recognition-software-moves-from-overseas-wars-to-local-police.html

[25] Kitchin, R. (2016) The ethics of smart cities and urban science. *Philosophical Transactions of the Royal Society A* 374(2083): 1–15. For an illustration of how detailed and extensive data traces of movements of smartphones are see the 'One Nation, Tracked' report by *The New York Times*. https://www.nytimes.com/interactive/2019/12/19/opinion/location-tracking-cell-phone.html

[26] Kitchin, R. and Fraser, A. (2020) *Slow Computing: How To Create More Balanced Digital Lives.* Bristol University Press, Bristol.

[27] Chan, K. (2019) Police, protesters clash in Hong Kong as demonstrators cut down smart lamppost. *Global News*, 24 Aug, https://globalnews.ca/news/5808861/hong-kong-protests-smart-lamppost/

[28] Aiken, S. (2019) Inside digital resistance in Cyberpunk Harbour. *CryptoPunks.* https://medium.com/crypto-punks/digital-resistance-security-privacy-tips-from-hong-kong-protesters-37ff9ef73129

[29] They will lock Telegram and also hide the app from the homepage, and restrict permissions related to the Camera, Contacts, Location, Microphone, Telephone and Storage. They will register a Telegram account using a prepaid SIM card that is not linked to user's ID. They'll use two-step authentication, set up a Passcode Lock to protect secret chats and adjust the privacy and security settings. Aiken (2019).

Chapter 21

[1] For a more straight academic discussion of themes in this story, see this paper that details an auto-ethnography of airport security. Kitchin, R. and Dodge, M. (2009) Airport code/spaces. In Cwerner, S., Kesselring, S. and Urry, U. (eds) *Aeromobilities: Theory and Research*. Routledge, London. pp 96–114.

[2] This did actually happen when I was waiting in a security queue at Stansted Airport.

Chapter 22

[1] The average new house price rose from €78,715 in Dublin and €66,914 for the country as a whole in 1991 to €416,225 in Dublin (a 429 per cent increase) and €322,634 for the country as a whole (a 382 per cent increase) in 2007. Second-hand homes followed the same trend, with rises in Dublin of 551 per cent and of 489 per cent outside the capital. See: Kitchin, R., Hearne, R. and O'Callaghan, C. (2016) Housing. In Roche, W.K., O'Connell, P. and Prothero, A. (eds) *Austerity and Recovery in Ireland: Europe's Poster Child and the Great Recession*. Oxford University Press, Oxford. pp 272–89.

[2] I have co-written a number of papers concerning the financial crisis in Ireland and its subsequent aftermath. See:

Kitchin, R., O'Callaghan, C., Boyle, M., Gleeson J. and Keaveney, K. (2012) Placing neoliberalism: The rise and fall of Ireland's Celtic Tiger. *Environment and Planning A: Economy and Space* 44(6): 1302–26.

Kitchin, R., O'Callaghan, C. and Gleeson, J. (2014) The new ruins of Ireland? Unfinished estates in the post-Celtic Tiger era. *International Journal of Urban and Regional Research* 38(3): 1069–80.

O'Callaghan, C., Boyle, M., Kelly, S. and Kitchin, R. (2015) Topologies and topographies of Ireland's neoliberal crisis. *Space and Polity* 19(1): 31–46.

O'Callaghan, C., Boyle, M. and Kitchin, R. (2014) Post-politics, crisis, and Ireland's ghost estates. *Political Geography* 42, September: 121–33.

Hearne, R., Kitchin, R. and O'Callaghan, C. (2014) Spatial justice and housing in Ireland. In Kearns, G., Meredith, D. and Morrissey, J. (eds) *Spatial Justice and the Irish Crisis*. Royal Irish Academy, Dublin. pp 57–77.

Hearne, R., O'Callaghan, C., Di Feliciantonio, C. and Kitchin, R. (2018) The relational articulation of housing crisis and activism in post-crash Dublin, Ireland. In Gray, N. (ed) *Rent and its Discontents: A Century of Housing Struggle*. Rowman & Littlefield, Lanham, MD. pp 153–67.

3   http://irelandafternama.wordpress.com/

4   For an account of our public scholarship blogging see: Kitchin, R., Linehan, D., O'Callaghan, C. and Lawton, P. (2013) Public geographies and social media. *Dialogues in Human Geography* 3(1): 56–72.

5   For an academic account of the story of this research and details of the practical process see: Kitchin, R. (2014) Engaging publics: Writing as praxis. *Cultural Geographies* 21(1): 153–7; Kitchin, R., Gleeson, J. and Dodge, M. (2013) Unfolding Mapping Practices: A New Epistemology for Cartography. *Transactions of the Institute of British Geographers* 38(3): 480–96.

6   PIIGS: Portugal, Ireland, Italy, Greece and Spain.

7   In total, I wrote 295 posts for *Ireland After NAMA* between 2009 and 2017, nearly all of them data stories.

8   Kitchin, R., Gleeson, J., Keaveney, K. and O'Callaghan, C. (2010) *A Haunted Landscape: Housing and Ghost Estates in Post-Celtic Tiger Ireland.* NIRSA Working Paper 59. http://eprints.maynoothuniversity.ie/2236/1/WP59-A-Haunted-Landscape.pdf

9   This was done by Justin Gleeson, Eoghan McCarthy and Aoife Dowling as part of their All-Island Research Observatory work, occasionally with supporting analysis by myself and others.

10 Most notably Professor Morgan Kelly of University College Dublin whose work suggested Ireland was heading for a major crash was publicly ridiculed by the Taoiseach, Bertie Ahern, TD.

11 Over a decade after the crash my salary is still less than it was in 2007. At one point my take-home pay was nearly 20 per cent less than it had been.

12 *The Irish Times* (2019) Number of people homeless in Ireland rises again, 30 Sept, https://www.irishtimes.com/news/social-affairs/number-of-people-homeless-in-ireland-rises-again-1.4034959

13 Rebuilding Ireland (2018) Annual Summary of Social Housing Assessments is Published. 26 Sept, https://rebuildingireland.ie/news/annual-summary-of-social-housing-assessments-is-published/

Chapter 23

1   Informationisbeautiful.net provides details on 185 data breaches, including the source and size of the breach. Over 100 of the incidents involve over 1 million customer accounts breached (with over 20 involving >100m records), with sensitive data stolen including names, addresses, social security numbers, credit card details, administrative and patient records. Data visualization: http://www.informationisbeautiful.net/visualizations/worlds-biggest-data-breaches-hacks/; Spreadsheet of data and sources: https://docs.google.com/spreadsheets/d/1Je-YUdnhjQJO_13r8iTeRxpU2pBKuV6RVRHoYCgiMfg

2   One study found that the average time for detection of a cybersecurity breach was 210 days, and in 92 per cent of cases the discovery was via an angry customer, law enforcement agency, or a contractor. Trustwave, cited in Goodman (2015).

3   The Ponemon Institute reported in 2014, based on a survey of 567 executives of US businesses, that 43 per cent of firms had experienced a data breach in the previous year involving the loss of more than 1,000 records. Ponemon Institute (2014) *Is Your Company Ready for a Big Data Breach? The Second Annual Study on Data Breach Preparedness.* Sept, http://www.experian.com/assets/data-breach/brochures/2014-ponemon-2nd-annual-preparedness.pdf

4   Collier, K. (2019) Crippling ransomware attacks targeting US cities on the rise. *CNN*, 11 May, https://edition.cnn.com/2019/05/10/politics/ransomware-attacks-us-cities/index.html

5   Goodman, M. (2015) *Future Crimes: A Journey to the Dark Side of Technology – and How to Survive It.* Bantam Press, New York.

6   12.6 million Americans were reportedly the victims of identity theft in 2012 at the collective loss of $21 billion. Finklea, K. (2014) Identity theft: Trends and issues. *Congressional Research Service*, 16 Jan, http://www.fas.org/sgp/crs/misc/R40599.pdf

Chapter 24

1   http://codeforireland.ie/

2   Such as Coding Grace (https://www.codinggrace.com/); PyLadies (https://www.facebook.com/PyladiesDublin); DCC Beta (http://www.dccbeta.ie/); and various hackathons. Perng, S-Y. (2019) Anticipating digital futures: ruins, entanglements and the possibilities of shared technology making, *Mobilities* 14(4): 418–34; Perng, S-Y. (2018) Promises, practices and problems of collaborative infrastructuring: The case of Dublin City Council (DCC) Beta and Code for Ireland. In Coletta, C., Evans, L., Heaphy, L. and Kitchin, R. (eds) *Creating Smart Cities.* Routledge, London. pp 155–68; Maalsen, S. and Perng, S-Y. (2018) Crafting code: Gender, coding and spatial hybridity in the events of Dublin Pyladies. In Luckman, S. and Thomas, N. (eds) *The Craft Economy: Making, Materiality and Meaning.* Bloomsbury, London. pp 223–32.

3   The 'myq.ie' domain is no longer operational. For an account of the project see Perng, S-Y. and Kitchin, R. (2018) Solutions and frictions in civic hacking: Collaboratively designing and building a queuing app for an immigration office. *Social and Cultural Geography* 19(1): 1–20.

4   Levitas, J. (2013) Defining civic hacking. *Code for America.* http://www.codeforamerica.org/blog/2013/06/07/defining-civic-hacking/

5   Haklay, M. (2015) *Citizen Science and Policy: A European Perspective.* Commons Lab, Woodrow Wilson International Center for Scholars. https://www.wilsoncenter.org/publication/citizen-science-and-policy-european-perspective

6   Bonney, R., Ballard, H., Jordan, R., McCallie, E., Phillips, T., Shirk, J. and Wilderman, C.C. (2009) *Public Participation in Scientific Research: Defining*

the Field and Assessing Its Potential for Informal Science Education. Center for Advancement of Informal Science Education (CAISE). Washington, D.C. https://www.informalscience.org/sites/default/files/PublicParticipationin ScientificResearch.pdf

7   For accounts of The Programmable City projects work on hackathons see: Perng, S-Y., Kitchin, R. and MacDonncha, D. (2018) Hackathons, entrepreneurial life and the making of smart cities. *Geoforum* 97: 189–97; Perng, S-Y. (2019) Hackathons and the Practices and Possibilities of Participation. In Cardullo, P., di Feliciantonio, C. and Kitchin, R. (eds) *The Right to the Smart City.* Emerald. pp 135–50; Maalsen, S. and Perng, S-Y. (2016) Encountering the city at hacking events. In Kitchin, R. and Perng, S-Y. (eds) *Code and the City.* Routledge, London. pp 190–9.

8   NDRC used to stand for National Digital Research Centre. However, since the centre no longer conducts research but acts as a business incubator it simply refers to itself as NDRC without ever stating what the acronym stands for. https://www.ndrc.ie/

9   Morozov, E. (2013) *To Save Everything, Click Here: Technology, Solutionism, and the Urge to Fix Problems That Don't Exist.* Allen Lane, New York.

10   Cardullo, P. and Kitchin, R. (2019) Being a 'citizen' in the smart city: Up and down the scaffold of smart citizen participation in Dublin, Ireland. *GeoJournal* 84(1): 1–13; Cardullo, P. and Kitchin, R. (2019) Smart urbanism and smart citizenship: The neoliberal logic of 'citizen-focused' smart cities in Europe. *Environment and Planning C: Politics and Space* 37(5): 813–30.

11   See Cardullo, P., di Feliciantonio, C. and Kitchin, R. (eds) (2019) *The Right to the Smart City.* Emerald. pp 1–24.

12   March, H. and Ribera-Fumaz, R. (2016) Smart contradictions: The politics of making Barcelona a self-sufficient city. *European Urban and Regional Studies* 23(4): 816–30.

13   Morozov, E. and Bria, F. (2018) *Rethinking Smart Cities: Democratizing Urban Technology.* Rosa Luxemburg Stiftung, New York. http://www.rosalux-nyc.org/rethinking-the-smart-city/

14   Galdon, G. (2017) Technological Sovereignty? Democracy, Data and Governance in the Digital Era. *CCCB Lab.* http://lab.cccb.org/en/technological-sovereignty-democracy-data-and-governance-in-the-digital-era/

15   Bria, F. (2017) Reclaiming Europe's digital sovereignty. https://www.acast.com/ft-tech-tonic/reclaimingeuropesdigitalsovereignty

16   McLaren, D. and Agyeman, J. (2015) *Sharing Cities: A Case for Truly Smart and Sustainable Cities.* MIT Press, Cambridge, MA.

17   Talvard, F. (2019) Can urban 'miracles' be engineered in laboratories? Turning Medellín into a model city for the Global South. In Coletta, C., Evans, L., Heaphy, L. and Kitchin, R. (eds) (2019) *Creating Smart Cities.* Routledge, London. pp 62–75.

18   This is a re-wording of a statement by Practical Action, a development organization, about technology justice. Heeks, R. and Renken, J. (2016)

Data justice for development: What would it mean? *Information Development* 34(1): 90–102.

19 https://www.aclu.org

20 https://www.amnesty.org/en/

21 https://www.eff.org/

22 https://www.libertyhumanrights.org.uk/

23 https://privacyinternational.org/

24 http://d4bl.org/

25 http://detroitdjc.org/data-justice/ and https://detroitcommunitytech.org/

26 https://practicalaction.org/

27 Slightly modified from 'information is power …' from: https://www.helpage.org/global-agewatch/blogs/caroline-dobbing-36/making-older-people-count-in-the-data-revolution-847/

Chapter 25

1 In the U.S. 99 per cent of killings by police from 2013 to 2019 have not resulted in officers being charged with a crime. http://mappingpoliceviolence.org/

2 http://mappingpoliceviolence.org/

3 Fatal Encounters (http://www.fatalencounters.org/), Killed by Police (http://killedbypolice.net/) and U.S. Police Shootings Database (https://docs.google.com/spreadsheets/d/1cEGQ3eAFKpFBVq1k2mZIy5mBPxC6nBTJHzuSWtZQSVw/edit)

4 WSB-TV2 (2020) Killer Mike: 'It is your duty to not burn your own house down for anger with an enemy', https://www.wsbtv.com/video/?id=4914290

5 http://detroitdjc.org/data-justice/

6 https://www.odbproject.org/

7 http://d4bl.org/

Chapter 26

1 Schumaker, E. (2020) Timeline: How coronavirus got started. *ABC News*, 23 April, https://abcnews.go.com/Health/timeline-coronavirus-started/story?id=69435165

2 Coronavirus (COVID-19) Dashboard, Datasets and other sources of information. Irish Government. Updated daily. https://data.gov.ie/blog/coronavirus-Covid-19

3 Chris Brunsdon, my co-PI on the Building City Dashboards project – see Chapter 11 – was drafted into the government's core modelling team.

4 *Financial Times* (2020) Coronavirus tracked: the latest figures as countries fight to contain the pandemic. Updated daily. https://www.ft.com/content/a26fbf7e-48f8-11ea-aeb3-955839e06441

5 https://www.worldometers.info/coronavirus/

6 https://twitter.com/Care2much18/status/1252819591090155523

7   Via the European Centre for Disease Prevention and Control's 'National information resources on COVID-19'. https://www.ecdc.europa.eu/en/COVID-19/sources-updated

8   Also see Rankin, J., Burgen, S., Willsher, K. and Walker, S. (2020) Is comparing Covid-19 death rates across Europe helpful? *The Guardian*, 24 April, https://www.theguardian.com/world/2020/apr/24/is-comparing-Covid-19-death-rates-across-europe-helpful-; Henriques, M. (2020) Coronavirus: Why death and mortality rates differ. *BBC Future*, 2 April, https://www.bbc.com/future/article/20200401-coronavirus-why-death-and-mortality-rates-differ

9   World Health Organization (2020) International guidelines for certification and classification (coding) of Covid-19 as cause of death, 16 April, https://www.who.int/classifications/icd/Guidelines_Cause_of_Death_COVID-19.pdf

10 Morris, C. and Reuben, A. (2020) Coronavirus: Why are international comparisons difficult? *BBC News*, 29 April, https://www.bbc.com/news/52311014; Kretchmer, H. (2020) 3 reasons we can't compare countries' coronavirus responses. *World Economic Forum*, 5 May, https://www.weforum.org/agenda/2020/05/compare-coronavirus-reponse-excess-deaths-rates/

11 Morris, C. and Reuben, A. (2020).

12 Sir David Spiegelhalter, Winton Professor of the Public Understanding of Risk, University of Cambridge, on *The Andrew Marr Show*, 10 May 2020, https://twitter.com/TobyonTV/status/1259416363556376576

13 Brewis, H. (2020) Government's 100,000 daily coronavirus test target missed for eighth day in a row at death toll jumps by 269. *Evening Standard*, 10 May, https://www.standard.co.uk/news/uk/coronavirus-tests-100000-target-missed-eighth-day-a4436566.html

14 Schraer, R. (2020) Coronavirus: Why did the UK need 100,000 tests a day? *BBC News*, 10 May, https://web.archive.org/web/20200510235645/https://www.bbc.com/news/health-51943612

15 Office of National Statistics, Coronavirus (COVID-19) https://www.ons.gov.uk/peoplepopulationandcommunity/healthandsocialcare/conditionsanddiseases

16 Krelle, H., Barclay, C. and Tallack, C. (2020) Understanding excess mortality: What is the fairest way to compare COVID-19 deaths internationally? *The Health Foundation*, 6 May, https://www.health.org.uk/news-and-comment/charts-and-infographics/understanding-excess-mortality-the-fairest-way-to-make-international-comparisons

17 Benedictus, L. (2020) What we know, and what we don't, about the true coronavirus death toll. *Full Fact*, 1 May, https://fullfact.org/health/covid-deaths/

18 EuroMOMO (2020) Graphs and maps. https://www.euromomo.eu/graphs-and-maps/

19 Burn-Murdoch, J., Romei, V. and Giles, C. (2020) Global coronavirus death toll could be 60% higher than reported, *Financial Times*, 26 April, https://www.ft.com/content/6bd88b7d-3386-4543-b2e9-0d5c6fac846c

20 Younge, G. (2020) We can't breathe. *New Statesman*, 3 June, https://www.newstatesman.com/politics/uk/2020/06/we-cant-breathe

21 Booth, R. and Barr, C. (2020) Black people four times more likely to die from Covid-19, ONS finds. *The Guardian*, 7 May, https://www.theguardian.com/world/2020/may/07/black-people-four-times-more-likely-to-die-from-covid-19-ons-finds

22 Younge, G. (2020).

23 Phillips, D. (2020) Brazil stops releasing Covid-19 death toll and wipes data from official site. *The Guardian*, 7 June, https://www.theguardian.com/world/2020/jun/07/brazil-stops-releasing-covid-19-death-toll-and-wipes-data-from-official-site

24 For an extensive discussion, see Kitchin, R. (2020) Civil liberties or public health, or civil liberties and public health? Using surveillance technologies to tackle the spread of the coronavirus. *Space and Polity*, doi: 10.1080/13562576.2020.1770587.

25 Also see: https://en.wikipedia.org/wiki/COVID-19_apps

26 Singer, N. and Sang-Hun, C. (2020) As Coronavirus Surveillance Escalates, Personal Privacy Plummets, *The New York Times*, 23 March, https://www.nytimes.com/2020/03/23/technology/coronavirus-surveillance-tracking-privacy.html

27 Goh, B. (2020) China rolls out fresh data collection campaign to combat coronavirus, *Reuters*, 26 Feb, https://www.reuters.com/article/us-china-health-data-collection/china-rolls-out-fresh-data-collection-campaign-to-combat-coronavirus-idUSKCN20K0LW

28 Stanley, J. and Granick, J.S. (2020) The limits of location tracking in an epidemic. ACLU. 8 April, https://www.aclu.org/sites/default/files/field_document/limits_of_location_tracking_in_an_epidemic.pdf

29 Nielsen, M. (2020) Privacy issues arise as governments track virus. *EU Observer*, 23 March, https://euobserver.com/coronavirus/147828

30 Url, S. (2020) Drones take Italians' temperature and issue fines. *Arab News*, 10 April, https://www.arabnews.com/node/1656576/world

31 Brandom, R. and Robertson, A. (2020) Apple and Google are building a coronavirus tracking system into iOS and Android. *The Verge*, 10 April, https://www.theverge.com/2020/4/10/21216484/google-apple-coronavirus-contract-tracing-bluetooth-location-tracking-data-app

32 Pollina, E. and Busvine, D. (2020) European mobile operators share data for coronavirus fight, *Reuters*, 18 March, https://www.reuters.com/article/us-health-coronavirus-europe-telecoms/european-mobile-operators-share-data-for-coronavirus-fight-idUSKBN2152C2

33 Fowler, G.A. (2020) Smartphone data reveal which Americans are social distancing (and not), *The Washington Post*, 24 March,

https://www.washingtonpost.com/technology/2020/03/24/social-distancing-maps-cellphone-location/

[34] Hoonhout, T. (2020) Kansas Says It's Using Residents' Cell-Phone Location Data to Fight Pandemic, *National Review*, 1 April, https://www.nationalreview.com/news/coronavirus-kansas-using-resident-cell-phone-location-data-fight-pandemic/

[35] Hatmaker, T. (2020) Palantir provides COVID-19 tracking software to CDC and NHS, pitches European health agencies. *Tech Crunch*, 1 April, https://techcrunch.com/2020/04/01/palantir-coronavirus-cdc-nhs-gotham-foundry/

[36] https://mooreinstitute.ie/2020/04/24/video-of-the-Covid-19-response-webinar-data-ethics-and-the-Covid-19-crisis/

[37] Kitchin, R. (2020) Using digital technologies to tackle the spread of the coronavirus: Panacea or folly? *The Programmable City* Working Paper 44. http://progcity.maynoothuniversity.ie/wp-content/uploads/2020/04/Digital-tech-spread-of-coronavirus-Rob-Kitchin-PC-WP44.pdf

[38] Kitchin, R. (2020) Will CovidTracker Ireland work? *The Programmable City* blog, 22 April, http://progcity.maynoothuniversity.ie/2020/04/will-covidtracker-ireland-work/

[39] Stanley and Granick (2020); Schwartz, A. and Crocker, A. (2020) Governments haven't shown location surveillance would help contain COVID-19, *Electronic Frontier Foundation*, 23 March, https://www.eff.org/deeplinks/2020/03/governments-havent-shown-location-surveillance-would-help-contain-Covid-19

[40] Leith, D.J. and Farrell, S. (2020) Coronavirus contact tracing: Evaluating the Potential of using Bluetooth received signal strength for proximity detection. 6 April, https://www.scss.tcd.ie/Doug.Leith/pubs/bluetooth_rssi_study.pdf

[41] Stanley and Granick (2020).

[42] Pew Research (2019) Mobile fact sheet. 12 June, https://www.pewresearch.org/internet/fact-sheet/mobile/

[43] Ada Lovelace Institute (2020); Guarglia, M. and Schwartz, A. (2020); Stanley, J. (2020) How to think about the right to privacy and using location data to fight COVID-19. Just Security, 30 March, https://www.justsecurity.org/69444/how-to-think-aboutthe-right-to-privacy-and-using-location-data-to-fight-covid-19/

[44] European Data Protection Board (2020) Guidelines 04/2020 on the use of location data and contact tracing tools in the context of the COVID-19 outbreak, 21 April, https://edpb.europa.eu/sites/edpb/files/files/file1/edpb_guidelines_20200420_contact_tracing_covid_with_annex_en.pdf

[45] Also of significance was the need to cooperate technically with the Apple/Google decentralized initiative.

[46] Agamben, G. (2005) *States of Exception*. University of Chicago Press, Chicago.

47 Avila, K. (2020) Coronavirus as a dispositive. *Open Democracy*, 4 May, https:// www.opendemocracy.net/en/democraciaabierta/coronavirus-dispositive/

48 Mosendz, P. and Melin, A. (2020) Bosses are panic-buying spy software to keep tabs on remote workers, *Los Angeles Times*, 27 March, https://www.latimes.com/business/technology/story/2020-03-27/ coronavirus-work-from-home-privacy

49 Weaver, M. (2020) Don't coerce public over contact-tracing app, say campaigners. *The Guardian*, 26 April, https://www.theguardian.com/law/ 2020/apr/26/dont-coerce-public-over-coronavirus-contract-tracing-app-say-campaigners

50 Sircar, S. and Sachdev, V. (2020) Not Just Red Zones, New Rules Make Aarogya Setu Mandatory For All. *The Quint*, 2 May, https://www.thequint. com/tech-and-auto/aarogya-setu-app-mandatory-for-containment-zone-red-zone-orange-zone-all-employees

Chapter 27

1 Kitchin, R. and Fraser, A. (2020) *Slow Computing: Why We Need Balanced Digital Lives.* Bristol University Press, Bristol.

2 Held, V. (2005) *The Ethics of Care.* Oxford University Press: Oxford; Tronto, J.C. (1993) *Moral Boundaries: A Political Argument for an Ethic of Care.* Routledge, New York.

3 Gilligan, C. (1987) Moral orientation and moral development. In Kittay, E. and Meyers, D. (eds) *Women and Moral Theory.* Rowman & Littlefield Publishers, Totowa, NJ. pp 19–33.

4 Tronto, J.C. (2005) An ethic of care. In Cudd, A.E. and Andreasen, R.O. (eds) *Feminist Theory: A Philosophical Anthology.* Blackwell, Oxford. pp 251–63.

5 Kukutai, T. and Taylor, J. (eds) (2016) *Indigenous Data Sovereignty: Toward An Agenda.* Australian National University Press, Acton; Mann, M. and Daly, A. (2019) (Big) Data and the North-in-South: Australia's Informational Imperialism and Digital Colonialism. *Television & New Media* 20(4): 379–95; Global Indigenous Data Alliance (GIDA) (2019) *CARE Principles for Indigenous Data Governance.* https://www.gida-global.org/care

6 Tauli-Corpuz, V. (2016) Preface. In Kukutai, T. and Taylor, J. (eds) *Indigenous Data Sovereignty: Toward An Agenda.* Australian National University Press, Acton. pp xxi–xxiii.

7 For example, browser plug-in tools such as 'Https Everywhere' (that always seeks to connect to sites using a secure and encrypted connection), Privacy Badger or Ghostery (that block trackers embedded into website code), various ad and pop-up blockers, and using non-tracking search engines such as DuckDuckGo, private (incognito) browser sessions, and actively managing/deleting cookies and browser history.

8   As designated by sites such as Web of Trust (https://www.mywot.com/), Norton Safe Web (https://safeweb.norton.com) or Trend Micro Site Safety Center (https://global.sitesafety.trendmicro.com/)

9   Brunton, F. and Nissenbaum, H. (2016) *Obfuscation: A User's Guide for Privacy and Protest*. MIT Press, Cambridge, MA.

10 For example, using a virtual private network (VPN) or a Tor browser.

11 Lustig, R. (2017) *The Hacking of The American Mind: The Science Behind the Corporate Takeover of Our Bodies and Brains*. Penguin, London.

12 Eyal, N. (2014) *Hooked: How to Build Habit Forming Products*. Portfolio Books, New York.

Index

A

abstraction 25, 29, 41, 104
accountability 64, 194, 215
Acxiom 117
Ada Lovelace Institute 215
Adams, Robin 88
addictive 226, 227
adverts 6, 117, 123, 125, 132
aggregation 29, 40, 51, 55, 64, 65,
    103, 104, 155, 211, 213
Airbnb 221
AIRO (All-Island Research
    Observatory) 16, 38, 70, 71, 72,
    73, 87, 188
airport security 13, 221, 169–74, 221
Alexa 5
Alipay 163
All-Island Research
    Observatory see AIRO
American Civil Liberties Union 106,
    195, 215, 225
Amnesty International 195, 225
An Foras Feasa 89, 91
analogue 6, 12, 111, 119, 167,
    225, 227
Android 115, 116, 167, 213
ANPR (Automatic Number Plate
    Recognition) 35, 106, 117
Apple 133, 134, 213
apps 4, 5, 18, 72, 106, 115, 116, 117,
    124, 128, 131, 133, 134, 139, 142,
    158, 161, 162, 167, 184, 188, 191,
    193, 203, 208, 212, 213, 214, 215,
    216, 221, 224, 225, 226, 227
archiving 10, 30, 85–93, 101–2,
    103–4, 105, 107, 129, 131, 163,
    199, 201
Arnstein, Sherry 192
Atlanta 185

ATM (Automatic Teller
    Machine) 112, 113
Australia 11, 12, 137–42, 146
Automatic Number Plate
    Recognition see ANPR
Automatic Teller Machine see ATM

B

Baltimore 185
BAME (Black, Asian, Minority
    Ethnic) 211
Barcelona 193
barcodes 113, 114, 169
BCD (Building City Dashboards) 10,
    39, 74–8
'Beyond 2022' 103–4
bias 9, 21, 41, 44, 130, 143, 147,
    148, 164
Big Brother 130, 157, 161–8, 216
biometric 208
    see also facial recognition
Black, Asian, Minority
    Ethnic see BAME
black-boxed 4, 171
Blogger 116, 133
Bluetooth 212, 214
Boston 12, 56–9
    Area Research Initiative 59
Brazil 212
Building City Dashboards see BCD

C

calibration 21, 24, 33, 41
Cambridge 57, 58, 59
    Analytica 4, 59
Campbell's Law 150
Cardiio 134
Cardullo, Paolo 191–2

CCTV (Closed Circuit
    Television) 43, 104, 106, 117,
    129, 155, 157, 162
census 10, 38, 42, 51, 53, 54, 72, 77,
    81, 103, 178, 179, 180, 199
Central Statistics Office *see* CSO
Charlton, Martin 55
Chicago 166
China 11, 13, 161–8, 207, 212, 216
Citistat 73
citizen science 189–90, 192, 200,
    201, 203
civic
    hacking 13, 189, 190, 192, 194
    tech 57, 69–78
civil
    rights 4, 106, 162
    liberties 213, 214, 215, 225
Closed Circuit Television *see* CCTV
Code for Ireland 187–9
Collins, Sandra 86, 92
completeness 9, 42, 43
consistency 9, 23, 43, 58, 70
Construction Industry Federation 179
consumption 5, 6, 12, 113, 114, 115,
    116, 119
contact tracing 208, 212, 213–4, 216
Cork 10, 43, 75, 77, 78, 89
coronavirus 207–17
coverage 9, 42, 43
crime 40, 41, 54, 69, 72, 105, 150,
    197, 199
Critical Data Studies 4, 8–9, 10, 91
cross-border 9, 51, 52, 54, 55,
    59, 178
crowdsourcing 72, 189, 193, 201, 202
CSO (Central Statistics Office) 11,
    38, 39, 40, 46, 48, 49, 51, 52, 54,
    93, 103, 179
curation 41, 76, 82, 124, 125, 132, 224
cybersecurity 183–6, 215, 224

D

dashboards 10, 12, 39, 43, 54, 55,
    69–78, 208
data
    access 9, 24, 29, 40, 42, 43, 53, 59,
        61, 62, 64, 74, 75, 83, 91, 104,
        105, 129, 130, 184, 189, 194, 201,
        215, 220
    activism 3, 194, 197–204
    analytics 3, 9, 12, 27, 57, 62, 74,
        75, 123, 187, 203, 208

assemblage 24–5, 29, 77, 220
big 3, 10, 28, 118, 168, 219
breaches 4, 13, 183–6
broker 3, 4, 12, 104, 106, 117, 118,
    132, 166, 213
cleaning 5, 9, 24, 29, 38, 43
cooked 5, 11, 21, 24, 78, 208, 211,
    216, 220
derived 27, 29, 30, 32, 34, 103,
    104, 105, 106, 117, 178
footprint 6, 12, 112, 113, 224
futures 6, 13, 85–93, 103, 219–28
indexical 112, 113, 134
infrastructure 3, 7, 10, 30, 59,
    61, 65, 69–78, 103, 166, 168,
    193, 219
journey 11, 31–6
justice 3, 13, 194–5, 213
lifecycle 5, 11, 30, 87, 101–7,
    208, 213
literacy 62, 75, 76, 194, 195,
    203, 223
management 62, 64, 78, 106, 107
market 6, 117
minimization 104–5, 194, 224
protection 6, 29, 42, 64, 65, 74,
    105, 106, 167, 195, 214, 215, 224
quality 9, 12, 21, 23, 40, 42, 43, 44,
    62, 74, 82, 220
real-time 28, 32, 43, 54, 66, 69,
    70, 72, 80, 104, 114, 134, 156,
    157, 158
science 3, 9, 12, 59
security 42, 65, 74, 183–6
shadow 6, 12, 106, 112, 113, 116
sharing 5, 6, 10, 29, 42, 58, 59, 62,
    64, 92, 114, 128, 131, 132, 134,
    135, 175, 214, 215, 219, 223,
    224, 227
sovereignty 167, 222–7
stories 7–11, 13, 76, 175, 177, 180,
    219, 227–8
transforming 5, 20, 24, 29, 30,
    39, 104
transitory 12, 32, 102
Data for Black Lives 195, 200
dataveillance 12, 117, 118, 119,
    219, 221
Dawkins, Oliver 39, 54
DBEI (Department of Business,
    Enterprise and Innovation) 85
DCC (Dublin City Council) 39, 71,
    72, 73, 74

DEHLG (Department of Environment, Heritage and Local Government) 38, 178, 179
deletion 5, 12, 30, 32, 102–7, 116, 155, 191, 193, 219
Deliveroo 140
democracy 13, 162
demographics 41, 53, 69, 72, 81, 85, 117, 209
Department of Business, Enterprise and Innovation *see* DBEI
Culture, Heritage and the Gaeltacht 85
Department of Education and Science *see* DES
Department of Environment, Heritage and Local Government *see* DEHLG
Department of Public Expenditure and Reform *see* DPER
Taoiseach 10
DES (Department of Education and Science) 85
Detroit
Community Technology Project 195
Digital Justice Coalition 195, 200
Deutsche Telekom 213
DHO (Dublin Humanities Observatory) 88
Digital Repository of Ireland *see* DRI
Digital Rights Ireland 213
Dodge, Martin 113, 128
DPER (Department of Public Expenditure and Reform) 45, 85
DRI (Digital Repository of Ireland) 10, 12, 85–93, 103, 188
Dublin 10, 37, 38, 39, 43, 56, 58, 70–4, 77, 103, 104, 176, 187, 188, 190, 192
Dublin City Council *see* DCC
Dublin Humanities Observatory *see* DHO
Dublinked 10, 39

E

ecological fallacy 41, 54
economy 3, 5, 25, 29, 52, 53, 54, 58, 64, 65, 67, 69, 97, 113, 140, 162, 163, 176, 177, 179, 181, 182, 188, 190, 193, 219, 221
efficiency 4, 29, 65, 66, 106, 118, 119, 139, 146, 148, 150, 151, 222

electoral division 53, 54
Electronic Frontier Foundation 106, 195, 215, 225
email 5, 40, 46, 73, 105, 112, 113, 114, 115, 116, 134, 139, 151, 161, 168, 216, 226
EPA (Environmental Protection Agency) 42
epistemology 12, 26, 27, 28
error 9, 12, 20, 21, 23, 24, 30, 37, 38, 39, 40, 41, 44, 46, 47, 49, 77
ethics 6, 12, 29, 83, 84, 130, 131, 135, 161, 168, 191, 195, 213, 221, 222, 223, 224, 226
ethics of digital care 222–3
European Central Bank 48, 179, 181
European Union 20, 48, 52, 53, 54, 58, 105, 179, 189, 224
Eurostat 48, 52, 53, 55
Evans, Leighton 150
evidence-informed policy 13, 63, 65, 66, 67, 180
Experian 166

F

Facebook 4, 34, 114, 116, 122, 123, 131, 132, 133, 156, 177
facial recognition 117, 155, 162, 165, 166, 167, 208
facts 3, 26, 63, 130
Fair Information Practice Principles *see* FIPPs
falsification 39, 41, 44, 81, 128, 130, 225
fertility 79–82
filter bubble 123, 125
finance 18, 45–9, 85–93, 106, 131, 177
Financial Times 208, 211
FIPPs (Fair Information Practice Principles) 104, 194, 224
Fitbit 127, 128
Flickr 114, 132
Foley, Peter 178
forgetting 130, 134
funding 24, 61, 62, 63, 66, 78, 85–93, 95, 96, 97, 144, 195

G

Gaeltacht 85, 96, 97, 98
Galleries, Libraries, Archives and Museums *see* GLAM
Garda National Immigration Bureau *see* GNIB

GDPR (General Data Protection
    Regulation) 3, 6, 105, 107, 224
gender 80, 81, 173, 224
General Data Protection
    Regulation *see* GDPR
General Government Debt *see* GGD
generalisation 29, 41, 104, 222
Geodirectory 38, 178
Geographic Information
    System *see* GIS
gerrymandering 98
GGD (General Government Debt) 46
ghost estates 177–8
GIS (Geographic Information
    System) 10, 52, 57, 58, 112
GLAM (Galleries, Libraries, Archives
    and Museums) 88, 90
Gleeson, Justin 51, 178, 208
Global Positioning System *see* GPS
GNIB (Garda National Immigration
    Bureau) 188, 189
Goodhart's Law 150
Goodreads 132, 133
Google 115–6, 133, 156, 187, 189,
    213, 224
governance 5, 56, 58, 59, 78, 91, 92,
    114, 115, 118, 145, 164, 191, 216
GPS (Global Positioning System) 115,
    116, 117, 133, 167, 213, 214
Gray, Jane 91
GSM (Global System for Mobile
    Communications) 20

H

hackathon 190–1, 192, 225
Hansen, Cordula 77
harmonization 12, 51–9
Harrower, Natalie 92
HEA (Higher Education
    Authority) 91, 147
health 5, 42, 52, 53, 54, 57, 69, 72,
    80, 81, 83, 103, 111, 117, 129,
    131, 132, 133, 134, 143, 156, 191,
    203, 207, 217, 220
Heeks, Richard 194
HFA (Housing Finance
    Agency) 46, 49
higher education 143–51
Higher Education Authority *see* HEA
h-index 133, 146
homelessness 138, 182, 191
Hong Kong 11, 16, 162, 164,
    167–8, 212

hook cycle 226–7
household survey 41, 52, 81
housing 37–8, 40, 54, 57, 63, 69, 72,
    77, 96, 163, 175–82, 181, 191,
    203, 221
Housing Finance Agency *see* HFA
HSIS (Humanities Serving Irish
    Society) 88, 89, 90

I

ideology 23, 78, 166, 193, 195, 221
IMF (International Monetary
    Fund) 48, 179, 181
immigration 176, 188–9
India 216
indicators 13, 54, 56, 70, 72, 73, 96,
    133, 143, 146, 150
indigenous communities 223–4
INSPIRE directive 55
Instagram 116, 131, 152, 198
integrity 4, 9, 22, 23, 24, 38, 44, 55,
    163, 194
intellectual property 24, 29, 91
International Monetary Fund *see* IMF
internet 10, 105, 112, 113, 114, 115,
    118, 124, 156, 162, 166, 167, 195
interoperability 12, 51–9
intimate technologies 131
iOS (iPhone Operating System) 213
IQDA (Irish Qualitative Data
    Archive) 10, 87, 89
Ireland After NAMA 11, 132, 177
Irish
    Council for Civil Liberties 213
    Qualitative Data Archive *see* IQDA
    Research Council 10
    Social Sciences Data Archive 11
    Social Sciences Platform *see* ISSP
ISO37120 55, 56, 71
ISSP (Irish Social Sciences
    Platform) 87, 88, 89

J

juking the stats 127, 128, 134

K

Kafkaesque 13, 171, 174
Keogh, Stephanie 54
Key Performance Indicator *see* KPI
Killer Mike 200
KPI (Key Performance
    Indicator) 143–5, 146, 147, 148

L

law 5, 6, 18, 25, 29, 30, 78, 105, 106, 115, 130, 135, 139, 194, 195, 197, 220, 221, 222, 223, 225, 226
LGBT (Lesbian, Gay, Bisexual and Transgender) 224
Liberty 106, 195
lifelog 106, 129–31, 134, 135, 161
lineage 42, 43
LinkedIn 132
London 43, 70, 75, 105–6, 166
Lyons, Ronan 38

M

Maalsen, Sophia 73, 188
MAC (Media Access Control) 117, 155, 166
machine learning 27, 28, 82
maintenance 65
management 13, 30, 31, 40, 42, 57, 58, 59, 60, 73, 78, 91, 118, 143–51, 163, 189, 216
MAPC 59
Mapping Police Violence 199
maps 25, 35, 38, 39, 40, 41, 52, 54, 62, 69, 72, 74, 76, 77, 80, 95, 96, 98, 99, 101, 102, 134, 177, 200, 201, 207, 225
marketing 28, 225
Mass GIS 58
McArdle, Gavin 39, 43, 56, 70
McCarthy, Eoghan 37
McGarrigle, Conor 77
Medellin 193
Media Access Control see MAC
memory 129, 130
meritocracy 147
metadata 29, 42, 43, 53, 59, 91, 105, 106, 116
methodology 12, 24, 40, 42, 43, 55, 99, 147, 166, 178
metrics 12, 78, 143–51, 216
mobile phone 4, 21, 104, 113, 115, 162
monetization 6, 66, 119, 132, 134, 167, 215, 225
Morozov, Evgeny 191
Moscow 104
movement 34, 35, 54, 116–7, 155, 158, 161, 166, 208, 212, 213, 216
Myq.ie 188–9

N

National Centre for Geocomputation 35
National Institute for Regional and Spatial Analysis see NIRSA
National Treasury Management Agency see NTMA
neoliberalism 151, 167
Netflix 121–5
neutral 5, 78, 211
New England StatNet 58–9
New Orleans 185
New Public Management see NPM
New York 75, 166
NIRSA (National Institute for Regional and Spatial Analysis) 87, 89, 91
NISRA (Northern Ireland Statistics and Research Agency) 51, 52, 54
noise 20, 23, 24, 41
Nomenclature des Unités Territoriales Statistiques see NUTS
Northern Ireland 12, 51–5
Northern Ireland Statistics and Research Agency see NISRA
NPM (New Public Management) 145, 146, 148, 149, 151
NTMA (National Treasury Management Agency) 46, 49
NUTS (Nomenclature des Unités Territoriales Statistiques) 52

O

objectivity 5, 7, 12, 19, 21, 23, 24, 96, 211
obfuscation 225
O'Carroll, Aileen 91
OECD (Organisation for Economic Co-operation and Development) 55, 146, 224
official statistics 9, 11, 38, 42, 43, 44, 53, 58, 65, 211
open data 3, 10, 11, 12, 29, 39, 43, 57, 58, 61–78, 86, 92, 119, 188, 193, 195, 203
open source software 70, 193, 224–5
Open Street Map 225
optimization 4, 32, 44, 75, 76
Ordnance Survey Ireland see OSI
Organisation for Economic Co-operation and Development see OECD

OSI (Ordnance Survey
    Ireland) 40, 77
Our Data Bodies 200

P

Palantir 213
Perng, Sung-Yueh 188
PIIGS (Portugal, Ireland, Italy, Greece
    and Spain) 179
planning 11, 51, 52, 58, 59, 66, 77,
    96, 118, 177–9, 180, 182
platform 4, 6, 75, 116, 123, 132, 163,
    213, 219, 221, 226
policing 40, 41, 53, 54, 104, 105,
    118, 130, 150, 159, 161, 164, 165,
    166, 167, 197, 198, 199, 201, 202,
    203, 204, 212
Portugal, Ireland, Italy, Greece and
    Spain *see* PIIGS
Practical Action 195
pre-criminal 197, 198
predictive policing 198
privacy 42, 43, 64, 132, 167–8, 195,
    214, 215, 221, 224, 225
Privacy International 106, 195, 225
PRO (Public Records Office) 103
productivity 4, 29, 65, 81, 119, 146,
    147, 148, 149, 151, 221
profiling 4, 6, 12, 57, 76, 117,
    118, 124, 132, 166, 167, 171,
    198
Programme for Research in
    Third Level
Institutions *see* PRTLI
Property Services Regulatory
    Authority *see* PSRA
protest 161, 164, 167–8
provenance 9, 42, 43, 224
proxies 41, 50, 147
PRTLI (Programme for Research in
    Third Level
Institutions) 87, 88, 89, 90
PSRA (Property Services Regulatory
    Authority) 37, 38
Public Records Office *see* PRO

Q

quality of life 55, 56, 65, 157, 189,
    191, 194
quantified self 127–35
quarantining 208, 212, 216

R

racism 13, 197–204
Radio Frequency
    Identification *see* RFID
Raidió Teilifís Éireann *see* RTE
Regional Research Laboratories 52
regulation 5, 24, 25, 42, 105, 106,
    118, 168, 208, 220, 221, 223, 226
reliability 9, 23
Renaissance 26, 27
Renken, Jaco 194
representativeness 8, 9, 23, 41, 81,
    82, 192
Research Excellence
    Framework 147–8
Residential Property Price
    Register *see* RPPR
Revenue Commissioners 38
RFID (Radio Frequency
    Identification) 113
RIA (Royal Irish Academy) 85,
    87, 89, 90
right to disconnect 151
Royal Irish Academy *see* RIA
RPPR (Residential Property Price
    Register) 37, 38
RTE (Raidió Teilifís Éireann) 147,
    178, 180

S

sampling 8, 20, 24, 29, 41, 42, 72,
    81, 83, 104, 147, 183, 210
SAPS (Small Area Population
    Statistics) 51
scale of economy 55
Schreibman, Susan 88
Science Foundation Ireland 75
scopophilic technologies 131
self-tracking 5, 135
sensors 12, 18, 19, 20, 21, 23, 39, 41,
    104, 114, 115, 116, 117, 119, 129,
    133, 139, 154, 155, 156, 157, 158,
    159, 166, 189, 193
SEUPB (Special European Union
    Programmes Body) 51
Siri 5
Sleep Cycle 134
slow computing 222–7
Small Area Population
    Statistics *see* SAPS
smart
    cards 117

city 9, 13, 56, 70, 153–9, 161, 190, 191, 192, 193, 194
district 153–9
Dublin 10
helmet 208
TV 5, 115
smartphone 5, 77, 106, 114, 115, 116, 124, 131, 155, 161, 163, 164, 165, 208, 212, 213, 214, 216, 227
Snapchat 131
Snowden leaks 4, 166
social
 credit scoring 13, 161, 162–6, 167, 168
 media 4, 5, 34, 73, 83, 117, 131, 132, 134, 135, 161, 162, 163, 168, 189, 197, 208, 214, 226
 sorting 6, 12, 117, 221
Social Science Assessment Instruments see SSAI
socio-technical system 5, 6, 24, 30, 220
Somerville 57, 59
sousveillance 12, 128, 131, 132
South Korea 212
Special European Union Programmes Body see SEUPB
SSAI (Social Science Assessment Instruments) 87
stakeholders 25, 56, 66, 68, 71, 73, 77, 78, 86, 88, 90, 153, 154, 168, 178, 180, 187, 212
standardization 20, 24, 29, 38, 40, 42, 43, 55, 56, 58, 59, 70, 71, 82, 91, 106, 144, 145, 147, 149, 222
standards 20, 23, 42, 43, 53, 55, 56, 58, 59, 70, 91, 106, 164, 168, 194, 222
storytelling 7–8, 11
surveillance 6, 13, 104, 115, 128, 161, 162, 165, 166, 167, 208, 212, 213, 215, 216
 capitalism 118, 167, 219

T

Taiwan 161, 162
TDR (Trusted Digital Repository) 10, 86, 91, 92, 103
technocratic 13, 78, 146, 148, 151, 191, 193, 219
technological sovereignty 193
Telecom Italia 213
teleology 6, 220

testbed 13, 153–9
TfL (Transport for London) 105, 106
thermal camera 208, 212
traffic management 12, 27, 30–6, 39, 41, 104, 118, 155, 157, 158
transparency 9, 55, 64, 146, 167, 178, 187, 210, 212, 215, 225
Transport for London see TfL
TRIPS (Travel-time Reporting and Integrated Performance System) 39
trust 4, 9, 37–44, 49, 55, 64, 82, 86, 91, 103, 139, 155, 163, 164, 165, 166, 220
Trusted Digital Repository see TDR
Twitter 34, 41, 80, 81, 82, 83, 84, 114, 122, 131, 132, 133, 209

U

Uber 140, 142, 221
Unacast 213
UNDRIP (United Nations Declaration on the Rights of Indigenous Peoples) 223
United Nations 55, 223

V

validity 9, 23, 28, 42, 43, 184
veracity 9, 12, 21, 23, 40, 42, 43, 74, 213
visualization 10, 26, 38, 52, 54, 69, 70, 72, 74, 75, 76, 77, 134, 208
Vodafone 213

W

Walkmeter 133–4
Walmart 41
wards 53, 54
wearables 129, 131, 208
Web 2.0 114–5
WeChat 163
Weeter, Jeffrey 77
welfare 42, 57, 72, 81, 111, 137–42, 191, 199
WhatsApp 116
WHO (World Health Organization) 207, 209
Wi-fi 115, 116, 157, 166
Wikipedia 225
Windtre 213
World Council of City Data 43, 56
World Health Organization see WHO

World Wide Web *see* WWW
Worldometer 209
WWW (World Wide Web) 112, 114

Y

Younge, Gary 211

YouTube 114, 116, 132, 167

Z

zero-sum game 148, 151